图书在版编目(CIP)数据

欧·亨利短篇小说选：英汉对照/(美)亨利(Henry,
O.)著；王永年译.—北京：商务印书馆，2012(2014.12重印)
(名著名译英汉对照读本丛书)
ISBN 978-7-100-07595-4

I.①欧···　II.①亨···②王···　III.①英语—汉语—
对照读物②短篇小说—作品集—美国—近代　IV.①
H319.4:I

中国版本图书馆 CIP 数据核字(2010)第 250232 号

名著名译英汉对照读本
欧·亨利短篇小说选
〔美〕欧·亨利　著
王永年　译

商　务　印　书　馆　出　版
(北京王府井大街36号　邮政编码 100710)
商　务　印　书　馆　发　行
北　京　冠　中　印　刷　厂　印　刷
ISBN 978-7-100-07595-4

2012 年 10 月第 1 版　　　　开本 850×1168　1/32
2014 年 12 月北京第 2 次印刷　　印张 8¾
定价：28.00 元

前　　言

　　这套丛书的名字比较长：名著名译英汉对照读本。还应该长一点儿才更准确，比如叫做"名著名译英汉对照翻译教程读本"，因为这更接近我们费尽周折编出这套书的全部用意和目的。下面简单地说明一下。

　　名著。外国文学名著成千上万，按说选出十种八种，做成英汉对照读物，奉献给读者，不应该是难事。但凡事怕讲条件。英汉对照读物不宜太长，最好在八九万字的篇幅；体裁要丰富，至少戏剧、长篇和短篇小说要照顾到；英语难易要兼顾，各个时期尽量不漏，写作风格多样化；译文优秀，确实可以作为翻译教程式的读本……这么多条件相加，名著挑选起来就有相当难度了。多亏了各家老字号出版社几十年来出版的外国文化和文学翻译作品十分丰厚，虽然花费了不少力气，但结果相当令人满意。且看我们所选作品的书目：剧本有《哈姆莱特》、《凯撒和克莉奥佩特拉》和《理想丈夫》；长篇小说有《名利场》和《简·爱》；中篇小说有《伊坦·弗洛美》和《黑暗的心》；随笔有《一间自己的房间》；短篇小说有《马克·吐温短篇小说选》和《欧·亨利短篇小说选》。

　　三个戏剧。流传下来的优秀戏剧作品是西方文学的重要组成部分。阅读西方文学作品，必须阅读优秀的戏剧作品。另外，戏剧是西方文学的重要形式之一。在小说形式没有出现之前，戏剧是文艺创作中最具包容量的形式。小

I

说出现后,戏剧除了不断丰富自己,仍然保持着所有文艺创作形式所无法取代的优势,那就是舞台演出。小说可以朗读,但是无法在舞台上演出。要想登台演出,还得改编成剧本。因此,戏剧仍然是阅读的主要对象。《哈姆莱特》不仅是莎士比亚的扛鼎之作,也是所有剧本中公认的代表之作,其深度、广度和厚度,只有亲自阅读才能领会。莎士比亚是戏剧发展史上的一座山,后来者只有仰望的,没有叫板的,偏偏出了个萧伯纳要与他试比高低。萧伯纳发愤读书(包括不列颠百科全书的全部),勤奋写作(共写了五十余部),还创办"费边社"。莎士比亚有个名剧叫《安东尼与克莉奥佩特拉》,写古罗马人的人性和爱情。萧伯纳说,不,古人更喜欢政治,不信你看我写的《凯撒和克莉奥佩特拉》。后者也成了名剧,还拍成了电影,成为电影经典。才子作家奥斯卡·王尔德却说,爱情和政治都重要,唯美主义更重要,我来写一出唯美剧本《理想丈夫》让你们看看。于是,《理想丈夫》集爱情、政治讽刺与社会风俗于一体,上演时轰动一时,也成了名剧。

长篇。为了适合英汉对照,我们只能选长篇小说名著的若干章节。萨克雷的《名利场》和夏洛特·勃朗特的《简·爱》我们各选了其中的八九万字,首先是因为这两部作品在西方文学史上具有独一无二的地位,其次是因为这个译本已经成了翻译外国文学作品的范本。所选的几章当然是其中最精彩的,完全可以当做短篇小说看,却又大体上窥见了全书中的几个主人公。萨克雷生前十分走红,许多后起作家都对他十分仰慕,夏洛特·勃朗特就是他的追星族,醉心文学,终写出一部《简·爱》献给他,勃朗特也从此成名。

两个中篇。实际上,英语文学里没有中篇小说这个明确概念。三四万字的短篇仍视为短篇,五六万字的作品就可以算作小长篇了。这里所选的两个中篇分别在八九万字,已经是名副其实的长篇了。康拉德的《黑暗的心》是公认的二十世纪文学经典,剥葱皮一样把殖民主义者的心态一层层刻画得淋漓尽致,其影响之大,先是在二十世纪三四十年代直接触动著名诗人托马斯·艾略特写出了《荒原》,后又在八十年代造就了轰动全球的电影大片《现代启示录》。美国心理派女作家伊迪丝·华顿以特有的细腻和力量,在她的最负盛名的《伊坦·弗洛美》里,写出了当初美国从农业国转向工业国时产生的物质问题和道德问题。

一则随笔。随笔是英语文学中非常重要的部分,但译得好的很少,只选了一篇。《一间自己的房间》,是英国女作家弗吉尼亚·吴尔夫的著名随笔,从一个思想相对开明的知识女性角度,把女性在社会上的地位问题进行了令人信服的阐述,被后来者誉为女性解放的宣言书。

最后是两位在中国读者群里最有声望的美国作家——马克·吐温和欧·亨利——的短篇小说选。马克·吐温的幽默讽刺和欧·亨利的巧妙构思,使他们跻身于世界文坛。我们选收时尽量照顾他们的创作特色,例如马克·吐温的《一张百万英镑钞票》和《腐蚀了哈德利堡镇居民的人》,欧·亨利的《麦琪的礼物》、《最后的常春藤叶》和《警察和赞美诗》,等等。

名译。"名译"的基点是译作出版后,经过一段时间考验,已经得到读者和专家的认可。大部分名译出自名家之手,如朱生豪、吕叔湘、杨宪益、杨必、黄雨石,自然算得上"名译"了。不过,这套丛书还特别强调了新中国成立以后文学翻译的历史与传统,变化与取向。新中国成立前的文学翻译是八仙过海各显神通，虽然不乏优秀的翻译作品，但是自由发挥随意删改的译风也确实存在，甚至在一些翻译作品中相当厉害。近几十年来，经过几代编辑的编辑和修订，共同努力，留住了一批新中国成立前的翻译作品，如朱生豪的《莎士比亚戏剧集》，吕叔湘的《伊坦·弗洛美》，徐霞村的《鲁滨孙飘流记》，等等。更重要的是通过淘汰、修改和碰撞，翻译界渐渐产生共识，形成了一种认真、严谨、准确、精当的译文标准取向，与当代白话文更加接轨了。读者通过每一种书的千把字的"翻译谈"，完全可以体会到这种变化和历史。

在这十种翻译作品里，《哈姆莱特》、《伊坦·弗洛美》、《名利场》可归为一类。它们更注重段落的信息，有时不惜打乱一点儿句序，力求更传神，更口语化，更接近白话文小说的味道与表达。译者能做到这点，靠的是雄厚的英文和汉语底子，尤其汉语。《凯撒和克莉奥佩特拉》是一种游刃有余的翻译，两种文字都照顾得很好；杨宪益、朱光潜、杨周翰、潘家洵，都算得上这种优秀的翻译的代表。《马克·吐温短篇小说选》的翻译，是一种更容易反映作者写作风格的译文。《简·爱》是目前英语作品之中汉译版本最多的。吴钧燮的译本是较早的，超过了过去的译本，后来的译本又无一可及，从此不难看出翻译不是谁都能做好的。《欧·亨利短篇小说选》、《一间自己的房间》、《黑暗的心》和《理想丈夫》的译文简朴、清顺，更贴近原文的原貌，代表了今后译文的走向。

英汉对照。译家和编辑有一句大白话：译文和原文对不上（或对得上）。这话往往代表一种翻译的优劣标准。这个系列的所有翻译都是"对得上的"，尽管程度上会出现差别。但是读者在对照英文和中文的时候，一定要琢磨一下，消化一下，发现有“对不上的”也切不要立即下结论，最好回头看看书前的那篇千把字的“翻译谈”，然后再下结论。你这样做了，无论发现什么结果，都会产生一种意想不到的飞跃，英文的和中文的。

读本。既然是读本，首先考虑的是为读者服务。无论英文中文，均有难易之分。按我们的设想，先读短篇，而后中篇，然后长篇，最后是戏剧。但是如果你只读英语，参考译文，那么先读戏剧中的对话倒是一个提高英语理解的有效捷径。

另外，前边说过，我们的这套书应该叫做“翻译教程读本”才更尽其意。我们知道，许多优秀的译家都承认他们从优秀的译本中获益颇多，翻译的经验和感受很重要，例如，“关键是‘信’‘达’”，“务使作者之命意豁然呈露”，“一仆二主”，“五点谈”，“首要原则是忠实，并力求神似”，“学会表达”，“拉住两个朋友的手”，等等，都在每一读本的前面作了具体而珍贵的详述。如果有什么东西可以称为翻译教程的话，这些类似“翻译谈”的东西才当之无愧。

苏福忠

一手要拉两个朋友

本书以人民文学出版社一九八六年出版的欧·亨利的《麦琪的礼物及其他故事》为基础,由于篇幅限制,抽掉了个别篇目。中外文对照的译本对翻译要求更为严格,因此,出版前译者又作了一次校订。

美国翻译理论家奈达认为译文读者对译文的反应如能与原文读者对原文的反应基本一致,翻译就可以说是成功的,奈达还主张翻译所传达的信息不仅包括思想内容,还应包括语言形式。

在翻译过程中,译者力求做到吃透原文含义,紧扣原作,在不损害汉语习惯的前提下,进行"功能对等"的转换,争取达到形似神似,希望译文读者一看就能领略原文意蕴,欣赏原著的魅力。换个通俗的说法,也就是译者一手要拉两个朋友,一方面要对得起原作者,如实介绍;另一方面心中要有读者,既不短斤缺两,糊弄读者,也不篡改原意,任意增删。

读欧·亨利的作品,细心的读者也许注意到,每篇开头几段多半有一些译注,这和欧·亨利出手不凡的开头有关。作者的风趣幽默、轻松活泼的开场白多与比喻联想、引经据典、人物刻画、抒情议论交融在一起,特别是能把抒情和阐理有机地结合起来,使读者精神为之一振,急于知道下文。

欧·亨利创作的另一个特点是文字简洁精练。他的短篇小说每篇很少超过五六千字,有的仅有二三千字。但短小的篇幅包含了丰富的内容,回味无穷。欧·亨利善于捕捉生活中令人啼笑皆非而富于哲理的戏剧性场景,用近似漫画的笔触勾勒人物,从细微之处抓住特点,用形象的语言加以描绘。

欧·亨利文笔生动活泼,经常运用俚语、双关语、讹音、谐音和旧典新意,美国是个多民族的国家,由大量移民组成,作品中经常出现德语、法语、西班牙语词汇,并引用希腊、罗马神话和《圣经》典故。《供应家具的房间》提到贫穷的房客们时说:"他们的葡萄藤是攀绕在阔边帽上的装饰,他们的无花果只是一株橡皮盆景",作者就在这里用了《圣经》的典故,《列王纪上》有"所罗门在世的日子……犹太人和以色列人都在自己的葡萄树下和无花果树下安然居住",葡萄树和无花果树是安定的家庭生活的象征。遇有这类情况,译者作了一些必要的注释,希望有助于读者阅读。

王永年

CONTENTS 目录

SELECTED
SHORT STORIES OF
O. HENRY
欧·亨利短篇小说选

The Gift of the Magi

ONE dollar and eighty-seven cents. That was all. And sixty cents of it was in pennies. Pennies saved one and two at a time by bulldozing the grocer and the vegetable man and the butcher until one's cheeks burned with the silent imputation of parsimony that such close dealing implied. Three times Della counted it. One dollar and eighty-seven cents. And the next day would be Christmas.

There was clearly nothing to do but flop down on the shabby little couch and howl. So Della did it. Which instigates the moral reflection that life is made up of sobs, sniffles, and smiles, with sniffles predominating.

While the mistress of the home is gradually subsiding from the first stage to the second, take a look at the home. A furnished flat at $ 8 per week. It did not exactly beggar description, but it certainly had that word on the lookout for the mendicancy squad.

In the vestibule below was a letter-box into which no letter would go, and an electric button from which no mortal finger could coax a ring. Also appertaining thereunto was a card bearing the name "Mr. James Dillingham Young".

The "Dillingham" had been flung to the breeze during a former period of prosperity when its possessor was being paid $ 30 per week. Now, when the income was shrunk to $ 20, the letters of "Dillingham" looked blurred, as though they were thinking seriously of contracting to a modest and unassuming D. But whenever

麦 琪 的 礼 物

一块八毛七分钱。全在这儿了。其中六毛钱还是铜子儿凑起来的。这些铜子儿是每次一个、两个向杂货铺、菜贩和肉店老板那儿死乞白赖地硬扣下来的；人家虽然没有明说，自己总觉得这种掂斤播两的交易未免太吝啬，当时脸都臊红了。德拉数了三遍。数来数去还是一块八毛七分钱，而第二天就是圣诞节了。

除了倒在那张破旧的小榻上号哭之外，显然没有别的办法。德拉就那样做了。这使得一种精神上的感慨油然而生，认为人生是由啜泣、抽噎和微笑组成的，而抽噎占了其中绝大部分。

这个家庭的主妇渐渐从第一阶段退到第二阶段，我们不妨抽空儿来看看这个家吧。一套连家具的公寓，房租每星期八块钱。虽不能说是绝对难以形容，其实跟贫民窟也相去不远。

下面门廊里有一个信箱，但是永远不会有信件投进去；还有一个电钮，除非神仙下凡才能把铃按响。那里还贴着一张名片，上面印有"詹姆斯·迪林汉·扬先生"几个字。

"迪林汉"这个名号是主人先前在每星期挣三十块钱的时候，一时高兴，加在姓名之间的。现在收入缩减到二十块钱，"迪林汉"几个字看来就有些模糊了，仿佛它们正在郑重考虑，是不是缩成一个质朴而谦逊的"迪"字为好。但每逢詹姆斯·迪林汉·扬先生回家上楼，走进房间的时候，詹姆斯·迪林汉·扬太太——就是刚才已经介绍给各位的德

Mr. James Dillingham Young came home and reached his flat above he was called "Jim" and greatly hugged by Mrs. James Dillingham Young, already introduced to you as Della. Which is all very good.

Della finished her cry and attended to her cheeks with the powder rag. She stood by the window and looked out dully at a gray cat walking a gray fence in a gray backyard. Tomorrow would be Christmas Day, and she had only $1.87 with which to buy Jim a present. She had been saving every penny she could for months, with this result. Twenty dollars a week doesn't go far. Expenses had been greater than she had calculated. They always are. Only $1.87 to buy a present for Jim. Her Jim. Many a happy hour she had spent planning for something nice for him. Something fine and rare and sterling—something just a little bit near to being worthy of the honor of being owned by Jim.

There was a pier-glass between the windows of the room. Perhaps you have seen a pier-glass in an $8 flat. A very thin and very agile person may, by observing his reflection in a rapid sequence of longitudinal strips, obtain a fairly accurate conception of his looks. Della, being slender, had mastered the art.

Suddenly she whirled from the window and stood before the glass. Her eyes were shining brilliantly, but her face had lost its color within twenty seconds. Rapidly she pulled down her hair and let it fall to its full length.

Now, there were two possessions of the James Dillingham Youngs in which they both took a mighty pride. One was Jim's gold watch that had been his father's and his grandfather's. The other was Della's hair. Had the Queen of Sheba lived in the flat across the

拉——总是管他叫做"吉姆",总是热烈地拥抱他。那当然是很好的。

德拉哭了之后,在脸颊上扑了些粉。她站在窗子跟前,呆呆地瞅着外面灰蒙蒙的后院里,一只灰猫正在灰色的篱笆上行走。明天就是圣诞节了,她只有一块八毛七分钱来给吉姆买一件礼物。好几个月来,她省吃俭用,能攒起来的都攒了,可结果只有这一点儿。一星期二十块钱的收入是不经用的。支出总比她预算的要多。总是这样的。只有一块八毛七分钱来给吉姆买礼物。她的吉姆。为了买一件好东西送给他,德拉自得其乐地筹划了好些日子。要买一件精致、珍奇而真有价值的东西——够得上为吉姆所有的东西固然很少,可总得有些相称才成呀。

房里两扇窗子中间有一面壁镜。诸位也许见过房租八块钱的公寓里的壁镜。一个非常瘦小灵活的人,从一连串纵的片断的映象里,也许可以对自己的容貌得到一个大致不差的概念。德拉全凭身材苗条,才精通了那种技艺。

她突然从窗口转过身,站到壁镜面前。她的眼睛晶莹明亮,可是她的脸在二十秒钟之内却失色了。她迅速地把头发解开,让它披落下来。

且说,詹姆斯·迪林汉·扬夫妇有两样东西特别引为自豪,一样是吉姆三代祖传的金表,另一样是德拉的头发。如果示巴女王①住在天井对面的公寓里,德拉总有一天会把她的头发悬在窗外去晾干,使那位女王的珠宝和礼物相

---

① 示巴古国在阿拉伯西南,即今之也门。《圣经·旧约·列王记上》载示巴女王带了许多香料、宝石和黄金去觐见所罗门王,用难题考验所罗门的智慧。

airshaft, Della would have let her hair hang out the window some day to dry just to depreciate Her Majesty's jewels and gifts. Had King Solomon been the janitor, with all his treasures piled up in the basement, Jim would have pulled out his watch every time he passed, just to see him pluck at his beard from envy.

So now Della's beautiful hair fell about her rippling and shining like a cascade of brown waters. It reached below her knee and made itself almost a garment for her. And then she did it up again nervously and quickly. Once she faltered for a minute and stood still while a tear or two splashed on the worn red carpet.

On went her old brown jacket; on went her old brown hat. With a whirl of skirts and with the brilliant sparkle still in her eyes, she fluttered out the door and down the stairs to the street.

Where she stopped the sign read: "Mme. Sofronie. Hair Goods of All Kinds." One flight up Della ran, and collected herself, panting. Madame, large, too white, chilly, hardly looked the "Sofronie".

"Will you buy my hair?" asked Della.

"I buy hair," said Madame. "Take yer hat off and let's have a sight at the looks of it."

Down rippled the brown cascade.

"Twenty dollars," said Madame, lifting the mass with a practised hand.

"Give it to me quick," said Della.

Oh, and the next two hours tripped by on rosy wings. Forget the hashed metaphor. She was ransacking the stores for Jim's present.

She found it at last. It surely had been made for Jim and no one else. There was no other like it in any of the

形见绌。如果所罗门王①当了看门人，把他所有的财富都堆在地下室里，吉姆每次经过那儿时准会掏出他的金表看看，好让所罗门妒忌得吹胡子瞪眼睛。

这当儿，德拉美丽的头发披散在身上，像一股褐色的小瀑布，奔泻闪亮。头发一直垂到膝盖底下，仿佛给她铺成了一件衣裳。她又神经质地赶快把头发梳好。她踌躇了一会儿，静静地站着，有一两滴泪水溅落在破旧的红地毯上。

她穿上褐色的旧外套，戴上褐色的旧帽子。她眼睛里还留着晶莹的泪光，裙子一摆，就飘然走出房门，下楼跑到街上。

她走到一块招牌前停住了，招牌上面写着："莎弗朗妮夫人——经营各种头发用品"。德拉跑上一段楼梯，气喘吁吁地让自己定下神来。那位夫人身躯肥大，肤色白得过分，一副冷冰冰的模样，同"莎弗朗妮"②这个名字不大相称。

"你要买我的头发吗？"德拉问道。

"我买头发。"夫人说。"脱掉帽子，让我看看头发的模样。"

那股褐色的小瀑布泻了下来。

"二十块钱。"夫人用行家的手法抓起头发说。

"赶快把钱给我。"德拉说。

噢，此后的两个钟头仿佛长了玫瑰色翅膀似地飞掠过去。诸位不必理会这种杂凑的比喻。总之，德拉正为了给吉姆的礼物在店铺里搜索。

德拉终于把它找到了。它准是专为吉姆，而不是为别

---

① 所罗门王为公元前约 973—公元前 933 年的以色列国王，以聪明豪富著称。

② 莎弗朗妮为意大利诗人塔索(1544—1595)以第一次十字军东征为题材的史诗《耶路撒冷的解放》中的人物，她为了拯救耶路撒冷全城的基督徒，承认了并未犯过的罪行，成为舍己救人的典型。

stores, and she had turned all of them inside out. It was a platinum fob chain simple and chaste in design, properly proclaiming its value by substance alone and not by meretricious ornamentation—as all good things should do. It was even worthy of The Watch. As soon as she saw it she knew that it must be Jim's. It was like him. Quietness and value—the description applied to both. Twenty-one dollars they took from her for it, and she hurried home with the 87 cents. With that chain on his watch Jim might be properly anxious about the time in any company. Grand as the watch was, he sometimes looked at it on the sly on account of the old leather strap that he used in place of a chain.

When Della reached home her intoxication gave way a little to prudence and reason. She got out her curling irons and lighted the gas and went to work repairing the ravages made by generosity added to love. Which is always a tremendous task, dear friends—a mammoth task.

Within forty minutes her head was covered with tiny, close-lying curls that made her look wonderfully like a truant schoolboy. She looked at her reflection in the mirror long, carefully, and critically.

"If Jim doesn't kill me," she said to herself, "before he takes a second look at me, he'll say I look like a Coney Island chorus girl. But what could I do—oh! what could I do with a dollar and eighty-seven cents?"

At 7 o'clock the coffee was made and the frying-pan was on the back of the stove hot and ready to cook the chops.

Jim was never late. Della doubled the fob chain in her hand and sat on the corner of the table near the door that he always entered. Then she heard his step on the

人制造的。她把所有店铺都兜底翻过,各家都没有像这样的东西。那是一条白金表链,式样简单朴素,只是以货色来显示它的价值,不凭什么装潢来炫耀——一切好东西都应该是这样的。它甚至配得上那只金表。她一看到就认为非给吉姆买下不可。它简直像他的为人。文静而有价值——这句话拿来形容表链和吉姆本人都恰到好处。店里以二十一块钱的价格卖给了她,她剩下八毛七分钱,匆匆赶回家去。吉姆有了那条链子,在任何场合都可以毫无顾虑地看看钟点了。那只表虽然华贵,可是因为只用一条旧皮带来代替表链,他有时候只是偷偷地瞥上一眼。

德拉回家以后,她的陶醉有一小部分被审慎和理智所替代。她拿出卷发铁钳,点燃煤气,着手补救由于爱情加上慷慨而造成的灾害。那始终是一件艰巨的工作,亲爱的朋友们——简直是了不起的工作。

不出四十分钟,她头上布满了紧贴着的小发卷,变得活像一个逃课的小学生。她对着镜子小心而苛刻地照了又照。

"如果吉姆看了一眼不把我宰掉才怪呢,"她自言自语地说,"他会说我像是康奈岛游乐场里的卖唱姑娘。我有什么办法呢?——唉!只有一块八毛七分钱,叫我有什么办法呢?"

到了七点钟,咖啡已经煮好,煎锅也放在炉子后面热着,随时可以煎肉排。

吉姆从没有晚回来过。德拉把表链对折着握在手里,在他进来时必经的门口的桌子角上坐了下来。接着,她听到楼下梯级上响起了他的脚步声。她脸色白了一忽儿。她

stair away down on the first flight, and she turned white for just a moment. She had a habit of saying little silent prayers about the simplest everyday things, and now she whispered: "Please God, make him think I am still pretty."

The door opened and Jim stepped in and closed it. He looked thin and very serious. Poor fellow, he was only twenty-two—and to be burdened with a family! He needed a new overcoat and he was without gloves.

Jim stopped inside the door, as immovable as a setter at the scent of quail. His eyes were fixed upon Della, and there was an expression in them that she could not read, and it terrified her. It was not anger, nor surprise, nor disapproval, nor horror, nor any of the sentiments that she had been prepared for. He simply stared at her fixedly with that peculiar expression on his face.

Della wriggled off the table and went for him.

"Jim, darling," she cried, "don't look at me that way. I had my hair cut off and sold it because I couldn't have lived through Christmas without giving you a present. It'll grow out again—you won't mind, will you? I just had to do it. My hair grows awfully fast. Say 'Merry Christmas!' Jim, and let's be happy. You don't know what a nice—what a beautiful, nice gift I've got for you."

"You've cut off your hair?" asked Jim, laboriously, as if he had not arrived at that patent fact yet even after the hardest mental labor.

"Cut it off and sold it," said Della. "Don't you like me just as well, anyhow? I'm me without my hair, ain't I?"

Jim looked about the room curiously.

有一个习惯，往往为了日常最简单的事情默祷几句，现在她悄声说："求求上帝，让他认为我还是美丽的。"

门打开了，吉姆走进来，随手把门关上。他很瘦削，非常严肃。可怜的人儿，他只有二十二岁——就负起了家庭的担子！他需要一件新大衣，手套也没有。

吉姆在门内站住，像一条猎狗嗅到鹌鹑气味似地纹丝不动。他的眼睛盯着德拉，所含的神情是她不能理解的，这使她大为惊慌。那既不是愤怒，也不是惊讶，又不是不满，更不是嫌恶，不是她所预料的任何一种神情。他只带着那种奇特的神情凝视着德拉。

德拉一扭腰，从桌上跳下来，走近他身边。

"吉姆，亲爱的，"她喊道，"别那样盯着我。我把头发剪掉卖了，因为不送你一件礼物，我过不了圣诞节。头发会再长出来的——你不会在意吧，是不是？我非这么做不可。我的头发长得快极啦。说句'恭贺圣诞'吧！吉姆，让我们快快乐乐的。我给你买了一件多么好——多么美丽的好东西，你怎么也猜不到的。"

"你把头发剪掉了吗？"吉姆吃力地问道，仿佛他绞尽脑汁之后，还没有把这个显而易见的事实弄明白似的。

"不但剪了，而且卖了。"德拉说。"不管怎样，你还是同样地喜欢我吗？虽然没了头发，我还是我，不是吗？"

吉姆好奇地向房里四下张望。

"You say your hair is gone?"he said, with an air almost of idiocy.

"You needn't look for it,"said Della. "It's sold, I tell you—sold and gone, too. It's Christmas Eve, boy. Be good to me, for it went for you. Maybe the hairs of my head were numbered," she went on with a sudden serious sweetness, "but nobody could ever count my love for you. Shall I put the chops on, Jim?"

Out of his trance Jim seemed quickly to wake. He enfolded his Della. For ten seconds let us regard with discreet scrutiny some inconsequential object in the other direction. Eight dollars a week or a million a year—what is the difference? A mathematician or a wit would give you the wrong answer. The magi brought valuable gifts, but that was not among them. This dark assertion will be illuminated later on.

Jim drew a package from his overcoat pocket and threw it upon the table.

"Don't make any mistake, Dell,"he said, "about me. I don't think there's anything in the way of a haircut or a shave or a shampoo that could make me like my girl any less. But if you'll unwrap that package you may see why you had me going a while at first. "

White fingers and nimble tore at the string and paper. And then an ecstatic scream of joy; and then, alas! a quick feminine change to hysterical tears and wails, necessitating the immediate employment of all the comforting powers of the lord of the flat.

For there lay The Combs—the set of combs, side and back, that Della had worshipped for long in a Broadway window. Beautiful combs, pure tortoise shell, with jewelled rims—just the shade to wear in the beautiful van-

"你说你的头发没有了吗?"他带着近乎白痴般的神情问道。

"你不用找啦。"德拉说。"我告诉你,已经卖了——卖了,没有了。今天是圣诞前夜,亲爱的。好好地对待我,我剪掉头发为的是你呀。我的头发也许数得清,"她突然非常温柔地接下去说,"但我对你的情爱谁也数不清。我把肉排煎上好吗,吉姆?"

吉姆好像从恍惚中突然醒了过来。他把德拉搂在怀里。我们不要冒昧,还是先花上十秒钟瞧瞧另一方面无关紧要的东西吧。每星期八块钱,或是每年一百万元——那有什么区别呢?一位数学家或是一位智者可能会给你不正确的答复。麦琪带来了宝贵的礼物①,但其中没有那件东西。对这句晦涩的话,下文将有所说明。

吉姆从大衣口袋里掏出一包东西,把它扔在桌上。

"别对我有什么误会,德尔。"他说,"不管是剪发、修脸,还是洗头,我对我姑娘的爱情是决不会减低的。但是只消打开那包东西,你就会明白,为什么刚才你使我愣住了。"

白皙的手指敏捷地撕开了绳索和包皮纸。接着是一声狂喜的呼喊;紧接着,哎呀!突然转变成女性神经质的眼泪和号哭,立刻需要公寓的主人用尽办法来安慰她。

因为摆在眼前的是那套插在头发上的梳子——全套的发梳,两鬓用的,后面用的,应有尽有;那原是百老汇路上的一个橱窗里,德拉渴望了好久的东西。纯玳瑁做的,边上镶着珠宝的美丽的发梳——来配那已经失去的美发,颜色真

---

① "麦琪"的英文原文也指基督初生时来送礼物的三贤人。一说是东方的三王:梅尔基奥尔(光明之王)赠送黄金表示尊贵,加斯帕(洁白者)赠送乳香象征神圣,巴尔撒泽赠送没药预示基督后来遭受迫害而死。

ished hair. They were expensive combs, she knew, and her heart had simply craved and yearned over them without the least hope of possession. And now, they were hers, but the tresses that should have adorned the coveted adornments were gone.

But she hugged them to her bosom, and at length she was able to look up with dim eyes and a smile and say: "My hair grows so fast, Jim!"

And then Della leaped up like a little singed cat and cried, "Oh, oh!"

Jim had not yet seen his beautiful present. She held it out to him eagerly upon her open palm. The dull precious metal seemed to flash with a reflection of her bright and ardent spirit.

"Isn't it a dandy, Jim? I hunted all over town to find it. You'll have to look at the time a hundred times a day now. Give me your watch. I want to see how it looks on it."

Instead of obeying, Jim tumbled down on the couch and put his hands under the back of his head and smiled.

"Dell," said he, "let's put our Christmas presents away and keep 'em a while. They're too nice to use just at present. I sold the watch to get the money to buy your combs. And now suppose you put the chops on."

The magi, as you know, were wise men—wonderfully wise men—who brought gifts to the Babe in the manger. They invented the art of giving Christmas presents. Being wise, their gifts were no doubt wise ones, possibly bearing the privilege of exchange in case of duplication. And here I have lamely related to you the uneventful chronicle of two foolish children in a flat who most unwisely sacrificed for each other the greatest treasures of

是再合适也没有了。她知道这套发梳是很贵重的,心向神往了好久,但从来没有存过占有它的希望。现在居然为她所有了,可是本可以用来使这令人向往已久的装饰品生色的头发却没有了。

但她还是把这套发梳搂在怀里不放,过了好久,她才能抬起迷濛的泪眼,含笑对吉姆说:"我的头发长得很快,吉姆!"

接着,德拉像一只给火烫着的小猫似地跳了起来,叫道:"喔!喔!"

吉姆还没有见到他的美丽的礼物呢。她热切地伸出摊开的手掌递给他。那无知觉的贵金属仿佛闪闪反映着她那快活和热诚的心情。

"漂亮吗,吉姆?我走遍全市才找到的。现在你每天要把表看上百来遍了。把你的表给我,我要看看它配在表上的样子。"

吉姆并没有照着她的话去做,却倒在榻上,双手枕着头,笑了起来。

"德尔,"他说,"我们把圣诞节礼物搁在一边,暂且保存起来。它们实在太好啦,现在用了未免可惜。我是卖掉了金表,换了钱去买你的发梳的。现在请你煎肉排吧。"

那三位麦琪,诸位知道,全是有智慧的人——非常有智慧的人——他们带来礼物,送给生在马槽里的圣子耶稣。他们首创了圣诞节馈赠礼物的风俗。他们既然有智慧,他们的礼物无疑也是聪明的,可能还附带一种碰巧收到同样的东西时可以交换的权利。我的拙笔在这里告诉了诸位一个没有曲折、不足为奇的故事;那两个住在一间公寓里的笨孩子,极不聪明地为对方牺牲了他们家里最宝贵的东西。

their house. But in a last word to the wise of these days let it be said that of all who give gifts these two were the wisest. Of all who give and receive gifts, such as they are wisest. Everywhere they are wisest. They are the magi.

但是，让我们对时下一班聪明人说最后一句话，在所有馈赠礼物的人当中，那两个人是最聪明的。在一切接受礼物的人当中，像他们这样的人也是最聪明的。无论在什么地方，他们都是最聪明的。他们就是麦琪。

A Service of Love

WHEN one loves one's Art no service seems too hard.

That is our premise. This story shall draw a conclusion from it, and show at the same time that the premise is incorrect. That will be a new thing in logic, and a feat in story-telling somewhat older than the great wall of China.

Joe Larrabee came out of the post-oak flats of the Middle West pulsing with a genius for pictorial art. At six he drew a picture of the town pump with a prominent citizen passing it hastily. This effort was framed and hung in the drug-store window by the side of the ear of corn with an uneven number of rows. At twenty he left for New York with a flowing necktie and a capital tied up somewhat closer.

Delia Caruthers did things in six octaves so promisingly in a pinetree village in the South that her relatives chipped in enough in her chip hat for her to go "North" and "finish". They could not see her f—, but that is our story.

Joe and Delia met in an atelier where a number of art and music students had gathered to discuss chiaroscuro, Wagner, music, Rembrandt's works, pictures, Waldteufel, wall paper, Chopin and Oolong.

Joe and Delia became enamored one of the other, or each of the other, as you please, and in a short time were married —for (see above), when one loves one's Art no service seems too hard.

爱 的 奉 献

当你爱好你的艺术时,就觉得没有什么奉献是难以忍受的。

那是我们的前提。这篇故事将从它那里得出一个结论,同时证明那个前提的谬误。从逻辑学的观点来说,这固然是一件新鲜事,可是从讲故事的观点来说,这却是一件比中国的万里长城更为古老的艺术。

乔·拉腊比来自中西部栎树参天的平原,浑身散发着绘画艺术的天才。他还只六岁时就画了一幅镇上抽水机的风景画,抽水机旁还画了一个匆匆走过的、有声望的居民。这件作品被配上架子,挂在药房的橱窗里,挨着一只留有几排参差不齐的玉米粒的穗棒。他二十岁时背井离乡来到纽约,束着一条飘拂的领带,带着一个更为飘拂的荷包。

迪莉娅·卡拉瑟斯生长在南方一个松林葱茏的小村里,她把六音阶之类的玩意儿搞得那样出色,以至亲戚们替她凑了一笔为数不多的款子,让她去北方"深造"。他们没有看到她成——,那就是我们要讲的故事。

乔和迪莉娅在一个画室里相遇了,有许多研究美术和音乐的人经常在那儿聚会,讨论明暗对比,瓦格纳,音乐,伦勃朗,绘画,瓦尔特费尔,糊墙纸,肖邦,奥朗①。

乔和迪莉娅互相——或者彼此,随你高兴怎么说——一见倾心,短期内就结了婚——因为(参看上文)当你爱好你的艺术时,就觉得没有什么奉献是难以忍受的。

---

① 瓦格纳(1813—1883),德国作曲家;伦勃朗(1606—1669),荷兰画家;瓦尔特费尔(1837—1915),法国作曲家;肖邦(1810—1849),波兰作曲家、钢琴家;"奥朗"为中国乌龙茶的粤音。

Mr. and Mrs. Larrabee began housekeeping in a flat. It was a lonesome flat—something like the A sharp way down at the left-hand end of the keyboard. And they were happy; for they had their Art, and they had each other. And my advice to the rich young man would be— sell all thou hast, and give it to the poor—janitor for the privilege of living in a flat with your Art and your Delia.

Flat-dwellers shall indorse my dictum that theirs is the only true happiness. If a home is happy it cannot fit too close —let the dresser collapse and become a billiard table; let the mantel turn to a rowing machine, the escritoire to a spare bedchamber, the washstand to an upright piano; let the four walls come together, if they will, so you and your Delia are between. But if home be the other kind, let it be wide and long—enter you at the Golden Gate, hang your hat on Hatteras, your cape on Cape Horn and go out by the Labrador.

Joe was painting in the class of the great Magister— you know his fame. His fees are high; his lessons are light—his high-lights have brought him renown. Delia was studying under Rosenstock—you know his repute as a disturber of the piano keys.

They were mighty happy as long as their money lasted. So is every—but I will not he cynical. Their aims were very clear and defined. Joe was to become capable very soon of turning out pictures that old gentlemen with thin sidewhiskers and thick pocketbooks would sandbag one another in his studio for the privilege of buying. Delia was to become familiar and then contemptuous with Music, so that when she saw the orchestra seats and boxes unsold she could have sore throat and lobster in a private dining-room and refuse to go on the stage.

　　拉腊比夫妇租了一套公寓,开始组织家庭。那是一个岑寂的地方——凄怆得像是钢琴键盘左端的升 A 调。可是他们很幸福;因为他们有了各自的艺术,又有了对方。我对有钱的年轻人的劝告是:为了争取同你的艺术以及你的迪莉娅住在公寓里的权利,赶快把你所有的东西都变卖掉,施舍给穷苦的看门人吧。

　　公寓生活是唯一真正的快乐,住公寓的人一定都赞成我的论断。家庭只要幸福,房间小又何妨——让梳妆台翻倒作为弹子桌;把火炉架改做练习划船用的器材;让写字桌充当备用的卧室;洗脸架充当竖式钢琴;如果可能,让四堵墙壁挤拢,你同你的迪莉娅仍旧在里面。可是倘若家庭不幸福,随它怎么宽敞——你从金门进去,把帽子挂在哈特勒斯,把披肩挂在合恩角,然后穿过拉布拉多出去①,到头来仍旧枉然。

　　乔在伟大的马吉斯特那儿学画——各位都知道他的声望。他取费高昂,课程轻松——他的昂贵轻松给他带来了声望。迪莉娅在罗森斯托克那儿学习,各位也知道他是一位出名的专跟钢琴键盘找麻烦的家伙。

　　只要他们的钱没用完,他们的生活是非常美满的。谁都是这样——算了吧,我不愿意说愤世嫉俗的话。他们的目标非常清晰明确。乔很快就能有佳作问世,那些鬓须稀疏而钱袋厚实的老先生就会争先恐后地挤到他的画室里来抢购他的作品。迪莉娅要同音乐搞熟,然后对它满不在乎;如果看到剧院正厅的位置和包厢不满座,她就推托喉咙痛,拒绝登台,在专用的餐室里吃龙虾。

---

　　① 金门是美国旧金山湾口的海峡;哈特勒斯是北卡罗来纳州海岸的海峡,与英文中"帽架"谐音;合恩角是南美智利的海峡,与"衣架"谐音;拉布拉多是赫德森湾与大西洋间的半岛,与"边门"谐音。

But the best, in my opinion, was the home life in the little flat—the ardent, voluble chats after the day's study; the cozy dinners and fresh, light breakfasts; the interchange of ambitions—ambitions interwoven each with the other's or else inconsiderable—the mutual help and inspiration; and—overlook my artlessness—stuffed olives and cheese sandwiches at 11 P. M.

But after a while Art flagged. It sometimes does, even if some switchman doesn't flag it. Everything going out and nothing coming in, as the vulgarians say. Money was lacking to pay Mr. Magister and Herr Rosenstock their prices. When one loves one's Art no service seems too hard. So, Delia said she must give music lessons to keep the chafing dish bubbling.

For two or three days she went out canvassing for pupils. One evening she came home elated.

"Joe, dear," she said, gleefully, "I've a pupil. And, oh, the loveliest people. General—General A. B. Pinkney's daughter—on Seventy-first street. Such a splendid house, Joe—you ought to see the front door! Byzantine I think you would call it. And inside! Oh, Joe, I never saw anything like it before.

"My pupil is his daughter Clementina. I dearly love her already. She's a delicate thing—dresses always in white; and the sweetest, simplest manners! Only eighteen years old. I'm to give three lessons a week; and, just think, Joe! $ 5 a lesson. I don't mind it a bit; for when I get two or three more pupils I can resume my lessons with Herr Rosenstock. Now, smooth out that wrinkle between your brows, dear, and let's have a nice supper."

"That's all right for you, Dele," said Joe, attacking a can of peas with a carving knife and a hatchet, "but how

　　但是依我说,最美满的还是那小公寓里的家庭生活:学习了一天之后的情话絮语;舒适的晚饭和新鲜清淡的早餐;关于志向的交谈——他们不但关心自己的,而且也关心对方的志向,否则就没有意义了——互助和灵感;还有——晚上十一点钟吃的菜裹肉片和奶酪三明治。

　　可是没多久,艺术就动摇了。即使没有人去碰它,有时它自己也会动摇的。俗话说得好,坐吃山空;应该付给马吉斯特和罗森斯托克两位先生的学费也没有着落了。当你爱好你的艺术时,就觉得没有什么奉献是难以忍受的。于是,迪莉娅说,她得教授音乐,以免断炊。

　　她在外面奔走了两三天,兜揽学生。一天晚上,她兴高采烈地回来了。

　　“乔,亲爱的,”她快活地说,“我有一个学生啦。哟,那家人真好。一位将军——艾·比·平克尼将军的小姐,住在第七十一号街。多么漂亮的房子,乔——你该看看那扇大门!我想就是你所说的那种拜占庭式①。还有屋子里面! 喔,乔,我从没见过那样豪华的装修。

　　“我的学生是他的女儿克莱门蒂娜。我见了她就欢喜极啦。她是个柔弱的小东西——老是穿白衣服;态度又那么朴实可爱! 她只有十八岁。我一星期教三次课;你想想看,乔! 每课五块钱。数目固然不大,可是我一点也不在乎。等我再找到两三个学生,我又可以到罗森斯托克先生那儿去学习了。现在,别皱眉头啦,亲爱的,让我们美美地吃一顿晚饭吧。”

　　“你倒不错,迪莉,”乔一面说,一面在用斧子和切肉刀

———————

　　① 拜占庭式:6世纪至15世纪间,在东罗马帝国风行的建筑式样,特点是圆屋顶,拱形门,细工镶嵌。

about me? Do you think I'm going to let you hustle for wages while I philander in the regions of high art? Not by the bones of Benvenuto Cellini! I guess I can sell papers or lay cobblestones, and bring in a dollar or two."

Delia came and hung about his neck.

"Joe, dear, you are silly. You must keep on at your studies. It is not as if I had quit my music and gone to work at something else. While I teach I learn. I am always with my music. And we can live as happily as millionaires on $15 a week. You mustn't think of leaving Mr. Magister."

"All right," said Joe, reaching for the blue scalloped vegetable dish. "But I hate for you to be giving lessons. It isn't Art. But you're a trump and a dear to do it."

"When one loves one's Art no service seems too hard," said Delia.

"Magister praised the sky in that sketch I made in the park," said Joe. "And Tinkle gave me permission to hang two of them in his window. I may sell one if the right kind of a moneyed idiot sees them."

"I'm sure you will," said Delia, sweetly. "And now let's be thankful for Gen. Pinkney and this veal roast."

During all of the next week the Larrabees had an early breakfast. Joe was enthusiastic about some morning-effect sketches he was doing in Central Park, and Delia packed him off breakfasted, coddled, praised and kissed at 7 o'clock. Art is an engaging mistress. It was most times 7 o'clock when he returned in the evening.

At the end of the week Delia, sweetly proud but languid, triumphantly tossed three five-dollar bills on the 8 ×10 (inches) centre table of the 8×10 (feet) flat parlor.

凿一个青豆罐头,"可是我该怎么办呢?你认为我能让你忙着挣钱,而我自己却在艺术的领域里追逐吗?我以本范努托·切利尼①的骨头赌咒,绝对不能!我想我能卖卖报纸,搬石子铺马路,多少也挣一两块钱回来。"

迪莉娅走过来,勾住他的脖子。

"乔,亲爱的,你真傻。你一定要坚持学习。我并不是抛弃了音乐去干别的事情。我一面教别人,自己一面也能学一些。我永远跟我的音乐在一起。何况我们一星期有十五块钱,可以过得像百万富翁那般快乐。你千万不要打算脱离马吉斯特先生。"

"好吧。"乔说,一面去拿那个贝壳形的蓝色菜碟子。"可我不愿意让你去教课。那不是艺术。你做出这样的奉献真了不起,真叫人钦佩。"

"当你爱好你的艺术时,就觉得没有什么奉献是难以忍受的。"迪莉娅说。

"我在公园里画的那幅素描,马吉斯特说上面的天空很好。"乔说。"廷克尔答应我在他的橱窗里挂上两幅。如果碰上一个合适的有钱的傻瓜,可能卖掉一幅。"

"我相信一定能卖掉。"迪莉娅亲切地说。"现在让我们先来感谢平克尼将军和这烤牛肉吧。"

下一个星期,拉腊比夫妇每天早餐都吃得很早。乔兴致勃勃地要到中央公园去在晨光下画几张速写。七点钟,迪莉娅在给了他早饭、拥抱、赞美和接吻之后,把他送出了门。艺术是个迷人的情妇。他回家时,多半已是晚上七点钟了。

周末,愉快自豪,但又疲惫不堪的迪莉娅得意洋洋地掏出三张五元的钞票,扔在那八英尺阔十英尺长的公寓客厅里的八英寸阔十英寸长的桌子上。

---

① 本范努托·切利尼(1500—1571):意大利著名雕刻家。

"Sometimes,"she said, a little wearily, "Clementina tries me. I'm afraid she doesn't practise enough, and I have to tell her the same things so often. And then she always dresses entirely in white, and that does get monotonous. But Gen. Pinkney is the dearest old man! I wish you could know him, Joe. He comes in sometimes when I am with Clementina at the piano—he is a widower, you know—and stands there pulling his white goatee. 'And how are the semiquavers and the demisemiquavers progressing?' he always asks.

"I wish you could see the wainscoting in that drawing room, Joe! And those Astrakhan rug portières. And Clementina has such a funny little cough. I hope she is stronger than she looks. Oh, I really am getting attached to her, she is so gentle and high bred. Gen. Pinkney's brother was once Minister to Bolivia."

And then Joe, with the air of Monte Cristo, drew forth a ten, a five, a two and a one—all legal tender notes—and laid them beside Delia's earnings.

"Sold that watercolor of the obelisk to a man from Peoria,"he announced, overwhelmingly.

"Don't joke with me,"said Delia—"not from Peoria!"

"All the way. I wish you could see him, Dele. Fat man with a woolen muffler and a quill toothpick. He saw the sketch in Tinkle's window and thought it was a windmill at first. He was game, though, and bought it anyhow. He ordered another—an oil sketch of the Lackawanna freight depot—to take back with him. Music lessons! Oh, I guess Art is still in it."

"I'm so glad you've kept on,"said Delia, heartily.

"有时候，"她有些厌倦地说，"克莱门蒂娜真叫我费劲。我想她大概练习得不充分，我得反反复复地教她。而且她老是穿白的，也叫人觉得单调。不过平克尼将军倒是个顶可爱的老头儿！我希望你能认识他，乔。我和克莱门蒂娜练习钢琴的时候，他偶尔走进来——他是个鳏夫，你知道——站在那儿捋他的白胡子。'十六分音符和三十二分音符教得怎么样啦?'他老是这样问道。

"我希望你能看到客厅里的护壁镶板，乔！还有那些阿斯特拉罕的呢门帘。克莱门蒂娜老是有点儿咳嗽。我希望她的身体比她外表看来的要结实些。喔，我实在是越来越喜欢她了，她多么温柔，多么有教养。平克尼将军的弟弟当过驻波利维亚的公使。"

接着，乔带着基督山伯爵的神气，掏出一张十元，一张五元，一张两元和一张一元的钞票——全是合法的货币——把它们摆在迪莉娅挣来的钱旁边。

"那幅方尖碑的水彩画卖给了一个从皮奥里亚①来的人。"他郑重其事地宣布说。

"别跟我开玩笑啦，"迪莉娅说，"不会是皮奥里亚那么远来的吧！"

"确实是那儿来的。我希望你能见到他，迪莉。一个胖子，围着羊毛围巾，衔着一根翎管牙签。他在廷克尔的橱窗里看到了那幅画，起先还以为是座风车呢。他倒很气派，不管三七二十一就把它买下了。他另外还预定了一幅——拉卡瓦纳货运车站的油画——准备带回去。我的画，加上你的音乐课！啊，我想艺术还是有前途的。"

"你坚持了下来，真使我高兴。"迪莉娅热切地说。"你

---

① 皮奥里亚:美国伊利诺伊州中部的城市。

"You're bound to win, dear. Thirty-three dollars! We never had so much to spend before. We'll have oysters to-night."

"And filet mignon with champignons," said Joe. "Where is the olive fork?"

On the next Saturday evening Joe reached home first. He spread his $18 on the parlor table and washed what seemed to be a great deal of dark paint from his hands.

Half an hour later Delia arrived, her right hand tied up in a shapeless bundle of wraps and bandages.

"How is this?" asked Joe after the usual greetings. Delia laughed, but not very joyously.

"Clementina," she explained, "insisted upon a Welsh rabbit after her lesson. She is such a queer girl. Welsh rabbits at 5 in the afternoon. The General was there. You should have seen him run for the chafing dish, Joe, just as if there wasn't a servant in the house. I know Clementina isn't in good health; she is so nervous. In serving the rabbit she spilled a great lot of it, boiling hot, over my hand and wrist. It hurt awfully, Joe. And the dear girl was so sorry! But Gen. Pinkney! —Joe, that old man nearly went distracted. He rushed downstairs and sent somebody—they said the furnace man or somebody in the basement—out to a drug store for some oil and things to bind it up with. It doesn't hurt so much now."

"What's this?" asked Joe, taking the hand tenderly and pulling at some white strands beneath the bandages.

"It's something soft," said Delia, "that had oil on it. Oh, Joe, did you sell another sketch?" she had seen the money on the table.

"Did I?" said Joe; "just ask the man from Peoria. He

一定会成功的,亲爱的。三十三块钱! 我们从来没有过这么多可花的钱。今晚我们买牡蛎吃。"

"加上炸嫩牛排和香菌。"乔说。"肉叉在哪儿?"

下个星期六的晚上,乔先回家。他把他的十八块钱摊在客厅的桌子上,然后把手上许多像是黑色颜料的东西洗掉。

半个钟点之后,迪莉娅来了,她的右手用棉纱和绷带包成一团,简直不成样子。

"这是怎么搞的?"乔照例打了招呼后问道。迪莉娅笑了,可笑得并不十分快活。

"克莱门蒂娜,"她解释说,"上了课以后一定要吃奶酪面包。她真是个古怪的姑娘。下午五点钟还要吃奶酪面包。将军也在场。你该看看他奔去拿烘锅时的样子,乔,仿佛家里没有佣人似的。我知道克莱门蒂娜身体不好;神经过敏。她浇奶酪的时候泼翻了许多,滚烫的,溅在我的手腕上。痛得要命,乔。那可爱的姑娘难过极了! 还有平克尼将军! ——乔,那老头儿急得几乎要发疯。他冲下楼去叫人——他们说是烧锅炉的或是地下室里的什么人——到药房里去买些油和别的什么东西来替我包扎。现在倒不十分痛了。"

"这是什么?"乔轻轻地握住那只手,扯扯绷带下面的几根白线,问道。

"那是涂了油的软纱。"迪莉娅说。"喔,乔,你又卖掉了一幅素描吗?"她看到了桌上的钱。

"可不是吗?"乔说,"只消问问那个从皮奥里亚来的人。

got his depot to-day, and he isn't sure but he thinks he wants another parkscape and a view on the Hudson. What time this afternoon did you burn your hand, Dele?"

"Five o'clock, I think," said Dele, plaintively. "The iron —I mean the rabbit came off the fire about that time. You ought to have seen Gen. Pinkney, Joe, when—"

"Sit down here a moment, Dele," said Joe. He drew her to the couch, sat beside her and put his arm across her shoulders.

"What have you been doing for the last two weeks, Dele?" he asked.

She braved it for a moment or two with an eye full of love and stubbornness, and murmured a phrase or two vaguely of Gen. Pinkney; but at length down went her head and out came the truth and tears.

"I couldn't get any pupils," she confessed. "And I couldn't bear to have you give up your lessons; and I got a place ironing shirts in that big Twenty-fourth Street laundry. And I think I did very well to make up both General Pinkney and Clementina, don't you, Joe? And when a girl in the laundry set down a hot iron on my hand this afternoon I was all the way home making up that story about the Welsh rabbit. You're not angry, are you, Joe? And if I hadn't got the work you mightn't have sold your sketches to that man from Peoria."

"He wasn't from Peoria," said Joe, slowly.

"Well, it doesn't matter where he was from. How clever you are, Joe—and—kiss me, Joe—and what made you ever suspect that I wasn't giving music lessons to Clementina?"

"I didn't," said Joe, "until to-night. And I wouldn't have then, only I sent up this cotton waste and oil from

他今天把他订的车站图取去了；他没有说定，可能还要一幅公园的和一幅赫德森河的风景。你今天下午什么时候烫痛手的，迪莉？"

"大概在五点钟吧。"迪莉娅可怜巴巴地说。"熨斗——我是说奶酪，大概在那时候烧好。你真该看到平克尼将军的样子，乔，他——"

"先坐一会儿，迪莉。"乔说。他把她拉到卧榻上，自己在她身边坐下，用胳臂围住了她的肩膀。

"这两个星期以来，你到底在干些什么，迪莉？"他问道。

她带着充满爱情和固执的眼神熬了一两分钟，含含混混地说着平克尼将军；但终于垂下了头，一边哭，一边说出实话来了。

"我找不到学生。"她供认说。"我又不忍心眼看你抛弃你的课程，所以在第二十四号街那家大洗衣店里找了一个熨衬衣的活儿。我以为我把平克尼将军和克莱门蒂娜两个人编造得很好呢，可不是吗，乔？今天下午，洗衣店里一个姑娘的热熨斗烫了我的手，我一路上就编出了那个烘奶酪的故事。你不会生我的气吧，乔？如果我不去做工，你也许不能把你的画卖给那个皮奥里亚来的人。"

"他不是从皮奥里亚来的。"乔慢吞吞地说。

"打哪儿来的都一样。你真行，乔——吻我吧，乔——你怎么会怀疑我不在教克莱门蒂娜的音乐课呢？"

"在今晚以前，我始终没有起疑。"乔说。"今晚本来也不会起疑的，可是今天下午，我替楼上一个给熨斗烫坏手的

the engine-room this afternoon for a girl upstairs who had her hand burned with a smoothing-iron. I've been firing the engine in that laundry for the last two weeks."

"And then you didn't—"

"My purchaser from Peoria," said Joe, "and Gen. Pinkney are both creations of the same art—but you wouldn't call it either painting or music."

And then they both laughed, and Joe began:

"When one loves one's Art no service seems—"

But Delia stopped him with her hand on his lips. "No," she said—"Just 'When one loves'."

姑娘找了一些机器房的油和废纱头。两星期来,我就在那家洗衣店的锅炉房里烧火。"

"那你并没有——"

"我的皮奥里亚来的主顾,"乔说,"和平克尼将军都是同一艺术的产物——只是你不会把那门艺术叫做绘画或音乐罢了。"

他们两个都笑了。乔开口说:

"当你爱好你的艺术时,就觉得没有什么奉献是——"

可是迪莉娅用手掩住了他的嘴。"别说啦,"她说,"只消说'当你爱的时候'。"

The Cop and the Anthem

ON his bench in Madison Square Soapy moved uneasily. When wild geese honk high of nights, and when women without sealskin coats grow kind to their husbands, and when Soapy moves uneasily on his bench in the park, you may know that winter is near at hand.

A dead leaf fell in Soapy's lap. That was Jack Frost's card. Jack is kind to the regular denizens of Madison Square, and gives fair warning of his annual call. At the corners of four streets he hands his pasteboard to the North Wind, footman of the mansion of All Out-doors, so that the inhabitants thereof may make ready.

Soapy's mind became cognizant of the fact that the time had come for him to resolve himself into a singular Committee of Ways and Means to provide against the coming rigor. And therefore he moved uneasily on his bench.

The hibernatorial ambitions of Soapy were not of the highest. In them were no considerations of Mediterranean cruises, of soporific Southern skies or drifting in the Vesuvian Bay. Three months on the Island was what his soul craved. Three months of assured board and bed and congenial company, safe from Boreas and bluecoats, seemed to Soapy the essence of things desirable.

For years the hospitable Blackwell's had been his winter quarters. Just as his more fortunate fellow New Yorkers had bought their tickets to Palm Beach and the Riviera each winter, so Soapy had made his humble arrangements for his annual hegira to the Island. And now

警察和赞美诗

苏贝躺在麦迪逊广场的长凳上，辗转反侧。当夜晚雁群引吭高鸣，当没有海豹皮大衣的女人对她们的丈夫亲热起来，或者当苏贝躺在广场的长凳上辗转反侧的时候，你就知道冬季已经逼近了。

一片枯叶飘落在苏贝的膝头。那是杰克·弗罗斯特①的名片。杰克对麦迪逊广场的老房客倒是体贴入微的，每年要来之前，总是预先通知。他在十字街头把他的名片交给"北风"——"幕天席地别墅"的门房——这样露天的居民就可以有所准备。

苏贝理会到，为了应付即将来临的严冬，由他来组织一个单人筹备委员会的时候已经到来了。因此，他在长凳上转侧不安。

苏贝对于冬令蛰居方面并没有什么奢望。他根本没去想地中海的游弋，或南方催人欲眠的风光，更没有想到在维苏威海湾②的游泳。他心向神往的只是到岛上③去住上三个月。三个月不愁食宿，既能摆脱北风神和巡警的干扰，又有意气相投的朋友共处，在苏贝的心目中，再没有比这更美满的事了。

多年来，好客的布莱克韦尔监狱成了他的冬季寓所。正如那些比他幸运得多的纽约人每年冬天买了车票到棕榈滩和里维埃拉④去消寒一样，苏贝也为他一年一度去岛上

---

① 杰克·弗罗斯特为英文对"寒霜"的拟人称呼。
② 位于意大利那不勒斯东南的海湾，气候温和。
③ 指在纽约和布鲁克林之间海峡中的布莱克韦尔岛，上有监狱和疯人院等。
④ 棕榈滩和里维埃拉均系美国南部城市，气候温和。

the time was come. On the previous night three Sabbath newspapers, distributed beneath his coat, a bout his ankles and over his lap, had failed to repulse the cold as he slept on his bench near the spurting fountain in the ancient square. So the Island loomed big and timely in Soapy's mind. He scorned the provisions made in the name of charity for the city's dependents. In Soapy's opinion the Law was more benign than Philanthropy. There was an endless round of institutions, municipal and eleemosynary, on which he might set out and receive lodging and food accordant with the simple life. But to one of Soapy's proud spirit the gifts of charity are encumbered. If not in coin you must pay in humiliation of spirit for every benefit received at the hands of philanthropy. As Cæsar had his Brutus, every bed of charity must have its toll of a bath, every loaf of bread its compensation of a private and personal inquisition. Wherefore it is better to be a guest of the law, which, though conducted by rules, does not meddle unduly with a gentleman's private affairs.

Soapy, having decided to go to the Island, at once set about accomplishing his desire. There were many easy ways of doing this. The pleasantest was to dine luxuriously at some expensive restaurant; and then, after declaring insolvency, be handed over quietly and without uproar to a policeman. An accommodating magistrate would do the rest.

Soapy left his bench and strolled out of the square and across the level sea of asphalt, where Broadway and Fifth Avenue flow together. Up Broadway he turned, and halted at a glittering café, where are gathered together nightly the choicest products of the grape, the silkworm,

的避难做了最低限度的准备。现在是时候了。昨晚，他在那古老的广场里，睡在喷泉池旁边的长凳上，用了三份星期日的厚报纸，衬在衣服里，遮着脚踝和膝盖，还是抵挡不住寒冷的侵袭。因此，布莱克韦尔岛在苏贝心中及时地涌现出来。他瞧不起那些以慈悲为名替地方上寄食者准备的布施。在苏贝看来，法律比慈善更为仁慈。他可以去的场所多得是，有的是市政府办的，有的是慈善机关办的，在哪儿他都可以谋得食宿，满足简单的生活要求。可是对苏贝这种性格高傲的人来说，慈善的恩赐是行不通的。从慈善家手里得到一点好处，固然不要你破费，但却要你承担精神上的屈辱。凡事有利必有弊①，要睡慈善机关的床铺，就先得被迫洗个澡；要吃一块面包，你个人的私事也就得给打破沙锅问到底。因此，还是做做法律的客人来得痛快，法律虽然铁面无私，照章办事，毕竟不去过分干涉一位大爷的私事。

既然打定了去岛上的主意，苏贝立刻准备实现他的愿望。轻而易举的办法倒有不少。最愉快的莫如在一家豪华的饭店里大模大样地吃上一顿；然后声明自己不名一文，就可以安安静静，不吵不闹地给交到警察手里。其余的事，自有一个知趣的地方法官来安排。

苏贝离开长凳，踱出广场，穿过了百老汇路和五马路交叉处的一片平坦的柏油路面。他拐到百老汇路上，在一家灯火辉煌的饭馆前停下来，那里每晚汇集着上好的美酒，华丽的衣服和有地位的人物。

---

① 此处原文是"有了凯撒，就有他的布鲁特斯"。凯撒（公元前100—公元前44）：罗马皇帝，为其好友布鲁特斯（公元前84—公元前42）所暗杀。

and the protoplasm.

Soapy had confidence in himself from the lowest button of his vest upward. He was shaven, and his coat was decent and his neat black, ready-tied four-in-hand had been presented to him by a lady missionary on Thanksgiving Day. If he could reach a table in the restaurant unsuspected success would be his. The portion of him that would show above the table would raise no doubt in the waiter's mind. A roasted mallard duck, thought Soapy, would be about the thing—with a bottle of Chablis, and then Camembert, a demi-tasse and a cigar. One dollar for the cigar would be enough. The total would not be so high as to call forth any supreme manifestation of revenge from the café management; and yet the meat would leave him filled and happy for the journey to his winter refuge.

But as Soapy set foot inside the restaurant door the head waiter's eye fell upon his frayed trousers and decadent shoes. Strong and ready hands turned him about and conveyed him in silence and haste to the sidewalk and averted the ignoble fate of the menaced mallard.

Soapy turned off Broadway. It seemed that his route to the coveted Island was not to be an epicurean one. Some other way of entering limbo must be thought of.

At a corner of Sixth Avenue electric lights and cunningly displayed wares behind plate-glass made a shop window conspicuous. Soapy took a cobblestone and dashed it through the glass. People came running around the corner, a policeman in the lead. Soapy stood still, with his hands in his pockets, and smiled at the sight of brass buttons.

"Where's the man that done that?" inquired the of-

苏贝对自己上半身的打扮颇有信心。他刮过脸,上衣还算体面,感恩节时一位女教士送给他的那个有活扣的黑领结也挺干净。只要他能走到饭馆里桌子边上而不引起别人的疑心,一切就可以如愿以偿了。他暴露在桌面以上的部分不至于使侍者起疑。一只烤野鸭,苏贝想道,也就够意思了——再加一瓶夏布利酒,卡门贝乳酪①——一小杯咖啡和一支雪茄。雪茄要一块钱一支的就行了。账单上的总数不要大得会引起饭馆掌柜的狠心报复;同时野鸭肉却使他在去冬季避难所的路上能吃得饱饱的而又快乐。

可是,苏贝刚踏进饭馆门口,侍者领班的眼光就落到了他的旧裤子和破皮鞋上。粗壮而利索的手把他推了一个转身,沉默而迅速地被撵到人行道上,从而改变了那只险遭暗算的野鸭的不体面的命运。

苏贝离开了百老汇路。到那想望之岛去,要采取满足口腹之欲的路线看来是行不通了。要进监狱,还得另想办法。

六马路的拐角上有一家铺子,玻璃橱窗里陈设精致的商品和灿烂的灯光很引人注目。苏贝捡起一块大圆石,砸穿了那块玻璃。人们从拐角上跑来,为首的正是一个警察。苏贝站定不动,双手插在口袋里,看到警察的铜纽扣时不禁笑了。

"砸玻璃的人在哪儿?"警察气急败坏地问道。

---

① 夏布利是法国以生产白葡萄酒而著名的地区。卡门贝是法国奥尼尔省地名,那里制作一种松软的干酪,享有盛名。

ficer,excitedly.

"Don't you figure out that I might have had something to do with it?"said Soapy,not without sarcasm,but friendly,as one greets good fortune.

The policeman's mind refused to accept Soapy even as a clue. Men who smash windows do not remain to parley with the law's minions. They take to their heels. The policeman saw a man halfway down the block running to catch a car. With drawn club he joined in the pursuit. Soapy,with disgust in his heart,loafed along,twice unsuccessful.

On the opposite side of the street was a restaurant of no great pretensions. It catered to large appetites and modest purses. Its crockery and atmosphere were thick; its soup and napery thin. Into this place Soapy took his accusive shoes and telltale trousers without challenge. At a table he sat and consumed beefsteak,flapjacks,doughnuts and pie. And then to the waiter he betrayed the fact that the minutest coin and himself were strangers.

"Now,get busy and call a cop,"said Soapy. "And don't keep a gentleman waiting."

"No cop for youse,"said the waiter,with a voice like butter cakes and an eye like the cherry in a Manhattan cocktail. "Hey. Con!"

Neatly upon his left ear on the callous pavement two waiters pitched Soapy. He arose joint by joint, as a carpenter's rule opens, and beat the dust from his clothes. Arrest seemed but a rosy dream. The Island seemed very far away. A policeman who stood before a drug store two doors away laughed and walked down the street.

Five blocks Soapy travelled before his courage per-

"难道你看不出我可能跟这事有关吗?"苏贝说,口气虽然带些讥讽,态度却很和善,仿佛是一个交上好运的人似的。

警察心里根本没把苏贝当做嫌疑犯。砸橱窗的人总是拔腿就跑,不会傻站在那儿跟法律的走卒打交道的。警察看到半条街前面有一个人跑着去赶搭一辆街车。他抽出警棍,追了上去。苏贝大失所望,垂头丧气地走开了。两次都不顺利。

对街有一家不怎么堂皇的饭馆。它迎合胃口大而钱包小的吃客的口味。它的盘碟和气氛都很粗厚;它的汤和餐巾却很稀薄。苏贝跨进这家饭馆,他那罪孽深重的鞋子和暴露隐秘的裤子倒没有被人注意到。他挑了个位子坐下,吃了牛排、煎饼、炸面饼圈和馅饼。然后他向侍者透露真相,说他一个子儿都没有。

"现在快去找警察来,"苏贝说,"别让大爷久等。"

"对你这种人不用找警察。"侍者的声音像奶油蛋糕,眼睛像曼哈顿鸡尾酒①里的红樱桃。他只嚷了一声:"嗨,阿康!"

两个侍者干净利落地把苏贝架出门外,他左耳贴地摔在坚硬的人行道上。像打开一支木工曲尺似的,他一节一节地撑了起来,掸去衣服上的尘土。被捕似乎只是一个美妙的梦想。那个岛仿佛非常遥远。站在隔了两家店铺远的药房门口的警察,笑了一笑,走到街上去了。

苏贝走过了五个街口之后,才有勇气再去追求被逮捕。

---

① 用威士忌、苦艾酒调成的混合酒,一般加一点苦味酒和一颗野樱桃。

mitted him to woo capture again. This time the opportunity presented what he fatuously termed to himself a "cinch". A young woman of a modest and pleasing guise was standing before a show window gazing with sprightly interest at its display of shaving mugs and inkstands, and two yards from the window a large policeman of severe demeanor leaned against a water plug.

It was Soapy's design to assume the rôle of the despicable and execrated "masher". The refined and elegant appearance of his victim and the contiguity of the conscientious cop encouraged him to believe that he would soon feel the pleasant official clutch upon his arm that would insure his winter quarters on the right little, tight little isle.

Soapy straightened the lady missionary's ready-made tie, dragged his shrinking cuffs into the open, set his hat at a killing cant and sidled toward the young woman. He made eyes at her, was taken with sudden coughs and "hems", smiled, smirked and went brazenly through the impudent and contemptible litany of the "masher". With half an eye Soapy saw that the policeman was watching him fixedly. The young woman moved away a few steps, and again bestowed her absorbed attention upon the shaving mugs. Soapy followed, boldly stepping to her side, raised his hat and said:

"Ah there, Bedelia! Don't you want to come and play in my yard?"

The policeman was still looking. The persecuted young woman had but to beckon a finger and Soapy would be practically en route for his insular haven. Already he imagined he could feel the cozy warmth of the station-house. The young woman faced him and, stretch-

他天真地暗忖着，这次是十拿九稳，不会再有闪失的了。一个衣着朴实，风姿可人的少妇站在一家店铺的橱窗前，出神地瞅着刮胡子用的杯子和墨水缸。离橱窗两码远的地方，一个大个子警察神气十足地靠在消防水龙头上。

苏贝打算扮演一个下流惹厌、调情求爱的浪子。他的受害者外表娴静文雅，而忠于职守的警察又近在咫尺；他有理由相信，马上就能痛痛快快地给逮住，保证可以在岛上的小安乐窝里逍遥过冬。

苏贝把女教士送给他的活扣领结拉拉挺，又把皱缩在衣服里面的衬衫袖管拖出来，风流自赏地把帽子歪戴在额头，向那少妇身边挨过去。他对她挤眉弄眼，嘴里哼哼哈哈，嬉皮笑脸地摆出浪子色胆包天、叫人恶心的架势。苏贝从眼角里看到警察正牢牢地盯着他。少妇让开了一步，仍旧全神贯注地瞅着那些刮胡子用的杯子。苏贝跟上去，大胆地走近她身边，掀起帽子说：

"啊喂，美人儿！要不要跟我一起去逛逛？"

警察仍旧盯着。受到纠缠的少妇只消举手一招，苏贝就可以毫无疑问地被送到他的安身之岛去了。他在想象中已经感到了警察局的舒适温暖。少妇扭过头来望着他，伸

ing out a hand, caught Soapy's coat sleeve.

"Sure, Mike," she said, joyfully, "if you'll blow me to a pail of suds. I'd have spoke to you sooner, but the cop was watching."

With the young woman playing the clinging ivy to his oak Soapy walked past the policeman overcome with gloom. He seemed doomed to liberty.

At the next corner he shook off his companion and ran. He halted in the district where by night are found the lightest streets, hearts, vows and librettos. Women in furs and men in greatcoats moved gaily in the wintry air. A sudden fear seized Soapy that some dreadful enchantment had rendered him immune to arrest. The thought brought a little of panic upon it, and when he came upon another policeman lounging grandly in front of a transplendent theatre he caught at the immediate straw of "disorderly conduct".

On the sidewalk Soapy began to yell drunken gibberish at the top of his harsh voice. He danced, howled, raved, and otherwise disturbed the welkin.

The policeman twirled his club, turned his back to Soapy and remarked to a citizen.

"'Tis one of them Yale lads celebratin' the goose egg they give to the Hartford College. Noisy; but no harm. We've instructions to lave them be."

Disconsolate, Soapy ceased his unavailing rachet. Would never a policeman lay hands on him? In his fancy the Island seemed an unattainable Arcadia. He buttoned his thin coat against the chilling wind.

In a cigar store he saw a well-dressed man lighting a cigar at a swinging light. His silk umbrella he had set by the door on entering. Soapy stepped inside, secured the

出手，抓住了苏贝的衣袖。

"当然啦，朋友，"她高兴地说，"只要你肯请我喝啤酒。不是警察望着的话，我早就招呼你了。"

少妇像常春藤攀住橡树般地偎依在苏贝身旁。苏贝心情阴郁，走过警察身边。他似乎注定是自由的。

一拐弯，他甩掉了同伴，撒腿就跑。他一口气跑到一个地方，那儿晚上有最明亮的街道，最愉快的心情，最轻率的盟誓和最轻松的歌声。披裘皮的女人和穿厚大衣的男人兴高采烈地冒着寒气走动。苏贝突然感到一阵恐惧，是不是一种可怕的魔力使他永远不会遭到逮捕了呢？这个念头带来了一些惊惶。当他看见另一个警察神气活现地在一家灯火辉煌的戏院门前巡逻时，他忽然想起了那个穷极无聊的办法——扰乱治安。

在人行道上，苏贝开始憋足劲尖声叫喊一些乱七八糟的醉话。他手舞足蹈，吆喝胡闹，想尽办法搅得天翻地覆。

警察挥旋着警棍，掉过身去，背对着苏贝，向一个市民解释说：

"那是耶鲁大学的学生，他在庆祝他们在赛球时给哈特福德学院吃了一个鸭蛋。虽然闹得凶，可是不碍事。我们接到指示，不必干涉。"

苏贝怏怏地停止了他那白费气力的嚷嚷。警察永远不来碰他了吗？在他的想象中，那个岛简直像是可望而不可即的世外桃源①了。他扣好单薄的上衣来抵挡刺骨的寒风。

在一家雪茄烟铺里，他看到一个衣冠楚楚的人正在摇曳的火上点雪茄。那人进去时将一把绸伞倚在门口。苏贝

---

① 此处原文为阿卡狄亚，是古希腊一个人情淳朴、风光明媚的理想乡。

umbrella and sauntered off with it slowly. The man at the cigar light followed hastily.

"My umbrella,"he said,sternly.

"Oh,is it?"sneered Soapy,adding insult to petit larceny. "Well,why don't you call a policeman? I took it. Your umbrella! Why don't you call a cop? There stands one on the corner."

The umbrella owner slowed his steps. Soapy did likewise, with a presentiment that luck would again run against him. The policeman looked at the two curiously.

"Of course,"said the umbrella man—"that is—well, you know how these mistakes occur—I—if it's your umbrella I hope you'll excuse me—I picked it up this morning in a restaurant—If you recognize it as yours,why —I hope you'll—"

"Of course it's mine,"said Soapy,viciously.

The ex-umbrella man retreated. The policeman hurried to assist a tall blonde in an opera cloak across the street in front of a street car that was approaching two blocks away.

Soapy walked eastward through a street damaged by improvements. He hurled the umbrella wrathfully into an excavation. He muttered against the men who wear helmets and carry clubs. Because he wanted to fall into their clutches,they seemed to regard him as a king who could do no wrong.

At length Soapy reached one of the avenues to the east where the glitter and turmoil was but faint. He set his face down this toward Madison Square,for the homing instinct survives even when the home is a park bench.

But on an unusually quiet corner Soapy came to a

跨进门,拿起伞,不慌不忙地扬长而去。点烟的人赶忙追出来。

"那是我的伞。"他厉声说。

"呵,是吗?"苏贝冷笑着说,在小偷的罪名上又加上侮辱。"那么,你干吗不叫警察呢?不错,是我拿的。你的伞!你干吗不叫警察?拐角上就有一个。"

伞主人放慢了脚步。苏贝也走慢了,预感到命运会再度跟他作对。拐角上的警察好奇地望着他们俩。

"当然,"伞主人说,"说起来——嗯,你知道这一类误会是怎么发生的——我——如果这把伞是你的,请你别见怪——我是今天早晨在一家饭馆里捡到的——如果你认出是你的,那么——请你——"

"当然是我的。"苏贝恶狠狠地说。

伞的前任主人退了下去。警察赶过去搀扶一个穿晚礼服的高身材的金发女郎,陪她穿过街道,以免一辆还在两个街口以外的车子碰上她。

苏贝往东走过一条因为修路而翻掘开来的街道。他愤愤地把伞扔进一个坑里。他咒骂那些头戴铜盔、手持警棍的人。他一心指望他们来逮捕他,他们却把他当做一贯正确的帝王。

最后,苏贝走到一条通向东区的路上,那里灯光黯淡,嘈杂声也低一些。他的方向是麦迪逊广场,因为他不知不觉地还是想回家,尽管这个家只是广场里的一条长凳。

但是当苏贝走到一个异常幽静的路角上时,他停了下

standstill. Here was an old church, quaint and rambling and gabled. Through one violet-stained window a soft light glowed, where, no doubt, the organist loitered over the keys, making sure of his mastery of the coming Sabbath anthem. For there drifted out to Soapy's ears sweet music that caught and held him transfixed against the convolutions of the iron fence.

The moon was above, lustrous and serene; vehicles and pedestrians were few; sparrows twittered sleepily in the eaves—for a little while the scene might have been a country churchyard. And the anthem that the organist played cemented Soapy to the iron fence, for he had known it well in the days when his life contained such things as mothers and roses and ambitions and friends and immaculate thoughts and collars.

The conjunction of Soapy's receptive state of mind and the influences about the old church wrought a sudden and wonderful change in his soul. He viewed with swift horror the pit into which he had tumbled, the degraded days, unworthy desires, dead hopes, wrecked faculties and base motives that made up his existence.

And also in a moment his heart responded thrillingly to this novel mood. An instantaneous and strong impulse moved him to battle with his desperate fate. He would pull himself out of the mire; he would make a man of himself again; he would conquer the evil that had taken possession of him. There was time; he was comparatively young yet; he would resurrect his old eager ambitions and pursue them without faltering. Those solemn but sweet organ notes had set up a revolution in him. To-morrow he would go into the roaring downtown district and find work. A fur importer had once offered him a place as

来。这儿有一座不很整齐的、砌着三角墙的、古色古香的老教堂。一丝柔和的灯火从紫罗兰色的玻璃窗里透露出来。无疑，里面的风琴师为了给星期日唱赞美诗伴奏正在反复练习。悠扬的乐声飘进了苏贝的耳朵，使他倚着螺旋形的铁栏杆而心醉神迷。

天上的月亮皎洁肃穆；车辆和行人都很稀少；冻雀在屋檐下睡迷迷地啁啾——这种境界使人不禁想起了乡村教堂的墓地。风琴师弹奏的赞美诗音乐把苏贝胶在了铁栏杆上，因为当他的生活中还有母爱、玫瑰、雄心、朋友、纯洁的思想和体面的衣着这类事物的时候，赞美诗的曲调对他曾是很熟悉的。

苏贝这时敏感的心情和老教堂环境的影响，使他在灵魂中突然起了奇妙的变化。他突然憎恶起他所坠入的深渊，堕落的生活，卑鄙的欲望，破灭了的希望，受到损害的才智和支持他生存的低下的动机。

一刹那间，他内心对这种新的感受起了深切的反应。一股迅疾而强有力的冲动促使他要向坎坷的命运奋斗。他要把自己拔出泥淖；他要重新做人；他要征服那已经控制了他的邪恶。时候还不晚；他算来还年轻；他要唤起当年那热切的志向，不含糊地去努力追求。庄严而亲切的风琴乐调使他内心有了转变。明天他要到热闹的市区去找工作做。

49

driver. He would find him to-morrow and ask for the position. He would be somebody in the world. He would—

Soapy felt a hand laid on his arm. He looked quickly around into the broad face of a policeman.

"What are you doin' here?"asked the officer.

"Nothin',"said Soapy.

"Then come along,"said the policeman.

"Three months on the Island,"said the Magistrate in the Police Court the next morning.

有个皮货进口商曾经叫他去当赶车的。明天他要去找那个商人,申请那个职务。他要做一个顶天立地的男子汉。他要——

苏贝觉得有一只手按在了他的胳臂上。他霍地扭过头去,看到了一个警察的阔脸。

"你在这儿干什么?"警察责问道。

"没干什么。"苏贝回答说。

"那么跟我来。"警察说。

第二天早晨,警庭的法官宣判说:"在布莱克韦尔岛上监禁三个月。"

An Unfinished Story

WE no longer groan and heap ashes upon our heads when the flames of Tophet are mentioned. For, even the preachers have begun to tell us that God is radium, or e- ther or some scientific compound, and that the worst we wicked ones may expect is a chemical reaction. This is a pleasing hypothesis; but there lingers yet some of the old, goodly terror of orthodoxy.

There are but two subjects upon which one may dis- course with a free imagination, and without the possibili- ty of being controverted. You may talk of your dreams; and you may tell what you heard a parrot say. Both Mor- pheus and the bird are incompetent witnesses; and your listener dare not attack your recital. The baseless fabric of a vision, then, shall furnish my theme—chosen with a- pologies and regrets instead of the more limited field of pretty Polly's small talk.

I had a dream that was so far removed from the higher criticism that it had to do with the ancient, re- spectable, and lamented bar-of-judgment theory.

Gabriel had played his trump; and those of us who could not follow suit were arraigned for examination. I noticed at one side a gathering of professional bondsmen in solemn black and collars that buttoned behind; but it seemed there was some trouble about their real estate ti- tles; and they did not appear to be getting any of us out.

A fly cop—an angel policeman—flew over to me

没有完的故事

　　如今人们提到地狱的火焰时,我们不再唉声叹气,把灰涂在自己头上了①。因为连传教的牧师也开始告诉我们说,上帝是镭锭,或者以太,或是某种科学的化合物;因此我们这伙坏人可能遭到的最恶的报应,无非只是个化学反应。这倒是一个可喜的假设;但是正教所启示的古老而巨大的恐怖,还有一部分依然存在。

　　你能海阔天空地信口开河,而不至于遭到驳斥的,只有两种话题。你可以叙说你梦见的东西;还可以谈谈从鹦哥那儿听来的话。摩耳甫斯②和鹦哥都不够证人资格,别人听到了你的高谈阔论也不敢指摘。我不在美丽的鹦哥的絮语中寻找素材,而挑了一个毫无根据的梦象作为主题,因为鹦哥说话的范围比较狭窄;那是我深感抱歉和遗憾的。

　　我做了一个梦,这个梦同《圣经》考证绝无关系,它只牵涉到那个历史悠久,值得敬畏,令人悲叹的末日审判问题。

　　加百列摊出了他的王牌;我们之中无法跟进的人只得被提去受审③。我看到一边是些穿着庄严的黑袍,反扣着硬领的职业保人④,但是他们自己的职权似乎出了一些问题,所以他们不像是保得了我们中间任何一个人的样子。

　　一个包探——也就是充当警察的天使——向我飞过

---

　　①　犹太风俗,悲切忏悔时,身穿麻衣,须发涂灰。
　　②　罗马神话中的梦神,为睡神之子。
　　③　加百列是希伯来神话中最高级的天使之一,上帝的主要传达吏,据说末日审判时的号角将由他吹响。原文中"王牌"与"号角"相同,原意是"天堂门开,天使吹响了他的号角"。
　　④　指教会的神职人员。

and took me by the left wing. Near at hand was a group of very prosperous-looking spirits arraigned for judgment.

"Do you belong with that bunch?" the policeman asked.

"Who are they?" was my answer.

"Why," said he, "they are—"

But this irrelevant stuff is taking up space that the story should occupy.

Dulcie worked in a department store. She sold Hamburg edging, or stuffed peppers, or automobiles, or other little trinkets such as they keep in department stores. Of what she earned, Dulcie received six dollars per week. The remainder was credited to her and debited to somebody else's account in the ledger kept by G—Oh, primal energy, you say, Reverend Doctor—Well, then, in the Ledger of Primal Energy.

During her first year in the store, Dulcie was paid five dollars per week. It would be instructive to know how she lived on that amount. Don't care? Very well; probably you are interested in larger amounts. Six dollars is a larger amount. I will tell you how she lived on six dollars per week.

One afternoon at six, when Dulcie was sticking her hat pin within an eighth of an inch of her *medulla oblongata*, she said to her chum, Sadie—the girl that waits on you with her left side:

"Say, Sade, I made a date for dinner this evening with Piggy."

"You never did!" exclaimed Sadie, admiringly. "Well, ain't you the lucky one? Piggy's an awful swell; and he always takes a girl to swell places. He took

来，挟了我的左臂就走。附近候审的是一群看上去境况极好的鬼灵。

"你是那一拨人里面的吗?"警察问道。

"他们是谁呀?"我反问说。

"嘿，"他说，"他们是——"

这些题外的闲话已经占去了正文应有的篇幅，我暂且先不谈它了。

达尔西在一家百货公司工作。她经售的可能是汉堡的花边，或是呢绒，或是汽车，或是百货公司常备的小饰物之类的商品。达尔西在她所创造的财富中，每星期只领到六块钱。其余的在上帝经管的总账上——哦，牧师先生，你说那叫"原始能量"吗？好吧，就算"原始能量总账"吧——记在某一个人名下的贷方，达尔西名下的借方。

达尔西进公司后的第一年，每星期只有五块钱工资。要研究她怎样靠那个数目来维持生活，倒是一件给人以启发的事。你不感兴趣吗？好吧，也许你对大一些的数目才感兴趣。六块钱是个较大的数目。我来告诉你，她怎样用六块钱来维持一星期的生活吧。

一天下午六点钟，达尔西在距离延髓八分之一英寸的地方插帽针时，对她的好友——老是侧着左身接待主顾的姑娘——萨迪说:

"喂，萨迪，今晚我跟皮吉约好了去吃饭。"

"真的吗!"萨迪羡慕地嚷道。"哼，你真运气。皮吉是个大阔佬;他总是带着姑娘上阔气的地方去。有一晚，他带

Blanche up to the Hoffman House one evening, where they have swell music, and you see a lot of swells. You'll have a swell time, Dulcie."

Dulcie hurried homeward. Her eyes were shining, and her cheeks showed the delicate pink of life's—real life's—approaching dawn. It was Friday; and she had fifty cents left of her last week's wages.

The streets were filled with the rush-hour floods of people. The electric lights of Broadway were glowing—calling moths from miles, from leagues, from hundreds of leagues out of darkness around to come in and attend the singeing school. Men in accurate clothes, with faces like those carved on cherry stones by the old salts in sailors' homes, turned and stared at Dulcie as she sped, unheeding, past them. Manhattan, the night-blooming cereus, was beginning to unfold its dead-white, heavy-odored petals.

Dulcie stopped in a store where goods were cheap and bought an imitation lace collar with her fifty cents. That money was to have been spent otherwise—fifteen cents for supper, ten cents for breakfast, ten cents for lunch. Another dime was to be added to her small store of savings; and five cents was to be squandered for licorice drops—the kind that made your cheek look like the toothache, and last as long. The licorice was an extravagance—almost a carouse—but what is life without pleasures?

Dulcie lived in a furnished room. There is this difference between a furnished room and a boarding-house. In a furnished room, other people do not know it when you go hungry.

Dulcie went up to her room—the third-floor-back in

了布兰奇上霍夫曼大饭店,那儿的音乐真棒,还可以看到许多阔佬。你准会玩得痛快的,达尔西。"

达尔西急急忙忙地赶回家去。她的眼睛闪闪发亮,她的脸颊泛出了生命的娇红——真正的生命的曙光。那天是星期五;她上星期的工资还剩下五毛钱。

街道上挤满了潮水般下班回家的人们。百老汇路的电灯光亮夺目,招致几英里、几里格①、甚至几百里格以外的飞蛾从黑暗中扑来,参加焦头烂额的锻炼。衣冠楚楚、面目模糊不清、像是海员养老院里的老水手在樱桃核上刻出来的男人们,扭过头来凝视着一意奔跑、打他们身边经过的达尔西。曼哈顿,这朵晚上开放的仙人掌花,开始展舒它那颜色死白、气味浓烈的花瓣了。

达尔西在一家卖便宜货的商店里停了一下,用她的五毛钱买了一条仿花边的纸衣领。那笔款子本来另有用途——晚饭一毛五,早饭一毛,中饭一毛。另外一毛是准备加进她那寒酸的储蓄里的;五分钱准备浪费在甘草糖上——那种糖能使你的脸颊鼓得像牙痛似的,含化的时间也像牙痛那么长。吃甘草糖是一种奢侈——几乎是狂欢——可是没有乐趣的生活又算是什么呢?

达尔西住的是一间连家具出租的房间。这种房间同包伙食的寄宿舍是有区别的。住在这种屋子里,挨饿的时候别人是不会知道的。

达尔西上楼到她的房间里去——西区一座褐石房屋的

---

① 里格:长度名,约合 3 英里。

a West Side brownstone-front. She lit the gas. Scientists tell us that the diamond is the hardest substance known. Their mistake. Landladies know of a compound beside which the diamond is as putty. They pack it in the tips of gas-burners; and one may stand on a chair and dig at it in vain until one's fingers are pink and bruised. A hairpin will not remove it; therefore let us call it immovable.

So Dulcie lit the gas. In its one-fourth-candle-power glow we will observe the room.

Couch-bed, dresser, table, washstand, chair—of this much the landlady was guilty. The rest was Dulcie's. On the dresser were her treasures—a gilt china vase presented to her by Sadie, a calendar issued by a pickle works, a book on the divination of dreams, some rice powder in a glass dish, and a cluster of artificial cherries tied with a pink ribbon.

Against the wrinkly mirror stood pictures of General Kitchener, William Muldoon, the Duchess of Marlborough, and Benvenuto Cellini. Against one wall was a plaster of Paris plaque of an O'Callahan in a Roman helmet. Near it was a violent oleograph of a lemon-colored child assaulting an inflammatory butterfly. This was Dulcie's final judgment in art; but it had never been upset. Her rest had never been disturbed by whispers of stolen copes; no critic had elevated his eyebrows at her infantile entomologist.

Piggy was to call for her at seven. While she swiftly makes ready, let us discreetly face the other way and gossip.

三楼后房。她点上煤气灯。科学家告诉我们,金刚石是世界上最坚硬的物质。他们错了。房东太太掌握了一种化合物,同它一比,连金刚石都软得像油灰了。她们把这种东西塞在煤气灯灯头上,任你站在椅子上挖得手指发红起泡,仍旧白搭。发针不能动它分毫,所以我们姑且管它叫做"牢不可移的"吧。

达尔西点燃了煤气灯。在那相当于四分之一支烛光的灯光下,我们来看看这个房间。

榻床,梳妆台,桌子,洗脸架,椅子——造孽的房东太太所提供的全在这儿了。其余是达尔西自己的。她的宝贝摆在梳妆台上:萨迪送给她的一个描金瓷瓶,腌菜作坊送的一组日历,一本详梦的书,一些盛在玻璃碟子里的扑粉,以及一束扎着粉红色缎带的假樱桃。

那面起皱的镜子前靠着基钦纳将军、威廉·马尔登、马尔伯勒公爵夫人①和本范努托·切利尼的相片。一面墙上挂着一个戴罗马式头盔的爱尔兰人的石膏像饰板,旁边有一幅色彩强烈的石印油画,画的是一个淡黄色的孩子在捉弄一只火红色的蝴蝶。达尔西认为那是登峰造极的艺术作品;也没有人对此提出过反对意见。从没有人私下议论这幅画的真赝而使她心中不安,也从没有批评家来奚落她的幼年昆虫学家。

皮吉说好七点钟来邀她。她正在迅速地打扮准备,我们不要冒昧,且掉过脸去,随便聊聊。

———————————

① 基钦纳将军(1850—1916)为第一次世界大战中英国的名将,曾任陆军元帅和陆军大臣。马尔伯勒公爵夫人:马尔伯勒系英国世袭公爵的称号,第一任约翰·丘吉尔(1650—1722)为第二次世界大战期间英国首相温斯顿·丘吉尔的祖先。

For the room, Dulcie paid two dollars per week. On weekdays her breakfast cost ten cents; she made coffee and cooked an egg over the gaslight while she was dressing. On Sunday mornings she feasted royally on veal chops and pineapple fritters at "Billy's" restaurant, at a cost of twenty-five cents —and tipped the waitress ten cents. New York presents so many temptations for one to run into extravagance. She had her lunches in the department-store restaurant at a cost of sixty cents for the week; dinners were $1.05. The evening papers—show me a New Yorker going without his daily paper! —came to six cents; and two Sunday papers—one for the personal column and the other to read—were ten cents. The total amounts to $4.76. Now, one has to buy clothes, and—

I give it up. I hear of wonderful bargains in fabrics, and of miracles performed with needle and thread; but I am in doubt. I hold my pen poised in vain when I would add to Dulcie's life some of those joys that belong to woman by virtue of all the unwritten, sacred, natural, inactive ordinances of the equity of heaven. Twice she had been to Coney Island and had ridden the hobby-horses. 'Tis a weary thing to count your pleasures by summers instead of by hours.

Piggy needs but a word. When the girls named him, an undeserving stigma was cast upon the noble family of swine. The words-of-three-letters lesson in the old blue spelling book begins with Piggy's biography. He was fat; he had the soul of a rat, the habits of a bat, and the magnanimity of a cat.... He wore expensive clothes; and was a connoisseur in starvation. He could look at a shop-girl and tell you to an hour how long it had been since she

达尔西这个房间的租金是每星期两块钱。平日,她早饭花一毛钱。她一面穿衣服,一面在煤气灯上煮咖啡,煎一只蛋。星期日早晨,她花上两毛五分钱在比利饭馆阔气地大吃小牛肉排和菠萝油煎饼——还给女侍者一毛钱的小账。纽约市有这么多的诱惑,很容易使人趋于奢华。她在百货公司的餐室里包了饭;每星期中饭是六毛钱,晚饭是一块零五分。那些晚报——你说有哪个纽约人不看报纸的!——要花六分钱;两份星期日的报纸——一份是买来看招聘广告栏的,另一份是预备细读的——要一毛钱。总数是四块七毛六分。然而,你总得添置些衣服,还有——

我没法算下去了。我常听说有便宜得惊人的衣料和针线做出来的奇迹;但是我始终表示怀疑。我很想在达尔西的生活里加上一些根据那神圣,自然,既无明文规定,又不生效的天理的法令而应该是属于女人的乐趣,可是我搁笔长叹,没法写了。她去过两次康奈岛,骑过轮转木马。一个人盼望乐趣要以年份而不是以钟点为期,也未免太乏味了。

形容皮吉只要一个词儿。姑娘们提到他时,高贵的猪族就蒙上了不应有的污名。在那本蓝封皮的老拼音读本中,用三个字母拼成生字的一课就是皮吉的外传。他长得肥胖,有着耗子的心灵,蝙蝠的习性和狸猫那爱戏弄捕获物的脾气①——他衣着华贵,是鉴别饥饿的专家。他只要朝一个女店员瞅上一眼,就能告诉你,她多久没有吃到比茶和

---

① "肥胖","耗子","蝙蝠","狸猫"在英语中都由三个字母组成。"皮吉"前三个字母意为"小猪"。

had eaten anything more nourishing than marshmallows and tea. He hung about the shopping districts, and prowled around in department stores with his invitations to dinner. Men who escort dogs upon the streets at the end of a string look down upon him. He is a type; I can dwell upon him no longer; my pen is not the kind intended for him; I am no carpenter.

At ten minutes to seven Dulcie was ready. She looked at herself in the wrinkly mirror. The reflection was satisfactory. The dark blue dress, fitting without a wrinkle, the hat with its jaunty black feather, the but-slightly-soiled gloves—all representing self-denial, even of food itself—were vastly becoming.

Dulcie forgot everything else for a moment except that she was beautiful, and that life was about to lift a corner of its mysterious veil for her to observe its wonders. No gentleman had ever asked her out before. Now she was going for a brief moment into the glitter and exalted show.

The girls said that Piggy was a "spender". There would be a grand dinner, and music, and splendidly dressed ladies to look at and things to eat that strangely twisted the girls' jaws when they tried to tell about them. No doubt she would be asked out again.

There was a blue pongee suit in a window that she knew—by saving twenty cents a week instead of ten in—let's see —Oh, it would run into years! But there was a second-hand store in Seventh Avenue where—

Somebody knocked at the door. Dulcie opened it. The landlady stood there with a spurious smile, sniffing for cooking by stolen gas.

"A gentleman's downstairs to see you," she said.

棉花糖更有营养的东西了,并且误差不会超出一小时。他老是在商业区徘徊,在百货公司里打转,相机邀请女店员们下馆子。连街上牵着绳子遛狗的人都瞧不起他。他是个典型;我不能再写他了;我的笔不是为他服务的;我不是木匠。

七点差十分时,达尔西准备停当了。她在那面起皱的镜子里照了一下。照出来的形象很称心。那套深蓝色的衣服非常合身,带着飘拂的黑羽毛的帽子,稍微有点脏的手套——这一切都代表苦苦地省吃俭用——都非常漂亮。

达尔西暂时忘了一切,只觉得自己是美丽的,生活就要把它神秘的帷幕揭开一角,让她欣赏它的神奇。以前从没有男人邀请她出去过。现在她居然就要投入那种绚烂夺目的高贵生活中去,在里面逗留片刻了。

姑娘们说,皮吉是舍得花钱的。一定会有一顿丰盛的大餐,音乐,还有服饰华丽的女人可以看,有姑娘们讲得下巴都要掉下来的好东西可以吃。无疑的,她下次还会被邀请出去。

在她所熟悉的一个橱窗里,有一件蓝色的柞蚕丝绸衣服——如果每星期的储蓄从一毛钱增加到两毛,在——让我们算算看——喔,得积上好几年呢!但是七马路有一家旧货商店,那儿——

有人敲门。达尔西把门打开。房东太太站在那儿,脸上堆着假笑,嗅嗅有没有偷用煤气烧食物的气味。

"楼下有一位先生要见你,"她说,"姓威金斯。"

"Name is Mr. Wiggins. "

By such epithet was Piggy known to unfortunate ones who had to take him seriously.

Dulcie turned to the dresser to get her handkerchief; and then she stopped still, and bit her underlip hard. While looking in her mirror she had seen fairyland and herself, a princess, just awakening from a long slumber. She had forgotten one that was watching her with sad, beautiful, stern eyes—the only one there was to approve or condemn what she did. Straight and slender and tall, with a look of sorrowful reproach on his handsome, melancholy face, General Kitchener fixed his wonderful eyes on her out of his gilt photograph frame on the dresser.

Dulcie turned like an automatic doll to the landlady.

"Tell him I can't go, "she said, dully. "Tell him I'm sick, or something. Tell him I'm not going out. "

After the door was closed and locked, Dulcie fell upon her bed, crushing her black tip, and cried for ten minutes. General Kitchener was her only friend. He was Dulcie's ideal of a gallant knight. He looked as if he might have a secret sorrow, and his wonderful moustache was a dream, and she was a little afraid of that stern yet tender look in his eyes. She used to have little fancies that he would call at the house sometime, and ask for her, with his sword clanking against his high boots. Once, when a boy was rattling a piece of chain against a lamp post she had opened the window and looked out. But there was no use. She knew that General Kitchener was away over in Japan, leading his army against the savage Turks; and he would never step out of his gilt frame for her. Yet one look from him had vanquished Piggy

　　对于那些把皮吉当做一回事的倒霉女人，皮吉总是用那个姓出面。

　　达尔西转向梳妆台去拿手帕；她突然停住了，使劲咬着下唇。先前她照镜子的时候，只看到仙境里的自己，仿佛刚从大梦中醒过来的公主。她忘了有一个人带着忧郁、美妙而严肃的眼神在瞅她——只有这个人关心她的行为，或是赞成，或是反对。他的身材颀长笔挺，他那英俊而忧郁的脸上带着伤心和谴责的神情，那是基钦纳将军从梳妆台上的描金镜框里在用他那奇妙的眼睛瞪着她。

　　达尔西像一个自动玩偶似地转过身来向着房东太太。

　　"对他说我不能去了。"她呆呆地说。"对他说我病了，或者随便找些理由。对他说我不出去了。"

　　等房门关上锁好之后，达尔西扑在床上，压坏了黑帽饰，哭了十分钟。基钦纳将军是她唯一的朋友。他是达尔西理想中的英武的男子汉。他好像怀有隐痛，他的胡髭美妙得难以形容，他眼睛里那严肃而温存的神色使她有些畏惧。她私下里常常幻想，但愿有一天他佩着碰在长靴上铿锵作响的宝剑，专程降临这所房屋来看她。有一次，一个小孩用一段铁链把灯柱擦得嘎嘎发响，她竟然打开窗子，伸出头去看看。可结果是大失所望。据她所知，基钦纳将军远在日本①，正率领大军同野蛮的土耳其人作战；他绝不会为了她从那描金镜框里踱出来的。可是那天晚上，基钦纳的

_____

　　①　基钦纳于1910年前后去澳大利亚及新西兰视察，先此，曾前往日本游历。

that night. Yes, or that night.

When her cry was over Dulcie got up and took off her best dress, and put on her old blue kimono. She wanted no dinner. She sang two verses of "Sammy". Then she became intensely interested in a little red speck on the side of her nose. And after that was attended to, she drew up a chair to the rickety table, and told her fortune with an old deck of cards.

"The horrid, impudent thing!" she said aloud. "And I never gave him a word or a look to make him think it!"

At nine o'clock Dulcie took a tin box of crackers and a little pot of raspberry jam out of her trunk and had a feast. She offered General Kitchener some jam on a cracker; but he only looked at her as the sphinx would have looked at a butterfly—if there are butterflies in the desert.

"Don't eat it if you don't want to," said Dulcie. "And don't put on so many airs and scold so with your eyes. I wonder if you'd be so superior and snippy if you had to live on six dollars a week."

It was not a good sign for Dulcie to be rude to General Kitchener. And then she turned Benvenuto Cellini face downward with a severe gesture. But that was not inexcusable; for she had always thought he was Henry VIII, and she did not approve of him.

At half-past nine Dulcie took a last look at the pictures on the dresser, turned out the light and skipped into bed. It's an awful thing to go to bed with a good-night look at General Kitchener, William Muldoon, the Duchess of Marlborough, and Benvenuto Cellini.

This story doesn't really get anywhere at all. The rest of it comes later—sometime when Piggy asks Dulcie

一瞥却把皮吉打垮了。是的，至少在那一晚是这样的。

达尔西哭过之后站起来，把身上那套外出时穿的衣服脱掉，换上蓝色的旧睡袍。她不想吃饭了。她唱了两节《萨美》歌曲。接着，她对鼻子旁边的一个小粉刺产生了强烈的兴趣。那桩事做完后，她把椅子拖到那张站不稳的桌子边，用一副旧纸牌替自己算命。

"可恶无礼的家伙！"她脱口说道。"我的谈吐和举止有哪些使他起意的地方！"

九点钟，达尔西从箱子里取出一盒饼干和一小罐木莓果酱，大吃了一顿。她敬了基钦纳将军一块涂好果酱的饼干；但是基钦纳却像斯芬克斯①望蝴蝶飞舞似地望着她——如果沙漠里也有蝴蝶的话。

"你不爱吃就别吃好啦。"达尔西说。"何必这样神气活现地瞪着眼责备我。如果你每星期也靠六块钱来维持生活，我倒想知道，你是不是仍旧这样优越，这样神气。"

达尔西对基钦纳将军不敬并不是个好现象。接着，她用严厉的姿态把本范努托·切利尼的脸翻了过去。那倒不是不可原谅的；因为她总把他当做亨利八世②，对他很不满意。

九点半钟，达尔西对梳妆台上的相片看了最后一眼，便熄了灯，跳上床去。临睡前还向基钦纳将军、威廉·马尔登、马尔巴勒公爵夫人和本范努托·切利尼行了一个晚安注目礼，真是不痛快的事情。

到这里为止，这个故事并不说明问题。其余的情节是

---

① 斯芬克斯：希腊的斯芬克斯是女首狮身展翅的石像；在埃及的是男首狮身无翼的石像，在大金字塔附近。

② 亨利八世（1491—1547）：英国国王，以多妻著称。

again to dine with him, and she is feeling lonelier than usual, and General Kitchener happens to be looking the other way; and then—

As I said before, I dreamed that I was standing near a crowd of prosperous-looking angels, and a policeman took me by the wing and asked if I belonged with them.

"Who are they?"I asked.

"Why,"said he,"they are the men who hired working-girls, and paid 'em five or six dollars a week to live on. Are you one of the bunch?"

"Not on your immortality,"said I. "I'm only a fellow that set fire to an orphan asylum, and murdered a blind man for his pennies. "

后来发生的——有一次,皮吉再请达尔西一起下馆子,她比平时更感到寂寞,而基钦纳将军的眼光碰巧又在望着别处;于是——

我在前面说过,我梦见自己站在一群境况很好的鬼灵旁边,一个警察挟着我的胳臂,问我是不是同那群人一起的。

"他们是谁呀?"我问。

"唷,"他说,"他们是那种雇佣女工,每星期给她们五六块钱维持生活的老板。你是那群人里面的吗?"

"对天起誓,我绝对不是。"我说。"我的罪孽没有那么重,我只不过是放火烧了一所孤儿院,并为了少许钱财而谋害了一个瞎子的性命。"

The Romance of
a Busy Broker

PITCHER, confidential clerk in the office of Harvey Maxwell, broker, allowed a look of mild interest and surprise to visit his usually expressionless countenance when his employer briskly entered at half past nine in company with his young lady stenographer. With a snappy "Good-morning, Pitcher". Maxwell dashed at his desk as though he were intending to leap over it, and then plunged into the great heap of letters and telegrams waiting there for him.

The young lady had been Maxwell's stenographer for a year. She was beautiful in a way that was decidedly unstenographic. She forewent the pomp of the alluring pompadour. She wore no chains, bracelets, or lockets. She had not the air of being about to accept an invitation to luncheon. Her dress was gray and plain, but it fitted her figure with fidelity and discretion. In her neat black turban hat was the gold-green wing of a macaw. On this morning she was softly and shyly radiant. Her eyes were dreamily bright, her cheeks genuine peach-blow, her expression a happy one, tinged with reminiscence.

Pitcher, still mildly curious, noticed a difference in her ways this morning. Instead of going straight into the adjoining room, where her desk was, she lingered, slightly irresolute, in the outer office. Once she moved over by Maxwell's desk, near enough for him to be aware of her presence.

The machine sitting at that desk was no longer a

忙碌经纪人的浪漫史

上午九点半，证券经纪人哈维·麦克斯韦尔事务所的机要秘书皮彻看到他的老板和那个年轻的女速记员一起匆匆进来，他那往常是毫无表情的脸上不禁露出一丝诧异和好奇。麦克斯韦尔飞快地说了声"早上好，皮彻"，就朝他的办公桌冲去，仿佛要跳过它似的。接着，他就埋头在一大堆等他处理的信件和电报里。

那个年轻姑娘已经替麦克斯韦尔当了一年速记员。她的美丽是一般速记员所没有的。她并不采用那种华丽诱人的庞巴杜式①的发型。也不戴什么项链，手镯，鸡心之类的东西。她根本没有那种准备接受人家邀请去吃饭的神气。她的灰色衣服虽然很朴素，但穿在她身上非但合适，而且文雅。她那俊俏的黑头巾帽上插了一支金绿色的鹦鹉羽毛。今天上午，她身上有一种温柔而羞怯的光辉。她的眼睛梦也似的晶莹，她的脸颊桃花般的娇艳，脸上还带着幸福的神色和追怀的情调。

皮彻仍旧有点好奇，注意到她今天早晨的举止有些异样。她不像往常那样，径直走进她办公桌所在的套间里去，却有点踌躇不决地逗留在外面的办公室里。有一次，她挨近麦克斯韦尔的办公桌，近得仿佛要让他知道自己在场。

坐在办公桌前的人简直成了一部机器；它是一个忙碌

---

① 庞巴杜式为 18 世纪盛行的一种从四面往上梳拢，松而高的头发式样，为法国国王路易十五的情妇庞巴杜首创。

man; it was a busy New York broker, moved by buzzing wheels and uncoiling springs.

"Well—what is it? Anything?" asked Maxwell, sharply. His opened mail lay like a bank of stage snow on his crowded desk. His keen gray eye, impersonal and brusque, flashed upon her half impatiently.

"Nothing," answered the stenographer, moving away with a little smile.

"Mr. Pitcher," she said to the confidential clerk, "did Mr. Maxwell say anything yesterday about engaging another stenographer?"

"He did," answered Pitcher. "He told me to get another one. I notified the agency yesterday afternoon to send over a few samples this morning. It's 9.45 o'clock, and not a single picture hat or piece of pineapple chewing gum has showed up yet."

"I will do the work as usual, then," said the young lady, "until some one comes to fill the place." And she went to her desk at once and hung the black turban hat with the gold-green macaw wing in its accustomed place.

He who has been denied the spectacle of a busy Manhattan broker during a rush of business is handicapped for the profession of anthropology. The poet sings of the "crowded hour of glorious life". The broker's hour is not only crowded, but minutes and seconds are hanging to all the straps and packing both front and rear platforms.

And this day was Harvey Maxwell's busy day. The ticker began to reel out jerkily its fitful coils of tape, the desk telephone had a chronic attack of buzzing. Men began to throng into the office and call at him over the railing, jovially, sharply, viciously, excitedly. Messenger

的纽约市的经纪人，由那些营营作响的齿轮和正在展开的发条推动着。

"哦——怎么？有事吗？"麦克斯韦尔粗声粗气地问道。那些拆开了的信件堆在杂乱的办公桌上，好像舞台上的假雪。他那锐利的灰色眼睛唐突而不近人情，有点不耐烦地扫了她一下。

"没事。"速记员回道，微笑着走开了。

"皮彻先生，"她对机要秘书说，"麦克斯韦尔先生昨天有没有对你说起另请一个速记员？"

"说过。"皮彻回道。"他吩咐我另找一位。昨天下午我就通知了介绍所，让他们今早送几个来看看。现在已经九点四十五分了，可是还没有哪一个戴花哨帽子或者嚼菠萝口香糖的来过。"

"那么，在有人顶替之前，"那年轻女人说，"我照常工作好啦。"她说罢走到自己的办公桌前，把那顶插着金绿色鹦鹉毛的黑头巾帽挂在老地方。

谁没见过一个生意大忙时的纽约经纪人，谁就没有资格当人类学家。诗人歌颂了"灿烂的生命中一个忙碌的时辰"①。对经纪人来说，不但时辰是忙碌的，他的每一分每一秒也都忙碌不堪，仿佛挤满了乘客的车厢，前后平台都没有立足的余地。

今天正是哈维·麦克斯韦尔的忙日。股票行情自动收录器开始痉挛地吐出一卷卷的纸条，电话机犯了不断营营发响的毛病。人们开始拥进事务所，在栏杆外探进身来向他呼唤，有的高兴，有的慌张，有的疾言厉色，有的刻薄狠

---

① 诗人指托马斯·莫当特(1730—1809)。他的《蜜蜂》一诗中有"灿烂的生命中一个忙碌的时辰，抵得上一世纪的默默无闻"。

boys ran in and out with messages and telegrams. The clerks in the office jumped about like sailors during a storm. Even Pitcher's face relaxed into something resembling animation.

On the Exchange there were hurricanes and landslides and snowstorms and glaciers and volcanoes, and those elemental disturbances were reproduced in miniature in the broker's offices. Maxwell shoved his chair against the wall and transacted business after the manner of a toe dancer. He jumped from ticker to 'phone, from desk to door with the trained agility of a harlequin.

In the midst of this growing and important stress the broker became suddenly aware of a high-rolled fringe of golden hair under a nodding canopy of velvet and ostrich tips, and imitation sealskin sacque and a string of beads as large as hickory nuts, ending near the floor with a silver heart. There was a self-possessed young lady connected with these accessories; and Pitcher was there to construe her.

"Lady from the Stenographer's Agency to see about the position," said Pitcher.

Maxwell turned half around, with his hands full of papers and ticker tape.

"What position?" he asked, with a frown.

"Position of stenographer," said Pitcher. "You told me yesterday to call them up and have one sent over this morning."

"You are losing your mind, Pitcher," said Maxwell. "Why should I have given you any such instructions? Miss Leslie has given perfect satisfaction during the year she has been here. The place is hers as long as she chooses to retain it. There's no place open here, madam.

毒。送信的小厮捧着信件和电报奔进奔出。事务所里的办事员跳来跳去，活像风暴发作时船上的水手。连皮彻那不露声色的脸上也泛起了近似有生气的神态。

交易所里有了飓风，山崩，暴风雪，冰川移动和火山爆发；自然界的剧变在经纪人的事务所里小规模地重演了。麦克斯韦尔把椅子往墙边一推，腾出身子来处理业务，忙得仿佛在跳脚尖舞。他从股票行情自动收录器跳到电话机旁，从办公桌边跳到门口，灵活得像是一个训练有素的小丑。

正在这个忙得不可开交，愈来愈紧张的当口，经纪人忽然瞥见一堆高耸的金黄色头发，上面是一顶颤动的丝绒帽子和鸵毛帽饰，一件充海豹皮的短外衣，一串几乎垂到地板、胡桃大的珠项链和一个银鸡心。同这些附属品有关联的是一个从容不迫的年轻姑娘，皮彻正准备介绍。

"速记员介绍所派来的小姐，来应聘的。"皮彻说。

麦克斯韦尔打了半个转身，双手还捧着一堆纸张和股票行情的纸条。

"应什么聘？"他皱皱眉头说。

"应聘当速记员。"皮彻说。"昨天你吩咐我打电话，叫他们今早晨派一个来。"

"你头脑搞糊涂了，皮彻。"麦克斯韦尔说。"我干吗要这样吩咐你？莱斯利小姐在这儿的一年里工作令人十分满意。只要她愿意继续干下去，这个职位永远是她的。对不起，小姐，这儿并没有空位置。皮彻，赶快向介绍所取消要

Countermand that order with the agency, Pitcher, and don't bring any more of 'em in here."

The silver heart left the office, swinging and banging itself independently against the office furniture as it indignantly departed. Pitcher seized a moment to remark to the bookkeeper that the "old man" seemed to get more absentminded and forgetful every day of the world.

The rush and pace of business grew fiercer and faster. On the floor they were pounding half a dozen stocks in which Maxwell's customers were heavy investors. Orders to buy and sell were coming and going as swift as the flight of swallows. Some of his own holdings were imperilled, and the man was working like some high-geared, delicate, strong machine—strung to full tension, going at full speed, accurate, never hesitating, with the proper word and decision and act ready and prompt as clockwork. Stocks and bonds, loans and mortgages, margins and securities—here was a world of finance, and there was no room in it for the human world or the world of nature.

When the luncheon hour drew near there came a slight lull in the uproar.

Maxwell stood by his desk with his hands full of telegrams and memoranda, with a fountain pen over his right ear and his hair hanging in disorderly strings over his forehead. His window was open, for the beloved janitress, Spring had turned on a little warmth through the waking registers of the earth.

And through the window came a wandering—perhaps a lost—odor—a delicate, sweet odor of lilac that fixed the broker for a moment immovable. For this odor

人的话，别再引谁进来啦。"

那个银鸡心晃晃荡荡，不听指挥地在办公室的家具上磕磕碰碰，愤愤离去。皮彻在百忙中对簿记员说，老板近来好像越发心不在焉，越发容易忘事了。

业务越来越忙，节奏越来越快。麦克斯韦尔的顾客投资很多的股票有五六种在市场上受到严重冲击。买进卖出的单据像飞燕穿帘般地递来递去。他自己持有的股票有几种也遭到了危险，他像一部高速运转，精巧坚固的机器——紧张万分，开足马力，正确精密，从不犹豫，言语、动作和决断都像钟表的机件那样恰当而迅速。证券和公债，借款和抵押，保证金和担保品——这是一个金融的世界，其中没有容纳人类世界或是自然世界的丝毫空隙。

将近午餐时间，喧嚣暂时平静下来。

麦克斯韦尔站在办公桌边，手里满是电报和备忘便条，右耳上夹着一支自来水笔，一绺绺的头发凌乱地垂在前额上。他的窗子是打开的，因为可爱的女门房，春天姑娘，已经在大地的暖气管里添了一些热气。

窗口飘进了一股迷惘的气息——或许是失落了的气息——一股紫丁香优雅的甜香，刹那间使经纪人动弹不得。因为这种气息是属于莱斯利小姐的；是她的，只是她一个人

belonged to Miss Leslie; it was her own, and hers only.

The odor brought her vividly, almost tangibly before him. The world of finance dwindled suddenly to a speck. And she was in the next room—twenty steps away.

"By George, I'll do it now," said Maxwell, half aloud. "I'll ask her now. I wonder I didn't do it long ago."

He dashed into the inner office with the haste of a short trying to cover. He charged upon the desk of the stenographer.

She looked up at him with a smile. A soft pink crept over her cheek, and her eyes were kind and frank. Maxwell leaned one elbow on her desk. He still clutched fluttering papers with both hands and the pen was above his ear.

"Miss Leslie," he began, hurriedly, "I have but a moment to spare. I want to say something in that moment. Will you be my wife? I haven't had time to make love to you in the ordinary way, but I really do love you. Talk quick, please—those fellows are clubbing the stuffing out of Union Pacific."

"Oh, what are you talking about?" exclaimed the young lady. She rose to her feet and gazed upon him, round-eyed.

"Don't you understand?" said Maxwell, restively. "I want you to marry me. I love you, Miss Leslie. I wanted to tell you, and I snatched a minute when things had slackened up a bit. They're calling me for the 'phone now. Tell 'em to wait a minute, Pitcher. Won't you, Miss Leslie?"

The stenographer acted very queerly. At first she seemed overcome with amazement; then tears flowed from her wondering eyes; and then she smiled sunnily

的。

那股气息使她的容貌栩栩如生地，几乎是触摸得到地显现在他眼前。金融的世界突然缩成了一个遥远的小黑点。她就在隔壁房间里——相去不到二十步。

"天啊，我现在就去。"麦克斯韦尔脱口说了出来。"我现在就去要求她。我不明白为什么早不去做。"

他一股劲儿冲进里面的办公室，像一个做空头的人急于补进一样①。他向速记员的办公桌冲过去。

她笑微微地抬眼望着他，面颊上泛起一抹淡淡的红晕，一双眼睛温和而坦率。麦克斯韦尔将一只胳臂撑在她的桌上。他两只手里仍然攥着那些窸窸窣窣的纸片，右耳上夹着那支自来水笔。

"莱斯利小姐，"他匆匆开口说，"我只有一点空闲。我利用它来说几句话。你愿意做我的妻子吗？我实在没有时间用普通的方式跟你谈情说爱，但是我确实爱你。请你快回答吧——那帮人正在抢购太平洋铁路的股票呢。"

"喔，你说什么？"年轻女人嚷道。她站了起来，眼睛睁得大大地盯着他。

"你不明白吗？"麦克斯韦尔着急地说。"我要求你跟我结婚。我爱你，莱斯利小姐。我早就想对你说了。所以事情稍微少一点时就抽空跑来。他们又打电话找我了。皮彻，让他们等一会儿。你肯不肯，莱斯利小姐？"

速记员的举动非常蹊跷。起先她似乎诧异得愣住了；接着，泪水从她惊讶的眼睛里流了下来；之后，她泪花晶莹

---

① 在证券交易中，行情看跌时，投机商大量抛出期货，等价格下落时再购进，以从中盈利；与"多头"相反。

through them, and one of her arms slid tenderly about the broker's neck.

"I know now," she said, softly. "It's this old business that has driven everything else out of your head for the time. I was frightened at first. Don't you remember, Harvey? We were married last evening at 8 o'clock in the Little Church around the Corner."

地愉快地笑了，一条胳臂温柔地勾住经纪人的脖子。

"我现在懂得啦，"她柔声说，"这种生意经使你把什么都忘了。起初我吓了一跳。难道你不记得了吗，哈维？我们昨晚八点钟在街角的小教堂里举行过婚礼啦。"

The Furnished Room

RESTLESS, shifting, fugacious as time itself is a certain vast bulk of the population of the red brick district of the lower West Side. Homeless, they have a hundred homes. They flit from furnished room to furnished room, transients forever—transients in abode, transients in heart and mind. They sing "Home, Sweet Home" in ragtime; they carry their *lares et penates* in a bandbox; their vine is entwined about a picture hat; a rubber plant is their fig tree.

Hence the houses of this district, having had a thousand dwellers, should have a thousand tales to tell, mostly dull ones, no doubt; but it would be strange if there could not be found a ghost or two in the wake of all these vagrant guests.

One evening after dark a young man prowled among these crumbling red mansions, ringing their bells. At the twelfth he rested his lean hand-baggage upon the step and wiped the dust from his hatband and forehead. The bell sounded faint and far away in some remote, hollow depths.

To the door of this, the twelfth house whose bell he had rung, came a housekeeper who made him think of an unwholesome, surfeited worm that had eaten its nut to a hollow shell and now sought to fill the vacancy with edible lodgers.

He asked if there was a room to let.

"Come in," said the housekeeper. Her voice came from her throat; her throat seemed lined with fur. "I

82

提供家具的房间

　　下西区那个全是红砖建筑物的地区,有一大批人像时间那样动荡不安,难以捉摸。说他们无家可归吧,他们又有几十、几百个家。他们从一个提供家具的房间搬到另一个提供家具的房间,永远是短暂的过客——在住家方面如此,在思想意识方面也是如此。他们用快拍子唱着《甜蜜的家庭》;把门神装在帽盒里随身携带;他们的葡萄藤是盘绕在阔边帽上的装饰;他们的无花果树只是一株橡皮盆景①。

　　这个地区的房屋既然有成千的住客,当然应该有成千的故事传奇。毫无疑问,这些故事大多是乏味的,不过在这许多飘零人的身后,如果找不出一两个幽灵来,那才叫怪呢。

　　某天晚上断黑的时候,有一个年轻人在这些摇摇欲坠的红砖房屋中间徘徊着,挨家挨户地拉门铃。到了第十二家的门口,他把他那寒酸的手提包放在台阶上,脱下帽子,擦擦帽圈和额头上的灰尘。铃声在冷静空洞的深处响了起来,显得微弱遥远。

　　他在第十二家的门口拉了铃,来了一个女房东,她的模样使他联想到一条不健康的、吃得太饱的蠕虫;蠕虫吃空了果仁,只留下一层空壳,现在想找一些可以充饥的房客来填满这个空间。

　　他打听有没有房间出租。

　　"进来。"女房东说。她的声音来自喉头,而喉头仿佛也

---

　　① 葡萄藤和无花果是安定的家庭生活的象征,典出《圣经·旧约·列王纪》(上)第 4 章第 25 节:"所罗门在世的日子,从但到别是巴的犹太人和以色列人,都在自己的葡萄树下和无花果树下安然居住。"

have the third-floor back, vacant since a week back. Should you wish to look at it?"

The young man followed her up the stairs. A faint light from no particular source mitigated the shadows of the halls. They trod noiselessly upon a stair carpet that its own loom would have forsworn. It seemed to have become vegetable; to have degenerated in that rank, sunless air to lush lichen or spreading moss that grew in patches to the stair-case and was viscid under the foot like organic matter. At each turn of the stairs were vacant niches in the wall. Perhaps plants had once been set within them. If so they had died in that foul and tainted air. It may be that statues of the saints had stood there, but it was not difficult to conceive that imps and devils had dragged them forth in the darkness and down to the unholy depths of some furnished pit below.

"This is the room," said the housekeeper, from her furry throat. "It's a nice room. It ain't often vacant. I had some most elegant people in it last summer—no trouble at all, and paid in advance to the minute. The water's at the end of the hall. Sprowls and Mooney kept it three months. They done a vaudeville sketch. Miss B'retta Sprowls—you may have heard of her—Oh, that was just the stage names—right there over the dresser is where the marriage certificate hung, framed. The gas is here, and you see there is plenty of closet room. It's a room everybody likes. It never stays idle long."

"Do you have many theatrical people rooming here?" asked the young man.

"They comes and goes. A good proportion of my lodgers is connected with the theatres. Yes, sir, this is the theatrical district. Actor people never stays long any-

长遍了舌苔。"我有一间三楼后房,刚空了一个星期。你想看看吗?"

年轻人跟她上楼。不知从哪儿来的一道微弱的光线冲淡了过道里的阴影。他们悄没声儿地踩在楼梯的毡毯上。那条毡毯已经完全走了样,就连原先制造它的织机也认不出它了。它仿佛变成了植物,在那腐臭阴暗的空气里化为一块腻滑的地衣或是蔓延的苔藓,附着在楼梯上,踩在脚下活像是黏糊糊的有机体。楼梯拐角的墙上都有空着的壁龛。以前,这里面也许搁过花草。果真这样的话,那些花草准是在污浊腐臭的空气中枯萎死去了。这里面也许搁过圣徒的塑像,但是不难想象,妖魔鬼怪早就在黑暗中把它们拉了下来,拖到底下某个提供家具的地窖里,让它们待在那邪恶的深渊了。

"就是这间。"女房东长满舌苔的喉咙里发出声音说。"很好的房间。难得空出来的。夏天,这里住过几个非常上等的客人——从来没有麻烦,总是先付后住,从不拖欠房租。过道尽头就有自来水龙头。斯普罗尔斯和穆尼租了三个月。她们是演歌舞杂耍的。布雷塔·斯普罗尔斯小姐——你也许听人说起过她——哦,那不过是艺名罢了——她的结婚证就是配好镜框挂在那儿的梳妆台上的。煤气灯在这儿,你瞧壁柜有多大。这个房间人人喜欢。从来没有空过很久。"

"你这里常有戏剧界的人来租房间吗?"年轻人问道。

"他们来来往往。我的房客中间许多人同剧院有关系。是啊,先生,这里是剧院区。当演员的人不会在一个地方待上很久。有许多就在我这里住过。是啊,他们是来来去去

where. I get my share. Yes, they comes and they goes."

He engaged the room, paying for a week in advance. He was tired, he said, and would take possession at once. He counted out the money. The room had been made ready, she said, even to towels and water. As the housekeeper moved away he put, for the thousandth time, the question that he carried at the end of his tongue.

"A young girl—Miss Vashner—Miss Eloise Vashner—do you remember such a one among your lodgers? She would be singing on the stage, most likely. A fair girl, of medium height and slender, with reddish, gold hair and dark mole near her left eyebrow."

"No, I don't remember the name. Them stage people has names they change as often as their rooms. They comes and they goes. No, I don't call that one to mind."

No. Always no. Five months of ceaseless interrogation and the inevitable negative. So much time spent by day in questioning managers, agents, schools and choruses; by night among the audiences of theatres from all-star casts down to music halls so low that he dreaded to find what he most hoped for. He who had loved her best had tried to find her. He was sure that since her disappearance from home this great, water-girt city held her somewhere, but it was like a monstrous quicksand, shifting its particles constantly, with no foundation, its upper granules of to-day buried to-morrow in ooze and slime.

The furnished room received its latest guest with a first glow of pseudo-hospitality, a hectic, haggard, perfunctory welcome like the specious smile of a demirep. The sophistical comfort came in reflected gleams from the decayed furniture, the ragged brocade upholstery of a

的。"

他租下这个房间,预付了一星期的租金。他说他累了,立刻就住下来,同时数出了钱。女房东说这个房间的一切早已准备就绪,连毛巾和洗脸水都是现成的。她要出去的时候,年轻人把那个带在舌尖,问了千百次的话说了出来。

"你可记得,你的房客中间有没有一个年轻的姑娘——瓦许纳小姐——埃洛伊丝·瓦许纳小姐?她多半会在剧院里唱歌。一个漂亮姑娘,个子不高不矮,细腰身,金红色头发,左眉毛旁边有颗黑痣。"

"不,我记不得那个姓名。演戏的人常常改名换姓,正像换房间一样。他们一会儿来一会儿去。不,我想不起那样一个人了。"

不。问来问去老是"不"。五个月来不断打听,结果总是落空。五个月来,白天在剧院经理、代理人、戏剧学校和歌唱团那儿打听,晚上混在观众里,从阵容坚强的剧院看起,直到那些低级得不能再低的,连他自己都害怕在那里找到心上人的游乐场为止。他对她一往情深,千方百计要找到她。自从她离家出走之后,他知道准是这个滨水的大城市留住了她,把她藏在什么地方;可这个城市像是一片无底的大流沙,不断地移动着它的沙粒,今天还在上层的沙粒,明天就沉沦到黏土污泥里去了。

这间屋子带着初次见面的假客气迎接了刚来到的客人,它那种强颜为欢,虚与委蛇的迎接像是妓女的假笑。破旧的家具反射出淡淡的光线,给人一种似是而非的慰藉;屋里有一张破旧的锦缎面睡榻和两把椅子,两扇窗户之间有

couch and two chairs, a foot-wide cheap pier glass between the two windows, from one or two gilt picture frames and a brass bedstead in a corner.

The guest reclined, inert, upon a chair, while the room, confused in speech as though it were an apartment in Babel, tried to discourse to him of its divers tenantry.

A polychromatic rug like some brilliant-flowered, rectangular, tropical islet lay surrounded by a billowy sea of soiled matting. Upon the gay-papered wall were those pictures that pursue the homeless one from house to house—The Huguenot Lovers, The First Quarrel, The Wedding Breakfast, Psyche at the Fountain. The mantel's chastely severe outline was ingloriously veiled behind some pert drapery drawn rakishly askew like the sashes of the Amazonian ballet. Upon it was some desolate flotsam cast aside by the room's marooned when a lucky sail had borne them to a fresh port—a trifling vase or two, pictures of actresses, a medicine bottle, some stray cards out of a deck.

One by one, as the characters of a cryptograph became explicit, the little signs left by the furnished rooms' procession of guests developed a significance. The threadbare space in the rug in front of the dresser told that lovely woman had marched in the throng. The tiny fingerprints on the wall spoke of little prisoners trying to feel their way to sun and air. A splattered stain, raying like the shadow of a bursting bomb, witnessed where a hurled glass or bottle had splintered with its contents against the wall. Across the pier glass had been scrawled with a diamond in staggering letters the name "Marie". It seemed that the succession of dwellers in the furnished room had turned in fury—perhaps tempted beyond for-

一面尺把宽的廉价壁镜,墙上有一两只描金镜框,角落里放着一张铜床。

客人有气无力地往椅子上一坐。这时,屋子像通天塔①里的一个房间似的,讷讷地想把以前各式各样住户的情况告诉给他。

肮脏的地席上有一块杂色斑驳的毯子,仿佛波涛汹涌的海洋中的一个长方形的、鲜花盛开的热带岛屿。花花绿绿的墙纸上贴着无家可归的人从东到西都能看见的画片:"法国新教徒的情侣","第一次口角","新婚的早餐"和"泉边的普赛克"。歪歪斜斜、不成体统的布帘,像歌剧里亚马逊妇女的腰带,遮住了壁炉架那道貌岸然的轮廓。壁炉架上有一些冷冷清清的零碎东西——一两只不值钱的花瓶,几张女艺人的相片,一只药瓶,几张不成套的纸牌。房间的住户有如船只失事后被困在孤岛上的旅客,侥幸遇到别的船而被搭救上来带往另一个港口,便把这些漂货给扔下了。

先前的住户们遗留下来的痕迹渐趋明朗,正如一篇密码被逐一破译一样。梳妆台前地毯上那块磨秃的地方说明有许多漂亮女人在上面踩过。墙上的小手印表示小囚徒们曾经摸索着寻求阳光与空气。一块像开花弹影子似的四散迸射的痕迹,证实有过玻璃杯或瓶子连同它所盛的东西给扔在了墙上。壁镜上被人用金刚钻歪歪扭扭地刻出了"玛丽"这个名字。看情形,这个提供家具的房间里的住户们,不论先后,总是怨气冲天——也许是被它的过分冷漠激惹

---

① 《圣经·旧约·创世记》第11章:巴比伦人要建造一座城和一座通天高塔,耶和华怒其狂妄,变乱了他们的口音,使他们彼此言语不通,无法取得协调,只得辍工。

bearance by its garish coldness—and wreaked upon it their passions. The furniture was chipped and bruised; the couch, distorted by bursting springs, seemed a horrible monster that had been slain during the stress of some grotesque convulsion. Some more potent upheaval had cloven a great slice from the marble mantel. Each plank in the floor owned its particular cant and shriek as from a separate and individual agony. It seemed incredible that all this malice and injury had been wrought upon the room by those who had called it for a time their home; and yet it may have been the cheated home instinct surviving blindly, the resentful rage at false household gods that had kindled their wrath. A hut that is our own we can sweep and adorn and cherish.

The young tenant in the chair allowed these thoughts to file, soft-shod, through his mind, while there drifted into the room furnished sounds and furnished scents. He heard in one room a tittering and incontinent, slack laughter; in others the monologue of a scold, the rattling of dice, a lullaby, and one crying dully; above him a banjo tinkled with spirit. Doors banged somewhere; the elevated trains roared intermittently; a cat yowled miserably upon a back fence. And he breathed the breath of the house—a dank savor rather than a smell—a cold, musty effluvium as from underground vaults mingled with the reeking exhalations of linoleum and mildewed and rotten woodwork.

Then suddenly, as he rested there, the room was filled with the strong, sweet odor of mignonette. It came as upon a single buffet of wind with such sureness and fragrance and emphasis that it almost seemed a living visitant. And the man cried aloud: "What, dear?" as if he

得忍无可忍——便拿它来出气。家具给搞得支离破碎,伤痕累累:弹簧已经脱颖而出的睡榻,活像一只在极度的痉挛中被杀死的可怕的怪物。大理石的壁炉架,由于某种猛烈得多的骚动,被砍落了一大块。地板上的每一块凹痕和每一条裂纹,都是一次特殊的痛苦的后果。强加于这间屋子的一切怨恨和伤害,都是那些在某一时期称它为"家"的人所干的,这种情况说来几乎难以使人相信;但是燃起他们的怒火的也许正是那种始终存在而不自觉的、无法满足的恋家的本能,是那种对于冒牌的家庭守护神的愤恨。如果是我们自己的家,即使换了一间茅舍,我们也会加以打扫、装饰和爱护的。

坐在椅子上的年轻住客让这些念头恍恍惚惚地掠过心头。这时,别的房间里飘来了各种声音和气息。他听到一间屋子里传来淫荡无力的吃吃笑声;另外的屋子里传来独自的咒骂、掷骰子声,催眠曲和啜泣抽噎;楼上却有起劲的五弦琴声。不知哪里在呼呼嘭嘭地关门;高架电车间歇地隆隆驶过;后院的篱笆上有一只猫在哀叫。他呼吸着屋子里的气息——与其说是气息,不如说是一股潮味儿——仿佛地窖里的油布和腐烂木头蒸发出来的那种冷冰冰的发霉的气味。

他正歇着的时候,屋里突然有了一阵浓烈、甜蜜的木犀草香味。它像是随着一股轻风飘来的,是那样确切、浓郁和强烈,以至像是一个有血有肉的来客。年轻人似乎听到有人在招呼他,便脱口嚷道:"什么事,亲爱的?"并且跳了起

had been called, and sprang up and faced about. The rich odor clung to him and wrapped him around. He reached out his arms for it, all his senses for the time confused and commingled. How could one be peremptorily called by an odor? Surely it must have been a sound. But, was it not the sound that had touched, that had caressed him?

"She has been in this room," he cried, and he sprang to wrest from it a token, for he knew he would recognize the smallest thing that had belonged to her or that she had touched. This enveloping scent of mignonette, the odor that she had loved and made her own—whence came it?

The room had been but carelessly set in odor. Scattered upon the flimsy dresser scarf were half a dozen hairpins—those discreet, indistinguishable friends of womankind, feminine of gender, infinite mood and uncommunicative of tense. These he ignored, conscious of their triumphant lack of identity. Ransacking the drawers of the dresser he came upon a discarded, tiny, ragged handkerchief. He pressed it to his face. It was racy and insolent with heliotrope; he hurled it to the floor. In another drawer he found odd buttons, a theatre programme, a pawnbroker's card, two lost marshmallows, a book on the divination of dreams. In the last was a woman's black satin hair bow, which halted him, poised between ice and fire. But the black satin hair bow also is femininity's demure, impersonal common ornament and tells no tales.

And then he traversed the room like a hound on the scent, skimming the walls, considering the corners of the bulging matting on his hands and knees, rummaging mantel and tables, the curtains and hangings, the drunken

来,四下张望着。那阵浓郁的香味依附在他身上,把他团团包围起来。他伸手去摸索,因为这时他所有的感觉都混杂紊乱了。气味怎么能断然招呼一个人呢?一定是声音。不过,刚才触摸他的,抚摩他的竟会是声音吗?

"她在这间屋子里待过。"他嚷道,立刻想在屋里找出一个证据。因为他知道,凡是属于她的或者经她触摸过的东西,无论怎样细小,他一看就认识。这股缭绕不散的木犀草香味,她所偏爱并已成为她个人特征的香味,究竟是从哪儿来的呢?

这间屋子收拾得很马虎。梳妆台那薄薄的台布上零乱地放着五六只发夹——一般女人的无声无息,无从区别的朋友,拿语法术语来说,就是阴性,不定式,不说明时间。他知道从这些发夹上是找不到线索的,便不加理会。搜寻梳妆台的抽屉时,他发现一方被抛弃的、破烂的小手帕。他拿起手帕,往脸上一按一股金盏草的香气直刺鼻子;他使劲把手帕摔在地上。在另一个抽屉里,他发现几枚零星的纽扣,一份剧院节目单,一张当铺的卡片,两颗遗漏的棉花糖和一本详梦的书。在最后一个抽屉里,有一个妇女用的黑缎子发结,使他一阵冷一阵热地踌躇了好一会儿。但是黑缎子发结只是妇女的一本正经,没有个性的普普通通的装饰品,并不说明问题。

接着,他像猎狗追踪臭迹似的在屋子里逡巡徘徊,扫视着墙壁,趴在地上察看角落里地席拱起的地方,搜索着壁炉架,桌子,窗帘,帷幔和屋角那只东倒西歪的柜子。他想找

cabinet in the corner for a visible sign, unable to perceive that she was there beside, around, against, within, above him, clinging to him, wooing him, calling him so poignantly through the finer senses that even his grosser ones became cognizant of the call. Once again he answered loudly: "Yes, dear!" and turned, wild-eyed, to gaze on vacancy, for he could not yet discern form and color and love and outstretched arms in the odor of mignonette. Oh, God! whence that odor, and since when have odors had a voice to call? Thus he groped.

He burrowed in crevices and corners, and found corks and cigarettes. These he passed in passive contempt. But once he found in a fold of the matting a half-smoked cigar, and this he ground beneath his heel with a green and trenchant oath. He sifted the room from end to end. He found dreary and ignoble small records of many a peripatetic tenant; but of her whom he sought, and who may have lodged there, and whose spirit seemed to hover there, he found no trace.

And then he thought of the housekeeper.

He ran from the haunted room downstairs and to a door that showed a crack of light. She came out to his knock. He smothered his excitement as best he could.

"Will you tell me, madam," he besought her, "who occupied the room I have before I came?"

"Yes, sir. I can tell you again. 'Twas Sprowls and Mooney, as I said. Miss B'retta Sprowls it was in the theatres, but Missis Mooney she was. My house is well known for respectability. The marriage certificate hung, framed, on a nail over—"

"What kind of a lady was Miss Sprowls—in looks, I mean?"

一个明显的迹象,却不理解她就在他身边,在他周围,在他心头,在他上空,偎依着他,追求着他,并且通过微妙的感觉在辛酸地呼唤他,以至他那迟钝的感觉也觉察到了这种呼唤。他又一次高声回答:"哎,亲爱的!"同时回过头来,干瞪着眼,凝视着空间。因为到目前为止,他还不能从木犀草香味中辨明形象、色彩、爱情和伸出来迎接他的胳臂。啊,老天哪!那股香味是从哪里来的呢?从什么时候开始,气味竟能发出声音呼唤呢?因此,他继续摸索着。

他在裂罅和角落里探查,找到了瓶塞和烟蒂。这些东西都被他鄙夷而默不作声地放过了。可是当在地席的皱褶里找到半支抽过的雪茄时,他狠狠地咒骂了一句,把它踩得粉碎。他把这间屋子从头到尾细细搜查了一遍。他发现了许多飘零的住户的凄凉的微细痕迹;可是关于他所寻找的,可能在这儿住过的,灵魂仿佛在这儿徘徊不散的她,却毫无端倪。

这时,他才想起了房东。

他从这间阴森森的房子跑下楼,来到一扇微露灯光的门口。女房东听到敲门声,便出来了。他尽可能控制住自己的激动。

"请问你,太太,"他恳求地说,"在我没来之前,谁住过这间屋子?"

"哎,先生。我可以再告诉你一遍。我早就说过,先前住在这儿的是斯普罗尔斯和穆尼。布雷塔·斯普罗尔斯小姐是剧院里的姓名,穆尼太太是真名。我的房子的正派是有名的。配了镜框的结婚证就挂在——"

"斯普罗尔斯小姐是什么样的——我是说长相怎么样?"

"Why, black-haired, sir, short, and stout, with a comical face. They left a week ago Tuesday."

"And before they occupied it?"

"Why, there was a single gentleman connected with the draying business. He left owing me a week. Before him was Missis Crowder and her two children, that stayed four months; and back of them was old Mr. Doyle, whose sons paid for him. He kept the room six months. That goes back a year, sir, and further I do not remember."

He thanked her and crept back to his room. The room was dead. The essence that had vivified it was gone. The perfume of mignonette had departed. In its place was the old, stale odor of mouldy house furniture, of atmosphere in storage.

The ebbing of his hope drained his faith. He sat staring at the yellow, singing gaslight. Soon he walked to the bed and began to tear the sheets into strips. With the blade of his knife he drove them tightly into every crevice around windows and door. When all was snug and taut he turned out the light, turned the gas full on again and laid himself gratefully upon the bed.

It was Mrs. McCool's night to go with the can for beer. So she fetched it and sat with Mrs. Purdy in one of those subterranean retreats where housekeepers foregather and the worm dieth seldom.

"I rented out my third-floor-back this evening," said Mrs. Purdy, across a fine circle of foam. "A young man took it. He went up to bed two hours ago."

"Now, did ye, Mrs. Purdy, ma'am?" said Mrs. McCool, with intense admiration. "You do be a wonder for

　　"唔,先生,黑头发,矮胖身段,一脸滑稽相。她们上星期二走的,已经一个星期了。"

　　"她们之前的房客是谁呢?"

　　"唔,一个做运货车生意的单身男人。他欠了我一星期的房租就走了。他之前是克劳德太太和她的两个孩子,他们住了四个月。再之前是多伊尔老先生,他的房钱是由他几个儿子付的。他住了六个月。这样已经推算到一年前了,再前面的我可记不清啦。"

　　他向她道了谢,垂头丧气地回到自己的屋子里。屋子里死气沉沉的。赋予它生命的要素已经消失了。木犀草的香味已经没有了。代替它的是发霉家具的腐臭的味道,是停滞的气氛。

　　希望的幻灭耗尽了他的信心。他坐在那儿,呆看着哑哑发响的煤气灯的黄光。过了片刻,他走到床边,把床单撕成一长条一长条的。他用小刀把这些布条结结实实地堵塞进窗框和门框的罅隙。安排停当后,他关掉煤气灯,再把它开足,却不去点火,然后死心塌地往床上一躺。

　　这晚轮到麦库尔太太去打啤酒。她去打了酒来,同珀迪太太一起坐在地下室里。那种地下室是房东太太们聚集的地方,也是蠕虫不会死的地方。①

　　"今晚我把三楼后房租出去了,"珀迪太太对着一圈薄薄的泡沫说。"房客是个年轻人。他上床已经两个钟头了。"

　　"真的吗,珀迪太太?"麦库尔太太极其羡慕地说。"你

---

　　①　参见《圣经·新约·马可福音》第 9 章 48 节:"在那里(地狱)虫是不死的,火是不灭的。"

rentin' rooms of that kind. And did ye tell him, then?" she concluded in a husky whisper laden with mystery.

"Rooms," said Mrs. Purdy, in her furriest tones, "are furnished for to rent. I did not tell him, Mrs. McCool."

"'Tis right ye are, ma'am; 'tis by renting rooms we kape alive. Ye have the rale sense for business, ma'am. There be many people will rayjict the rentin' of a room if they be tould a suicide has been after dyin' in the bed of it."

"As you say, we has our living to be making," remarked Mrs. Purdy.

"Yis, ma'am; 'tis true. 'Tis just one wake ago this day I helped ye lay out the third-floor-back. A pretty slip of a colleen she was to be killin' herself wid the gas—a swate little face she had, Mrs. Purdy, ma'am."

"She'd a-been called handsome, as you say," said Mrs. Purdy, assenting but critical, "but for that mole she had a-growin' by her left eyebrow. Do fill up your glass again, Mrs. McCool."

能把那种房间租出去,真不简单。那你有没有告诉他呢?"
她非常神秘地哑着嗓子低声说了一些话。

"房间嘛,"珀迪太太用舌苔非常腻厚的音调说,"本来是备好家具出租的。我没有告诉他,麦库尔太太。"

"你做得对,太太;我们是靠房租过活的。你真有生意头脑,太太。人们如果知道床上有人自杀过,多半就不愿意租那间房子。"

"就是嘛,我们要靠房租过活呀。"珀迪太太说。

"是啊,太太,一点儿不错。就是上星期的今天,我还帮你收拾三楼后房来着。这么漂亮的一个姑娘,想不到竟用煤气自杀——她那张小脸真惹人爱,珀迪太太。"

"就是嘛,她称得上漂亮,"珀迪太太表示同意,可又有点儿吹毛求疵地说,"可惜左眉毛旁边长了那么一颗黑痣。你把杯子再满上吧,麦库尔太太。"

Telemachus, Friend

RETURNING from a hunting trip, I waited at the little town of Los Piños, in New Mexico, for the southbound train, which was one hour late. I sat on the porch of the Summit House and discussed the functions of life with Telemachus Hicks, the hotel proprietor.

Perceiving that personalities were not out of order, I asked him what species of beast had long ago twisted and mutilated his left ear. Being a hunter, I was concerned in the evils that may befall one in the pursuit of game.

"That ear," says Hicks, "is the relic of true friendship."

"An accident?" I persisted.

"No friendship is an accident," said Telemachus; and I was silent.

"The only perfect case of true friendship I ever knew," went on my host, "was a cordial intent between a Connecticut man and a monkey. The monkey climbed palms in Barranquilla and threw down cocoanuts to the man. The man sawed them in two and made dippers, which he sold for two *reales* each and bought rum. The monkey drank the milk of the nuts. Through each being satisfied with his own share of the graft, they lived like brothers.

"But in the case of human beings, friendship is a transitory art, subject to discontinuance without further notice.

"I had a friend once, of the entitlement of Paisley Fish, that I imagined was sealed to me for an endless

100

刎 颈 之 交

　　我狩猎归来,在新墨西哥州的洛斯比尼奥斯小镇等候南下的火车。火车误点,迟了一小时。我便坐在"顶点"客栈的阳台上,同客栈老板泰勒马格斯·希克斯闲聊,议论生活的意义。

　　我发现他的性情并不乖戾,不像是爱打架斗殴的人,便问他是哪种野兽伤残了他的左耳。作为猎人,我认为狩猎时很容易遇到这类不幸的事。

　　"那只耳朵,"希克斯说,"是真挚友情的纪念。"

　　"一件意外吗?"我追问道。

　　"友情怎么能说是意外呢?"泰勒马格斯反问道,这下子可把我问住了。

　　"我所知道的仅有的一对亲密无间、真心实意的朋友,"客栈老板接着说,"要算是一个康涅狄格州人和一只猴子了。猴子在巴兰基利亚①爬椰子树,把椰子摘下来扔给那人。那人把椰子锯成两片,做成水勺,每只卖两个雷阿尔②,换了钱来沽酒。椰子汁归猴子喝。他们两个坐地分赃,各得其所,像兄弟一般,生活得非常和睦。

　　"换了人类,情况就不同了;友情变幻无常,随时可以宣告失效,不再另行通知。

　　"以前我有个朋友,名叫佩斯利·菲什,我认为我同他的交情是地久天长、牢不可破的。有七年,我们一起挖矿,

---

　　① 巴兰基利亚为哥伦比亚北部马格达莱纳河口的港市。

　　② 雷阿尔:旧时西班牙和拉丁美洲某些国家用的辅币,有银质的,也有镍质的。

space of time. Side by side for seven years we had mined, ranched, sold patent churns, herded sheep, took photographs and other things, built wire fences, and picked prunes. Thinks I, neither homicide nor flattery nor riches nor sophistry nor drink can make trouble between me and Paisley Fish. We was friends an amount you could hardly guess at. We was friends in business, and we let our amicable qualities lap over and season our hours of recreation and folly. We certainly had days of Damon and nights of Pythias.

"One summer me and Paisley gallops down into these San Andrés mountains for the purpose of a month's surcease and levity, dressed in the natural store habiliments of man. We hit this town of Los Piños, which certainly was a roof-garden spot of the world, and flowing with condensed milk and honey. It had a street or two, and air, and hens, and a eating-house; and that was enough for us.

"We strikes the town after supper-time, and we concludes to sample whatever efficacy there is in this eating-house down by the railroad tracks. By the time we had set down and pried up our plates with a knife from the red oil-cloth, along intrudes Widow Jessup with the hot biscuit and fried liver.

"Now, there was a woman that would have tempted an anchovy to forget his vows. She was not so small as she was large; and a kind of welcome air seemed to mitigate her vicinity. The pink of her face was the *in hoc signo* of a culinary temper and a warm disposition, and her smile would have brought out the dogwood blossoms in December.

"Widow Jessup talks to us a lot of garrulousness

办牧场,兜销专利的搅乳器,放羊,摄影,打桩拉铁丝网,摘水果当临时工,碰到什么就干什么。我想,我同佩斯利两人的感情是什么都离间不了的,不管它是凶杀,谄谀,财富,诡辩或者老酒。我们交情之深简直使你难以想象。干事业的时候,我们是朋友;休息娱乐的时候,我们也让这种和睦相好的特色持续下去,给我们的生活增添了不少乐趣。不论白天黑夜,我们都难舍难分,好比达蒙和皮西厄斯①。

"一年夏天,我和佩斯利两人打扮得整整齐齐,骑马来到这圣安德烈斯山区,打算休养一个月,消遣消遣。我们到了这个洛斯比尼奥斯小镇,这里简直算得上是世界的屋顶花园,是流炼乳和蜂蜜之地②。这里空气新鲜,有一两条街道,有鸡可吃,有客栈可住;我们需要的也就是这些东西。

"我们进镇时,天色已晚,便决定在铁路旁边的这家客栈里歇歇脚,尝尝它所能供应的任何东西。我们刚坐定,用刀把粘在红油布上的盘子撬起来,寡妇杰塞普就端着刚出炉的热面包和炸肝尖进来了。

"哎呀,这个女人叫鳗鱼看了都会动心。她长得不肥不瘦,不高不矮,一副和蔼的样子,使人觉得分外可亲。红润的脸颊是她喜爱烹调和为人热情的标志,她的微笑叫山茱萸在寒冬腊月里都会开花。

"寡妇杰塞普谈锋很健地同我们扯了起来,聊着天气,

---

① 达蒙和皮西厄斯:公元前四世纪锡拉丘兹的两个朋友。皮西厄斯被暴君狄奥尼西斯判处死刑,要求回家料理后事,由达蒙代受监禁。执行死刑之日,皮西厄斯及时赶回,狄奥尼西斯为他们崇高的友谊所感动,便赦免了他们。

② 《圣经·旧约》记载:上帝遣摩西率领以色列人出埃及,前往丰饶的迦南,即流奶与蜜之地。

about the climate and history and Tennyson and prunes and the scarcity of mutton, and finally wants to know where we came from.

"'Spring Valley,' says I.

"'Big Spring Valley,' chips in Paisley, out of a lot of potatoes and knuckle-bone of ham in his mouth.

"That was the first sign I noticed that the old *fidus Diogenes* business between me and Paisley Fish was ended forever. He knew how I hated a talkative person, and yet he stampedes into the conversation with his amendments and addendums of syntax. On the map it was Big Spring Valley; but I had heard Paisley himself call it Spring Valley a thousand times.

"Without saying any more, we went out after supper and set on the railroad track. We had been pardners too long not to know what was going on in each other's mind.

"'I reckon you understand,' says Paisley, 'that I've made up my mind to accrue that widow woman as part and parcel in and to my hereditaments forever, both domestic, sociable, legal, and otherwise, until death us do part.'

"'Why, yes,' says I, 'I read it between the lines, though you only spoke one. And I suppose you are aware,' says I, 'that I have a movement on foot that leads up to the widow's changing her name to Hicks, and leaves you writing to the society column to inquire whether the best man wears a japonica or seamless socks at the wedding!'

"'There'll be some hiatuses in your program,' says Paisley, chewing up a piece of a railroad tie. 'I'd give in to you,' says he, 'in 'most any respect if it was secular

历史，丁尼生①，梅干，以及不容易买到羊肉等等，最后才问我们是从哪儿来的。

"'春谷。'我回答说。

"'大春谷。'佩斯利嘴里塞满了土豆和火腿骨头，突然插进来说。

"我注意到，这件事的发生标志着我同佩斯利·菲什的忠诚友谊的结束。他明知我最恨多嘴的人，可他还是冒冒失失地插了嘴，替我作了一些措辞上的修正和补充。地图上的名称固然是大春谷；然而佩斯利自己也管它叫春谷，我听过不下一千遍。

"我们也不多话，吃了晚饭便走出客栈，在铁轨上坐定。我们合伙的时间太长了，不可能不了解彼此的心情。

"'我想你总该明白，'佩斯利说，'我已经打定主意，要让那位寡妇太太永远成为我的不动产的主要部分，在家庭、社会、法律等等方面都是如此，到死为止。'

"'当然啦，'我说，'你虽然只说了一句话，我已经听到了弦外之音。不过我想你也该明白，'我说，'我准备采取步骤，让那位寡妇改姓希克斯，我劝你还是等着写信给报纸的社会新闻栏，问问举行婚礼时，男傧相是不是在纽扣孔里插了山茶花，穿了无缝丝袜！'

"'你的如意算盘打错了。'佩斯利嚼着一片铁路枕木屑说。'遇到世俗的事情，'他说，'我几乎什么都可以让步，这件事可不行。女人的笑靥，'佩斯利继续说，'是海葱和含铁

---

① 丁尼生(1809—1892)：英国桂冠诗人。

affairs, but this is not so. The smiles of woman,' goes on Paisley, 'is the whirlpool of Squills and Chalybeates, into which vortex the good ship Friendship is often drawn and dismembered. I'd assault a bear that was annoying you,' says Paisley, 'or I'd indorse your note, or rub the place between your shoulder-blades with opodeldoc the same as ever; but there my sense of etiquette ceases. In this fracas with Mrs. Jessup we play it alone. I've notified you fair.'

"And then I collaborates with myself, and offers the following resolutions and by-laws:

"'Friendship between man and man,' says I, 'is an ancient historical virtue enacted in the days when men had to protect each other against lizards with eighty-foot tails and flying turtles. And they've kept up the habit to this day, and stand by each other till the bellboy comes up and tells them the animals are not really there. I've often heard,' I says, 'about ladies stepping in and breaking up a friendship between men. Why should that be? I'll tell you, Paisley, the first sight and hot biscuit of Mrs. Jessup appears to have inserted a oscillation into each of our bosoms. Let the best man of us have her. I'll play you a square game, and won't do any underhanded work. I'll do all of my courting of her in your presence, so you will have an equal opportunity. With that arrangement I don't see why our steamboat of friendship should fall overboard in the medicinal whirlpools you speak of, whichever of us wins out.'

"'Good old hoss!' says Paisley, shaking my hand. 'And I'll do the same,' says he. 'We'll court the lady synonymously, and without any of the prudery and bloodshed usual to such occasions. And we'll be friends

矿泉的漩涡①，友谊之船虽然结实，碰上它也往往要撞碎沉
没。我像以前一样，'佩斯利说，'愿意同一头招惹你的狗熊
拼命，替你的借据担保，用肥皂樟脑搽剂替你擦脊梁；但是
在这件事情上，我可不能讲客气。在同杰塞普太太打交道
这件事上，我们只能各干各的了。我丑话说在前头，先跟你
讲清楚。'

　　"于是，我暗自寻思一番，提出了下面的结论和附则：

　　"'男人与男人的友谊，'我说，'是一种古老的，具有历
史意义的美德。当男人们互相保护，共同对抗尾巴有八十
英尺长的蜥蜴和会飞的海鳖时，这种美德就已经制定了。
他们把这种习惯一直保留到今天，一直在互相支持，直到旅
馆侍者跑来告诉他们说，这种动物实际上并不存在。我常
听人说，'我说，'女人牵涉进来之后，男人之间的交情就破
裂了。为什么要这样呢？我告诉你吧，佩斯利，杰塞普太太
的出现和她的热面包，仿佛使我们两人的心都怦然跳动了。
让我们中间更棒的一个去赢得她吧。我要跟你公平交易，
决不搞不光明正大的小动作。我追求她的时候，一举一动
都要当着你的面，那你的机会也就均等了。这样安排，无论
哪一个得手，我想我们的友谊大轮船决不至于翻在你所说
的药水气味十足的漩涡里了。'

　　"'这才够朋友！佩斯利握握我的手说。'我一定照样
行事。我们齐头并进，同时追求那位太太，不让通常那种虚
假和流血的事情发生。无论成败，我们仍是朋友。'

――――――――

　　①　"海葱和含铁矿泉的漩涡"原文是"the Whirlpool of Squills and Chalybeates"。英文成语有"between Scylla and Charybdis"，意为危险之地。
"Scylla"是意大利墨西拿海峡的岩礁，读音与海葱的拉丁名"scilla"相近；
"Charybdis"是它对面的大漩涡，读音与含铁矿泉"Chalybeate"相近，作者故意
混淆了这两个字。

still, win or lose. '

"At one side of Mrs. Jessup's eating-house was a bench under some trees where she used to sit in the breeze after the south-bound had been fed and gone. And there me and Paisley used to congregate after supper and make partial payments on our respects to the lady of our choice. And we was so honorable and circuitous in our calls that if one of us got there first we waited for the other before beginning any gallivantery.

"The first evening that Mrs. Jessup knew about our arrangement I got to the bench before Paisley did. Supper was just over, and Mrs. Jessup was out there with a fresh pink dress on, and almost cool enough to handle.

"I sat down by her and made a few specifications about the moral surface of nature as set forth by the landscape and the contiguous perspective. That evening was surely a case in point. The moon was attending to business in the section of sky where it belonged, and the trees was making shadows on the ground according to science and nature, and there was a kind of conspicuous hullabaloo going on in the bushes between the bullbats and the orioles and the jack-rabbits and other feathered insects of the forest. And the wind out of the mountains was singing like a jew's-harp in the pile of old tomato-cans by the railroad track.

"I felt a kind of sensation in my left side—something like dough rising in a crock by the fire. Mrs. Jessup had moved up closer.

"'Oh, Mr. Hicks,' says she, 'when one is alone in the world, don't they feel it more aggravated on a beautiful night like this?'

"I rose up off the bench at once.

　　"杰塞普太太客栈旁的几株树下有一条长凳,等南行火车上的乘客打过尖,离开之后,她就坐在那里乘凉。晚饭后,我和佩斯利在那里集合,分头向我们的意中人献殷勤。我们追求的方式很光明正大,瞻前顾后,如果一个先到,非得等另一个也来了之后才开始调情。

　　"杰塞普太太知道我们的安排后的第一晚,我比佩斯利先到了长凳那儿。晚饭刚开过,杰塞普太太换了一套干净的粉红色的衣服在那儿乘凉,并且凉得几乎可以对付了。

　　"我在她身边坐下,稍稍发表了一些意见,谈到自然界通过近景和远景所表现出来的精神面貌。那晚确实是一个典型的环境。月亮升到空中应有的地方来应景凑趣,树木根据科学原理和自然规律把影子洒在地上,灌木丛中的小美洲夜鹰、金莺、长耳兔和别的有翅的昆虫此起彼伏地发出一片喧嘈声。山间吹来的微风,掠过铁轨旁边一堆旧番茄酱罐头,发出了小口琴似的声音。

　　"我觉得左边有什么东西在蠢蠢欲动——正如火炉旁瓦罐里的面团在发酵。原来是杰塞普太太挨近了一些。

　　"'哦,希克斯先生,'她说,'一个举目无亲、孤独寂寞的人,在这样一个美丽的夜晚,是不是更会感到凄凉?'

　　"我赶紧从长凳上站起来。

"'Excuse me, ma'am,' says I, 'but I'll have to wait till Paisley comes before I can give a audible hearing to leading questions like that.'

"And then I explained to her how we was friends cinctured by years of embarrassment and travel and complicity, and how we had agreed to take no advantage of each other in any of the more mushy walks of life, such as might be fomented by sentiment and proximity. Mrs. Jessup appears to think serious about the matter for a minute, and then she breaks into a species of laughter that makes the wildwood resound.

"In a few minutes Paisley drops around, with oil of bergamot on his hair, and sits on the other side of Mrs. Jessup, and inaugurates a sad tale of adventure in which him and Pieface Lumley has a skinning-match of dead cows in '95 for a silver-mounted saddle in the Santa Rita valley during the nine months' drought.

"Now, from the start of that courtship I had Paisley Fish hobbled and tied to a post. Each one of us had a different system of reaching out for the easy places in the female heart. Paisley's scheme was to petrify 'em with wonderful relations of events that he had either come across personally or in large print. I think he must have got his idea of subjugation from one of Shakespeare's shows I see once called 'Othello'. There is a colored man in it who acquires a duke's daughter by disbursing to her a mixture of the talk turned out by Rider Haggard, Lew Dockstader, and Dr. Parkhurst. But that style of courting don't work well off the stage.

"Now, I give you my own recipe for inveigling a woman into that state of affairs when she can be referred to as '*née* Jones'. Learn how to pick up her hand

　　"'对不起,夫人,'我说,'对于这样一个富于诱导性的问题,我得等佩斯利来了以后,才能公开答复。'

　　"接着,我向她解释,我和佩斯利·菲什是老朋友,多年的甘苦与共、浪迹江湖和同谋关系,已经使我们的友谊牢不可破;如今我们正处在生活的缠绵阶段,我们商妥决不乘一时感情冲动和近水楼台的机会互相钻空子。杰塞普太太仿佛郑重其事地把这件事考虑了一会儿,忽然哈哈大笑,周围的林子都响起了回声。

　　"没几分钟,佩斯利也来了,他头上抹了香柠檬油,在杰塞普太太的另一边坐下,开始讲一段悲惨的冒险事迹:一八九五年圣丽塔山谷连旱了九个月,牛群一批批地死去,他同扁脸拉姆利比赛剥牛皮,赌一只镶银的马鞍。

　　"那场追求一开头,我就比垮了佩斯利·菲什,弄得他束手无策。我们两人各有一套打动女人内心弱点的办法。佩斯利的办法是讲一些他亲身体验的,或是从通俗书刊里看来的惊险事迹,吓唬女人。我猜想,他准是从莎士比亚的一出戏里学到那种慑服女人的主意的。那出戏叫'奥瑟罗',我以前也看过,里面是说一个黑人,把赖德·哈格德、卢·多克斯塔德和帕克赫斯特博士①三个人的话语混杂起来,讲给一位公爵的女儿听,把她弄到了手。可是那种求爱方式下了舞台就不中用了。

　　"现在,我告诉你,我自己是怎样迷住一个女人,使她落到改姓的地步的。你只要懂得怎么抓起她的手,把它握住,

①　赖德·哈格德(1856—1925):英国小说家,作品多以南非蛮荒为背景;帕克赫斯特博士(1842—1933):美国长老会牧师,攻击纽约腐败的市政甚力,促使市长改选。

and hold it, and she's yours. It ain't so easy. Some men grab at it so much like they was going to set a dislocation of the shoulder that you can smell the arnica and hear 'em tearing off bandages. Some take it up like a hot horseshoe, and hold it off at arm's length like a druggist pouring tincture of asafoetida in a bottle. And most of 'em catch hold of it and drag it right out before the lady's eyes like a boy finding a baseball in the grass, without giving her a chance to forget that the hand is growing on the end of her arm. Them ways are all wrong.

"I'll tell you the right way. Did you ever see a man sneak out in the backyard and pick up a rock to throw at a tomcat that was sitting on a fence looking at him? He pretends he hasn't got a thing in his hand, and that the cat don't see him, and that he don't see the cat. That's the idea. Never drag her hand out where she'll have to take notice of it. Don't let her know that you think she knows you have the least idea she is aware you are holding her hand. That was my rule of tactics; and as far as Paisley's serenade about hostilities and misadventure went, he might as well have been reading to her a timetable of the Sunday trains that stop at Ocean Grove, New Jersey.

"One night when I beat Paisley to the bench by one pipeful, my friendship gets subsidized for a minute, and I asks Mrs. Jessup if she didn't think a 'H' was easier to write than a 'J'. In a second her head was mashing the oleander flower in my button-hole, and I leaned over and—but I didn't.

"'If you don't mind,' says I, standing up, 'we'll wait for Paisley to come before finishing this. I've never done anything dishonorable yet to our friendship, and this

她就成了你的人。讲讲固然容易,做起来并不简单。有的男人使劲拉住女人的手,仿佛要把脱臼的肩胛骨复位一样,简直叫你可以闻到山金车酊剂的气味,听到撕绷带的声音了。有的男人像拿一块烧烫的马蹄铁那样握着女人的手,又像药剂师把阿魏酊往瓶里灌时那样,伸直手臂,隔得远远的。大多数男人握到了女人的手,便把它拉到她眼皮下面,像小孩在草里寻找棒球似的,不让她忘掉她的手长在胳臂上。这种种方式都是错误的。

"我把正确的方式告诉你吧。你可曾见过一个人偷偷地溜进后院,捡起一块石头,想扔一只蹲在篱笆上盯着他直瞧的公猫?他假装手里没有东西,假装猫没有看见他,他也没有看见猫。就是那么一回事。千万别把她的手拉到她自己注意得到的地方。你虽然清楚她知道你握着她的手,可是你得装出没事的样子,别露痕迹。那就是我的策略。至于佩斯利用战争和灾祸的故事来博得她的欢心,正像把星期日的火车时刻表念给她听一样。那天的火车连新泽西州欧欣格罗夫①之类的小地方也要停站的。

"有一晚,我先到长凳那儿,比佩斯利早了一袋烟的工夫。我的友谊出了一会儿毛病,我竟然问杰塞普太太是不是认为'希'字要比'杰'字好写一点儿。她的头立刻压坏了我纽扣孔里的夹竹桃,我也凑了过去——可是我没有干。

"'假如你不在意的话,'我站起来说,'我们等佩斯利来了之后再完成这件事吧。到目前为止,我还没有干过对不起我们朋友交情的事,这样不很光明。'

---

① 欧欣格罗夫为新泽西州的滨海小镇,当时人口只有三千左右。

won't be quite fair.'

"'Mr. Hicks,' says Mrs. Jessup, looking at me peculiar in the dark, 'if it wasn't for but one thing, I'd ask you to hike yourself down the gulch and never disresume your visits to my house.'

"'And what is that, ma'am?' I asks.

"'You are too good a friend not to make a good husband,' says she.

"In five minutes Paisley was on his side of Mrs. Jessup.

"'In Silver City, in the summer of '98,' he begins, 'I see Jim Bartholomew chew off a Chinaman's ear in the Blue Light Saloon on account of a crossbarred muslin shirt that—what was that noise?'

"I had resumed matters again with Mrs. Jessup right where we had left off.

"'Mrs. Jessup,' says I, 'has promised to make it Hicks. And this is another of the same sort.'

"Paisley winds his feet around a leg of the bench and kind of groans.

"'Lem,' says he, 'we been friends for seven years. Would you mind not kissing Mrs. Jessup quite so loud? I'd do the same for you.'

"'All right,' says I. 'The other kind will do as well.'

"'This Chinaman,' goes on Paisley, 'was the one that shot a man named Mullins in the spring of '97, and that was —'

"'Paisley interrupted himself again.

"'Lem ,' says he, 'if you was a true friend you wouldn't hug Mrs. Jessup quite so hard. I felt the bench shake all over just then. You know you told me you

　　"'希克斯先生,'杰塞普太太说,她在黑暗里瞅着我,神情有点异样,'如果不是另有原因的话,我早就请你走下山谷,永远别来见我啦。'

　　"'请问是什么原因呢,夫人?'我问道。

　　"'你既然是这样忠诚的朋友,当然也能成为忠诚的丈夫。'她说。

　　"五分钟之后,佩斯利也坐在杰塞普太太身边了。

　　"'一八九八年夏天,'他开始说,'我在锡尔弗城见到吉姆·巴塞洛缪在蓝光酒馆里咬掉了一个中国人的耳朵,起因只是一件横条花纹的平布衬衫——那是什么声音呀?'

　　"我跟杰塞普太太重新做起了刚才中断的事。

　　"'杰塞普太太,已经答应改姓希克斯了。'我说,'这只不过是再证实一下而已。'

　　"佩斯利把他的两条腿盘在长凳脚上,呻吟起来。

　　"'勒姆,'他说,'我们已经交了七年朋友。你能不能别跟杰塞普太太吻得这么响?以后我也保证不这么响。'

　　"'好吧,'我说,'轻一点儿也可以。'

　　"'这个中国人,'佩斯利继续说,'在一八九七年春天枪杀了一个名叫马林的人,那是——'

　　"佩斯利又打断了他自己的故事。

　　"'勒姆,'他说,'假如你真是个仗义的朋友,你就不该把杰塞普太太搂得这么紧。刚才我觉得整个长凳都在晃。你明白,你对我说过,只要还有机会,你总是同我平分秋色

would give me an even chance as long as there was any.'

"'Mr. Man,'says Mrs. Jessup, turning around to Paisley, 'if you was to drop in to the celebration of mine and Mr. Hicks's silver wedding, twenty-five years from now, do you think you could get it into that Hubbard squash you call your head that you are *nix cum rous* in this business? I've put up with you a long time because you was Mr. Hicks's friend; but it seems to me it's time for you to wear the willow and trot off down the hill.'

"'Mrs. Jessup,'says I, without losing my grasp on the situation as fiancé, 'Mr. Paisley is my friend, and I offered him a square deal and a equal opportunity as long as there was a chance.'

"'A chance!'says she. 'Well, he may think he has a chance; but I hope he won't think he's got a cinch, after what he's been next to all the evening.'

"Well, a month afterwards me and Mrs. Jessup was married in the Los Piños Methodist Church; and the whole town closed up to see the performance.

"When we lined up in front and the preacher was beginning to sing out his rituals and observances, I looks around and misses Paisley. I calls time on the preacher. 'Paisley ain't here,'says I. 'We've got to wait for Paisley. A friend once, a friend always—that's Telemachus Hicks,'says I. Mrs. Jessup's eyes snapped some; but the preacher holds up the incantations according to instructions.

"In a few minutes Paisley gallops up the aisle, putting on a cuff as he comes. He explains that the only dry-goods store in town was closed for the wedding, and he couldn't get the kind of a boiled shirt that his taste called for until he had broke open the back window of the store

的。'

"'你这个家伙,'杰塞普太太转身向佩斯利说,'再过二十五年,假如你来参加我和希克斯先生的银婚纪念,你那个南瓜脑袋还认为你在这件事上有希望吗？只因为你是希克斯先生的朋友,我才忍了好久;不过我认为现在你该死了这条心,下山去啦。'

"'杰塞普太太,'我说,不过我并没有丧失未婚夫的立场,'佩斯利先生是我的朋友,只要有机会,我总是同他公平交易,利益均等的。'

"'机会!'她说。'好吧,让他自以为还有机会吧;今晚他在旁边看到了这一切,我希望他别自以为很有把握。'

"一个月之后,我和杰塞普太太在洛斯比尼奥的卫理公会教堂结婚了;全镇的人都跑来看结婚仪式。

"当我们并排站在最前面,牧师开始替我们主持婚礼的时候,我四下里扫了一眼,没找到佩斯利。我请牧师等一会儿。'佩斯利不在这儿。'我说。'我们非等佩斯利不可。交朋友要交到老——泰勒马格斯·希克斯就是这种人。'我说。杰塞普太太的眼睛里有点儿冒火;但是牧师遵照我的吩咐,没有立即诵读经文。

"过了几分钟,佩斯利飞快地跑进过道,一边跑,一边还在安上一只硬袖口。他说镇上唯一的卖服装的铺子关了门来看婚礼,他搞不到他所喜欢的上过浆的衬衫,只得撬开铺

and helped himself. Then he ranges up on the other side of the bride, and the wedding goes on. I always imagined that Paisley calculated as a last chance that the preacher might marry him to the widow by mistake.

"After the proceedings was over we had tea and jerked antelope and canned apricots, and then the populace hiked itself away. Last of all Paisley shook me by the hand and told me I'd acted square and on the level with him and he was proud to call me a friend.

"The preacher had a small house on the side of the street that he'd fixed up to rent; and he allowed me and Mrs. Hicks to occupy it till the ten-forty train the next morning, when we was going on a bridal tour to El Paso. His wife had decorated it all up with hollyhocks and poison ivy, and it looked real festal and bowery.

"About ten o'clock that night I sets down in the front door and pulls off my boots a while in the cool breeze, while Mrs. Hicks was fixing around in the room. Right soon the light went out inside; and I sat there a while, reverberating over old times and scenes. And then I heard Mrs. Hicks call out, 'Ain't you coming in soon, Lem?'

"'Well, well!' says I, kind of rousing up. 'Durn me if I wasn't waiting for old Paisley to—

"But when I got that far," concluded Telemachus Hicks, "I thought somebody had shot this left ear of mine off with a forty-five. But it turned out to be only a lick from a broomhandle in the hands of Mrs. Hicks."

子的后窗,自己取了一件。接着,他站到新娘的那一边去,婚礼继续进行。我一直在琢磨,佩斯利还在等最后一个机会,盼望牧师万一搞错,替他同寡妇成亲呢。

"婚礼结束后,我们吃了茶、羚羊肉干和罐头杏子,镇上的居民便纷纷散去。最后同我握手的是佩斯利,他说我为人光明磊落,同我交朋友脸上有光。

"牧师在街边有一幢专门出租的小房子;他让我和希克斯太太占用到第二天早晨十点四十分,那时候,我们就乘火车去埃尔帕索度蜜月旅行。牧师太太用蜀葵和毒藤把那幢房子打扮起来,看上去喜气洋洋的,并且有凉亭的风味。

"那晚十点钟左右,我在门口坐下,脱掉靴子凉快凉快,希克斯太太在屋里张罗。没有多久,里面的灯熄了;我还坐在那儿,回想以前的时光和情景。我听到希克斯太太招呼说:'你就进来吗,勒姆?'

"'哎,哎!'我仿佛惊醒似地说。'我刚才在等老佩斯利——'

"可是这句话还没说完,"泰勒马格斯·希克斯结束他的故事说,"我觉得仿佛有人用四五口径的手枪把我这只左耳朵打掉了。后来我才知道,那只是希克斯太太用扫帚把揍了一下。"

Two Thanksgiving
Day Gentlemen

THERE is one day that is ours. There is one day
when all we Americans who are not self-made go back to
the old home to eat saleratus biscuits and marvel how
much nearer to the porch the old pump looks than it used
to. Bless the day. President Roosevelt gives it to us. We
hear some talk of the Puritans, but don't just remember
who they were. Bet we can lick 'em, anyhow, if they try
to land again. Plymouth Rocks? Well, that sounds more
familiar. Lots of us have had to come down to hens since
the Turkey Trust got its work in. But somebody in Washington is leaking out advance information to 'em about
these Thanksgiving proclamations.

The big city east of the cranberry bogs has made
Thanksgiving Day an institution. The last Thursday in
November is the only day in the year on which it recog-
nizes the part of America lying across the ferries. It is the
one day that is purely American. Yes, a day of celebration, exclusively American.

And now for the story which is to prove to you that
we have traditions on this side of the ocean that are becoming older at a much rapider rate than those of England are—thanks to our git-up and enterprise.

Stuffy Pete took his seat on the third bench to the
right as you enter Union Square from the east, at the
walk opposite the fountain. Every Thanksgiving Day for
nine years he had taken his seat there promptly at 1
o'clock. For every time he had done so things had hap-

两位感恩节的绅士

有一天是属于我们的。到了那一天,只要不是从石头里迸出来的美国人都回到自己的老家,吃苏打饼干,看着门口的旧抽水机,觉得它仿佛比以前更靠近门廊,不禁暗自纳闷。祝福那一天吧。罗斯福总统把它给了我们。我们听到过一些有关清教徒的传说①,可是记不清他们是什么样的人了。不用说,假如他们再想登陆的话,我们准能把他们揍得落花流水。普利茅斯岩石②吗?唔,这个名称听来倒有些耳熟。自从火鸡托拉斯垄断了市场以后,我们有许多人不得不降格以求,改吃母鸡了。不过华盛顿又有人走漏消息,把感恩节公告预先通知了他们。

越橘沼泽地东面的那个大城市③使感恩节成了法定节日。一年之中,惟有在十一月的最后一个星期四,那个大城市才承认渡口以外的美国。惟有这一天才纯粹是美国的。是的,它是独一无二的美国的庆祝日。

现在有一个故事可以向你们证明:在大洋此岸的我们,也有一些日趋古老的传统,并且由于我们的奋发和进取精神,这些传统趋向古老的速度比在英国要快得多。

斯塔弗·皮特坐在联合广场喷水泉对面人行道旁边东入口右面的第三条长凳上。九年来,每逢感恩节,他总是不

---

① 1620年,英国清教徒因不堪宗教压迫,首批乘坐"五月花号"轮船来到美洲,次年,为庆祝第一次收获,感谢上帝的恩惠,制定了感恩节,后成为美国法定节日,一般在每年11月的最后一个星期四。这里的罗斯福总统指西奥多·罗斯福(1858—1919),在任期为1901年至1909年。

② 普利茅斯岩石在马萨诸塞州普利茅斯港口,相传为首批清教徒登陆之处,其实登陆地点是在普罗文斯敦的科德角。

③ 指纽约市。

pened to him—Charles Dickensy things that swelled his
waistcoat above his heart,and equally on the other side.

But to-day Stuffy Pete's appearance at the annual
trysting place seemed to have been rather the result of
habit than of the yearly hunger which,as the philanthro-
pists seem to think,afflicts the poor at such extended in-
tervals.

Certainly Pete was not hungry. He had just come
from a feast that had left him of his powers barely those
of respiration and locomotion. His eyes were like two
pale gooseberries firmly imbedded in a swollen and gra-
vy-smeared mask of putty. His breath came in short
wheezes;a senatorial roll of adipose tissue denied a fashionable set to his upturned coat collar. Buttons that had
been sewed upon his clothes by kind Salvation fingers a
week before flew like popcorn,strewing the earth around
him.Ragged he was,with a split shirt front open to the
wishbone;but the November breeze,carrying fine snow-
flakes,brought him only a grateful coolness. For Stuffy
Pete was overcharged with the caloric produced by a su-
per-bountiful dinner,beginning with oysters and ending
with plum pudding,and including (it seemed to him) all
the roast turkey and baked potatoes and chicken salad
and squash pie and ice cream in the world.Wherefore he
sat,gorged,and gazed upon the world with after-dinner
contempt.

The meal had been an unexpected one.He was passing a red brick mansion near the beginning of Fifth
Avenue,in which lived two old ladies of ancient family
and a reverence for traditions.They even denied the existence of New York, and believed that Thanksgiving
Day was declared solely for Washington Square.One of

早不迟,在一点钟的时候坐在老地方。他每次这样一坐,总有一些意外的遭遇——查尔斯·狄更斯式的遭遇,使他的坎肩胀过心口,背后也是如此。

但是,斯塔弗·皮特今天出现在一年一度的约会地点,似乎是出于习惯,而不是出于一年一度的饥饿。据慈善家们的看法,穷苦人仿佛要隔那么长的时间才会遭到饥饿的折磨。

当然啦,皮特一点儿也不饿。他来这儿之前刚刚大吃了一顿,如今只剩下呼吸和挪动的气力了。他的眼睛活像两颗淡色的醋栗,牢牢地嵌在一张浮肿的、油水淋漓的油灰面具上。他短促地、呼哧呼哧地喘着气;脖子上一圈参议员似的脂肪组织,使他翻上来的衣领失去了时髦的派头。一星期以前,救世军修女的仁慈的手指替他缝在衣服上的纽扣,像玉米花似地爆开来,在他身边撒了一地。他的衣服固然褴褛,衬衫前襟一直豁到心口,可是夹着雪花的十一月的微风只给他带来一种可喜的凉爽。因为那顿特别丰富的饭菜所产生的热量,使得斯塔弗·皮特不胜负担。那顿饭以牡蛎开始,以葡萄干布丁结束,包括了他所认为的全世界的烤火鸡、煮土豆、鸡肉色拉、南瓜馅饼和冰淇淋。因此,他肚子塞得饱饱的坐着,带着撑得慌的神情看着周围的一切。

那顿饭完全出乎他意料之外。他路过五马路起点附近的一幢红砖住宅,那里面住有两位家系古老、尊重传统的老太太。她们甚至不承认纽约的存在,并且认为感恩节只是为了华盛顿广场才制定的。她们的传统习惯之一,是派一

their traditional habits was to station a servant at the postern gate with orders to admit the first hungry way-farer that came along after the hour of noon had struck, and banquet him to a finish. Stuffy Pete happened to pass by on his way to the park, and the seneschals gathered him in and upheld the custom of the castle.

After Stuffy Pete had gazed straight before him for ten minutes he was conscious of a desire for a more var-ied field of vision. With a tremendous effort he moved his head slowly to the left. And then his eyes bulged out fearfully, and his breath ceased, and the rough-shod ends of his short legs wriggled and rustled on the gravel.

For the Old Gentleman was coming across Fourth Avenue toward his bench.

Every Thanksgiving Day for nine years the Old Gentleman had come there and found Stuffy Pete on his bench. That was a thing that the Old Gentleman was try-ing to make a tradition of. Every Thanksgiving Day for nine years he had found Stuffy there, and had led him to a restaurant and watched him eat a big dinner. They do those things in England unconsciously. But this is a young country, and nine years is not so bad. The Old Gentleman was a stanch American patriot, and considered himself a pioneer in American tradition. In order to become pic-turesque we must keep on doing one thing for a long time without ever letting it get away from us. Something like collecting the weekly dimes in industrial insurance. Or cleaning the streets.

The Old Gentleman moved, straight and stately, to-ward the Institution that he was rearing. Truly, the annu-al feeling of Stuffy Pete was nothing national in its char-acter, such as the Magna Charta or jam for breakfast was

个用人等在侧门口,吩咐他在正午过后把第一个饥饿的过路人请进来,让他大吃大喝,饱餐一顿。斯塔弗·皮特去公园时,碰巧路过那里,给管家们请了进去,成全了城堡里的传统。

斯塔弗·皮特朝前面直瞪瞪地望了十分钟之后,觉得很想换换眼界。他费了好大的劲,才慢慢把头扭向左面。这当儿,他的眼球惊恐地鼓了出来,他的呼吸也停止了,他那穿着破皮鞋的短脚在沙砾地上簌簌地扭动着。

因为那位老先生正穿过四马路,朝他坐着的长凳方向走来。

九年来,每逢感恩节的时候,这位老先生总是来这儿寻找坐在长凳上的斯塔弗·皮特。老先生想把这件事形成一个传统。九年来的每一个感恩节,他总是在这儿找到了斯塔弗,总是带他到一家饭馆里去,看他美餐一顿。这类事在英国是做得很自然的。然而美国是个年轻的国家,坚持九年已经算是不坏了。那位老先生是忠实的美国爱国者,并且自认为是创立美国传统的先驱之一。为了引起人们注意,我们必须长期坚持一件事情,一步也不放松。比如收集每周几毛钱的工人保险费啦,打扫街道啦,等等。

老先生庄严地朝着他所培植的制度笔直地走去。不错,斯塔弗·皮特一年一度的感觉并不像英国的大宪章或者早餐的果酱那样具有国家性。不过它至少是向前迈了一

in England. But it was a step. It was almost feudal. It showed, at least, that a Custom was not impossible to New Y—ahem! —America.

The Old Gentleman was thin and tall and sixty. He was dressed all in black, and wore the old-fashioned kind of glasses that won't stay on your nose. His hair was whiter and thinner than it had been last year, and he seemed to make more use of his big, knobby cane with the crooked handle.

As his established benefactor came up Stuffy wheezed and shuddered like some woman's over-fat pug when a street dog bristles up at him. He would have flown, but all the skill of Santos-Dumont could not have separated him from his bench. Well had the myrmidons of the two old ladies done their work.

"Good morning," said the Old Gentleman. "I am glad to perceive that the vicissitudes of another year have spared you to move in health about the beautiful world. For that blessing alone this day of thanksgiving is well proclaimed to each of us. If you will come with me, my man, I will provide you with a dinner that should make your physical being accord with the mental."

That is what the Old Gentleman said every time. Every Thanksgiving Day for nine years. The words themselves almost formed an Institution. Nothing could be compared with them except the Declaration of Independence. Always before they had been music in Stuffy's ears. But now he looked up at the Old Gentleman's face with tearful agony in his own. The fine snow almost sizzled when it fell upon his perspiring brow. But the Old Gentleman shivered a little and turned his back to the wind.

步。它几乎有点儿封建意味。它至少证明了要在纽约——唔！——在美国树立一种习俗并不是不可能的。

老先生又高又瘦，年过花甲。他穿着一身黑衣服，鼻子上架着一副不稳当的老式眼镜。他的头发比去年白一点儿，稀一点儿，并且好像比去年更借重那支粗而多节的曲柄拐杖。

斯塔弗·皮特眼看他的老恩人走近，不禁呼吸短促，直打哆嗦，正如某位太太的过于肥胖的狮子狗看到一条野狗对它龇牙竖毛时所会做的那样。他很想跳起来逃跑，可是即使桑托斯－杜蒙特①施展出全部本领，也无法使他同长凳分开。那两位老太太的忠心的家仆办事可着实彻底。

"你好。"老先生说。"我很高兴见到，又一年的变迁对你并没有什么影响，你仍旧很健旺地在这个美好的世界上逍遥自在。仅仅为了这一点儿幸福，今天这个感恩节对我们两人都有很大的意义。假如你愿意跟我一起来，朋友，我预备请你吃顿饭，让你的身心取得协调。"

老先生每次都说这番同样的话。九年来的每一个感恩节都是这样的。这些话本身几乎成了一个制度。除了《独立宣言》之外，没有什么可以同它相比了。以前在斯塔弗听来，它们像音乐一般美妙。现今他却愁眉苦脸，眼泪汪汪地抬头看着老先生的脸。细雪落到斯塔弗的汗水淋漓的额头上，几乎嗞嗞发响。但是老先生却在微微打战，他掉转身子，背朝着风。

---

① 桑托斯－杜蒙特（1873—1932）：巴西气球驾驶员，1901 年乘气球从法国的圣克卢至埃菲尔铁塔往返飞行一次，1906 和 1909 年又试飞过双翼飞机和单翼飞机。

Stuffy had always wondered why the Old Gentleman spoke his speech rather sadly. He did not know that it was because he was wishing every time that he had a son to succeed him. A son who would come there after he was gone—a son who would stand proud and strong before some subsequent Stuffy, and say: "In memory of my father." Then it would be an Institution.

But the Old Gentleman had no relatives. He lived in rented rooms in one of the decayed old family brownstone mansions in one of the quiet streets east of the park. In the winter he raised fuchsias in a little conservatory the size of a steamer trunk. In the spring he walked in the Easter parade. In the summer he lived at a farmhouse in the New Jersey hills, and sat in a wicker armchair, speaking of a butterfly, the ornithoptera amphrisius, that he hoped to find some day. In the autumn he fed Stuffy a dinner. These were the Old Gentleman's occupations.

Stuffy Pete looked up at him for a half minute, stewing and helpless in his own self-pity. The Old Gentleman's eyes were bright with the giving-pleasure. His face was getting more lined each year, but his little black necktie was in as jaunty a bow as ever, and his linen was beautiful and white, and his gray mustache was curled gracefully at the ends. And then Stuffy made a noise that sounded like peas bubbling in a pot. Speech was intended; and as the Old Gentleman had heard the sounds nine times before, he rightly construed them into Stuffy's old formula of acceptance.

"Thankee, sir. I'll go with ye, and much obliged. I'm very hungry, sir."

The coma of repletion had not prevented from enter-

　　斯塔弗一向纳闷,老先生说这番话时的神情为什么相当悲哀。他不明白,因为老先生每次都在希望有一个儿子来继承他的事业。他希望自己去世后有一个儿子能来到这个地方——一个壮实自豪的儿子,站在以后的斯塔弗一类的人面前说:"为了纪念家父。"那一来,一个制度就形成了。

　　然而老先生没有亲属。他在公园东面一条冷僻街道的一座败落的褐石住宅里租了几间屋子。冬天,他在一个不比衣箱大多少的温室里种些倒挂金钟。春天,他参加复活节的游行。夏天,他在新泽西州山间的农舍里寄宿,坐在柳条扶手椅上,谈着他希望总有一天能找到的某种扑翼蝴蝶。秋天,他请斯塔弗吃顿饭。老先生干的事就是这些。

　　斯塔弗抬着头,瞅了他一会儿,自怨自艾,好不烦恼,可是又束手无策。老先生的眼睛里闪现出为善最乐的光亮。他脸上的皱纹一年比一年深,但他那小小的黑领结依然非常神气,他的衬衫又白又漂亮,他那两撇灰胡髭典雅地翘着。斯塔弗发出一种像是锅里煮豌豆的声音。他原想说些什么;这种声音老先生已经听过九次了,他理所当然地把它当成斯塔弗表示接受的老一套话。

　　"谢谢你,先生。非常感谢,我跟你一起去。我饿极啦,先生。"

　　饱胀引起的昏昏沉沉的感觉,并没有动摇斯塔弗脑子

ing Stuffy's mind the conviction that he was the basis of an Institution. His Thanksgiving appetite was not his own; it belonged by all the sacred rights of established custom, if not by the actual Statute of Limitations, to this kind old gentleman who had preëmpted it. True, America is free; but in order to establish tradition some one must be a repetend—a repeating decimal. The heroes are not all heroes of steel and gold. See one here that wielded only weapons of iron, badly silvered, and tin.

The Old Gentleman led his annual protégé southward to the restaurant, and to the table where the feast had always occurred. They were recognized.

"Here comes de old guy," said a waiter, "dat blows dat same bum to a meal every Thanksgiving."

The Old Gentleman sat across the table glowing like a smoked pearl at his corner-stone of future ancient Tradition. The waiters heaped the table with holiday food—and Stuffy, with a sigh that was mistaken for hunger's expression, raised knife and fork and carved for himself a crown of imperishable bay.

No more valiant hero ever fought his way through the ranks of an enemy. Turkey, chops, soups, vegetables, pies, disappeared before him as fast as they could be served. Gorged nearly to the uttermost when he entered the restaurant, the smell of food had almost caused him to lose his honor as a gentleman, but he rallied like a true knight. He saw the look of beneficent happiness on the Old Gentleman's face—a happier look than even the fuchsias and the ornithoptera amphrisius had ever brought to it—and he had not the heart to see it wane.

In an hour Stuffy leaned back with a battle won.

"Thankee kindly, sir," he puffed like a leaky steam

里的那个信念：他是某种制度的基石。他的感恩节的胃口并不属于他自己，而属于这位占有优先权的慈祥的老先生；因为即使不根据实际的起诉期限法①，也得考虑到既定习俗的全部神圣权利。不错，美国是一个自由的国家；可是为了建立传统，总得有人充当循环小数呀，英雄们不一定非得使用钢铁和黄金不可。瞧，这儿就有一位英雄，光是挥弄着马马虎虎地镀了银的铁器和锡器②。

老先生带着他的一年一度的受惠者，朝南去到那家饭馆和那张年年举行盛宴的桌子旁。他们给认出来了。

"老家伙来啦，"一个侍者说，"他每年感恩节都请那个穷汉吃上一顿。"

老先生坐在桌子对面，朝着他的将要成为古老传统的基石，脸上发出像熏黑的珠子似的光芒。侍者在桌子上摆满了节日的食物——斯塔弗叹了口气（别人还以为这是饥饿的表示呢），举起了刀叉，替自己刻了一顶不朽的桂冠。

在敌军人马中杀开一条血路的英雄都没有他这样勇敢。火鸡、肉排、汤、蔬菜、馅饼，一端到他面前就不见了。他跨进饭馆的时候，肚子里已经塞得实实足足，食物的气味几乎使他丧失绅士的荣誉，但他却像一个真正的骑士，打起精神，坚持到底。他看到老先生脸上的行善的快乐——倒挂金钟和扑翼蝴蝶带来的快乐都不能与此相比——他实在不忍扫他老人家的兴。

一小时之后，斯塔弗往后一靠，这一仗已经打赢了。

"多谢你，先生，"他像一根漏气的蒸汽管子那样呼哧呼

---

① 起诉期限法：当时的英美法律规定，不动产遭受侵害的起诉期限为20年，动产为6年，犯法行为为2年；超过上述期限后原告不得提出诉讼。

② 指吃饭用的刀叉盘碟。

pipe;"thankee kindly for a hearty meal."

Then he arose heavily with glazed eyes and started toward the kitchen. A waiter turned him about like a top,and pointed him toward the door. The Old Gentleman carefully counted out ＄1.30 in silver change,leaving three nickels for the waiter.

They parted as they did each year at the door,the Old Gentleman going south,Stuffy north.

Around the first corner Stuffy turned,and stood for one minute. Then he seemed to puff out his rags as an owl puffs out his feathers,and fell to the sidewalk like a sunstricken horse.

When the ambulance came the young surgeon and the driver cursed softly at his weight. There was no smell of whiskey to justify a transfer to the patrol wagon,so Stuffy and his two dinners went to the hospital. There they stretched him on a bed and began to test him for strange diseases,with the hope of getting a chance at some problem with the bare steel.

And lo! an hour later another ambulance brought the Old Gentleman. And they laid him on another bed and spoke of appendicitis,for he looked good for the bill.

But pretty soon one of the young doctors met one of the young nurses whose eyes he liked,and stopped to chat with her about the cases.

"That nice old gentleman over there,now,"he said, "you wouldn't think that was a case of almost starvation. Proud old family,I guess. He told me he hadn't eaten a thing for three days."

哧地说,"多谢你赏了一顿称心的中饭。"

接着,他两眼发直,费劲地站起身来,向厨房走去。一个侍者把他像陀螺似地打了一个转,推他走向门口。老先生仔仔细细地数出一块三毛钱的小银币,另外给了侍者三枚镍币作小账。

他们像往年那样,在门口分了手,老先生往南,斯塔弗往北。

在第一个拐角上,斯塔弗转过身,站了一会儿。接着,他的破旧衣服像猫头鹰的羽毛似地鼓了起来,他自己则像一匹中暑的马那样,倒在人行道上。

救护车开到了,年轻的医师和司机低声咒骂他的笨重。既然没有威士忌的气息,也就没有理由把他移交给警察局的巡逻车,于是斯塔弗和他肚子里的双份饭就给带到医院里去了。他们把他抬到医院里的床上,开始检查他是不是得了某些怪病,希望有机会用尸体解剖来发现一些问题。

瞧呀!过了一小时,另一辆救护车把老先生送来了。他们把他放在另一张床上,谈论着阑尾炎,因为从外表看来,他是付得起钱的。

但是不多久,一个年轻的医师碰到一个眼睛讨他欢喜的年轻的护士,便停住脚步,跟她谈谈病人的情况。

"那个体面的老先生,"他说,"你怎么都猜不到,他几乎要饿死了。从前大概是名门世家,如今落魄了。他告诉我说,他已经三天没有吃东西了。"

The Last Leaf

IN a little district west of Washington Square the streets have run crazy and broken themselves into small strips called "places". These "places" make strange angles and curves. One street crosses itself a time or two. An artist once discovered a valuable possibility in this street. Suppose a collector with a bill for paints, paper and canvas should, in traversing this route, suddenly meet himself coming back, without a cent having been paid on account!

So, to quaint old Greenwich Village the art people soon came prowling, hunting for north windows and eighteenth-century gables and Dutch attics and low rents. Then they imported some pewter mugs and a chafing dish or two from Sixth Avenue, and became a "colony."

At the top of a squatty, three-story brick Sue and Johnsy had their studio. "Johnsy" was familiar for Joanna. One was from Maine; the other from California. They had met at the *table d'hôte* of an Eighth Street "Delmonico's", and found their tastes in art, chicory salad and bishop sleeves so congenial that the joint studio resulted.

That was in May. In November a cold, unseen stranger, whom the doctors called Pneumonia, stalked about the colony, touching one here and there with his icy fingers. Over on the east side this ravager strode boldly, smiting his victims by scores, but his feet trod slowly through the maze of the narrow and moss-grown

134

最后的常春藤叶

在华盛顿广场西面的一个小区里,街道仿佛发了狂似的,分成了许多叫做"巷子"的小胡同。这些"巷子"形成许多奇特的角度和曲线。一条街本身往往交叉一两回。有一次,一个艺术家发现这条街也有它的可贵之处。如果一个商人去收颜料、纸张和画布的账款,在这条街上转弯抹角、大兜圈子的时候,突然碰上一文钱也没收到,空手而回的他自己,那才有意思呢!

因此,搞艺术的人不久都到这个古色古香的格林尼治村[①]来了。他们逛来逛去,寻找朝北的窗户,十八世纪的三角墙,荷兰式的阁楼,以及低廉的房租。接着,他们又从六马路买来了一些锡镴杯子和一两只烘锅,组成了一个"艺术区"。

苏艾和琼珊在一座矮墩墩的三层砖屋的顶楼设立了她们的画室。"琼珊"是琼娜的昵称。两人一个是从缅因州来的;另一个的家乡是加利福尼亚州。她们是在八马路上一家"德尔蒙尼戈饭馆"里吃客饭时碰到的,彼此一谈,发现她们对于艺术、饮食和衣着的口味十分相投,结果便联合租下了那间画室。

那是五月间的事。到了十一月,一个冷酷无情,肉眼看不见,医生管他叫"肺炎"的不速之客,在艺术区里潜蹑着,用他的冰冷的手指这儿碰碰那儿摸摸。在广场的东面,这个坏家伙明目张胆地走动着,每闯一次祸,受害的人总有几十个。但是,在这错综复杂,狭窄而苔藓遍地的"巷子"里,

---

① 格林尼治村:美国纽约市西区的一个地名,住在这里的多半是作家、艺术家等。

"places".

Mr. Pneumonia was not what you would call a chivalric old gentleman. A mite of a little woman with blood thinned by California zephyrs was hardly fair game for the red-fisted, short-breathed old duffer. But Johnsy he smote; and she lay, scarcely moving, on her painted iron bedstead, looking through the small Dutch window-panes at the blank side of the next brick house.

One morning the busy doctor invited Sue into the hallway with a shaggy, gray eyebrow.

"She has one chance in—let us say, ten," he said, as he shook down the mercury in his clinical thermometer. "And that chance is for her to want to live. This way people have of lining-up on the side of the undertaker makes the entire pharmacopoeia look silly. Your little lady has made up her mind that she's not going to get well. Has she anything on her mind?"

"She—she wanted to paint the Bay of Naples some day," said Sue.

"Paint? —bosh! Has she anything on her mind worth thinking about twice—a man, for instance?"

"A man?" said Sue, with a jew's-harp twang in her voice. "Is a man worth—but, no, doctor; there is nothing of the kind."

"Well, it is the weakness, then," said the doctor. "I will do all that science, so far as it may filter through my efforts, can accomplish. But whenever my patient begins to count the carriages in her funeral procession I subtract 50 per cent, from the curative power of medicines. If you will get her to ask one question about the new winter styles in cloak sleeves I will promise you a one-in-five chance for her, instead of one in ten."

他的脚步却放慢了。

"肺炎先生"并不是你们所谓的扶弱济困的老绅士。一个弱小的女人,已经被加利福尼亚的西风吹得没有什么血色了,当然经不起那个有着红拳头,气吁吁的老家伙的赏识。但他竟然打击了琼珊;她躺在那张漆过的铁床上,一动也不动,望着荷兰式小窗外对面砖屋的墙壁。

一天早晨,那位忙碌的医生扬扬他那蓬松的灰眉毛,招呼苏艾到过道上去。

"依我看,她的病只有一成希望。"他说,一面把体温表里的水银甩下去。"那一成希望在于她自己要不要活下去。人们不想活,情愿照顾殡仪馆的生意,这种精神状态使医药一筹莫展。你的这位小姐满肚子以为自己不会好了。她有什么心事吗?"

"她——她希望有一天能去画那不勒斯①海湾。"苏艾说。

"绘画?——别扯淡了!她心里有没有值得想两次的事情——比如说,男人?"

"男人?"苏艾像吹小口琴似地哼了一声说。"难道男人值得——别说啦,不,大夫;根本没有那种事。"

"那么,一定是身体虚弱的关系。"医生说。"我一定尽我所知,用科学所能达到的一切方法来治疗她。可是每逢我的病人开始盘算有多少辆马车送他出殡的时候,我就得把医药的治疗力量减去百分之五十。要是你能使她对冬季大衣的袖子式样发生兴趣,提出一个问题,我就可以保证,她恢复的机会准能从十分之一提高到五分之一。"

---

① 意大利南部的海港。

After the doctor had gone Sue went into the workroom and cried a Japanese napkin to a pulp. Then she swaggered into Johnsy's room with her drawing board, whistling ragtime.

Johnsy, lay, scarcely making a ripple under the bedclothes, with her face toward the window. Sue stopped whistling, thinking she was asleep.

She arranged her board and began a pen-and-ink drawing to illustrate a magazine story. Young artists must pave their way to Art by drawing pictures for magazine stories that young authors write to pave their way to Literature.

As Sue was sketching a pair of elegant horseshow riding trousers and a monocle on the figure of the hero, an Idaho cowboy, she heard a low sound, several times repeated. She went quickly to the bedside.

Johnsy's eyes were open wide. She was looking out the window and counting—counting backward.

"Twelve," she said, and a little later "eleven"; and then "ten", and "nine"; and then "eight" and "seven", almost together.

Sue looked solicitously out of the window. What was there to count? There was only a bare, dreary yard to be seen, and the blank side of the brick house twenty feet away. An old, old ivy vine, gnarled and decayed at the roots, climbed half way up the brick wall. The cold breath of autumn had stricken its leaves from the vine until its skeleton branches clung, almost bare, to the crumbling bricks.

"What is it, dear?" asked Sue.

"Six," said Johnsy, in almost a whisper. "They're falling faster now. Three days ago there were almost a

医生离去之后，苏艾到工作室里哭了一场，把一张日本纸餐巾擦得一团糟。然后，她拿起画板，吹着拉格泰姆音乐调子，昂首阔步地走进琼珊的房间。

琼珊躺在被窝里，脸朝着窗口，一点动静也没有。苏艾以为她睡着了，赶紧不吹口哨。

她架好画板，开始替杂志社画一幅短篇小说的钢笔画插图。青年画家不得不以杂志小说的插图来铺平通向艺术的道路，而这些小说则是青年作家为了铺平文学道路而创作的。

苏艾正为小说里的主角，一个爱达荷州的牧人，画上一条在马匹展览会里穿的漂亮的马裤和一片单眼镜，忽然听到一个微弱的声音重复了几遍。她赶紧走到床边。

琼珊的眼睛睁得大大的。她望着窗外，在计数——倒数上来。

"十二，"她说，过了一会儿，又说"十一"；接着是"十"、"九"；再接着是几乎连在一起的"八"和"七"。

苏艾关切地向窗外望去。有什么可数的呢？外面见到的只是一个空荡荡、阴沉沉的院子，和二十英尺外的一幢砖屋的墙壁。一株极老极老的常春藤，纠结的根已经枯萎，攀在半墙上。秋季的寒风把藤上的叶子差不多全吹落了，只剩下几根几乎是光秃秃的藤枝依附在那堵松动残缺的砖墙上。

"怎么回事，亲爱的？"苏艾问道。

"六。"琼珊说，声音低得像是耳语。"它们现在掉得快些了。三天前差不多有一百片。数得我头昏眼花。现在可

hundred. It made my head ache to count them. But now it's easy. There goes another one. There are only five left now."

"Five what, dear? Tell your Sudie."

"Leaves. On the ivy vine. When the last one falls I must go, too. I've known that for three days. Didn't the doctor tell you?"

"Oh, I never heard of such nonsense," complained Sue, with magnificent scorn. "What have old ivy leaves to do with your getting well? And you used to love that vine, so, you naughty girl. Don't be a goosey. Why, the doctor told me this morning that your chances for getting well real soon were—let's see exactly what he said—he said the chances were ten to one! Why, that's almost as good a chance as we have in New York when we ride on the street cars or walk past a new building. Try to take some broth now, and let Sudie go back to her drawing, so she can sell the editor man with it, and buy port wine for her sick child, and pork chops for her greedy self."

"You needn't get any more wine," said Johnsy, keeping her eyes fixed out the window. "There goes another. No, I don't want any broth. That leaves just four. I want to see the last one fall before it gets dark. Then I'll go, too."

"Johnsy, dear," said Sue, bending over her, "will you promise me to keep your eyes closed, and not look out the window until I am done working? I must hand those drawings in by to-morrow. I need the light, or I would draw the shade down."

"Couldn't you draw in the other room?" asked Johnsy, coldly.

"I'd rather be here by you," said Sue. "Besides, I

容易了。喏，又掉了一片。只剩下五片了。"

"五片什么，亲爱的？告诉你的苏艾。"

"叶子。常春藤上的叶子。等最后一片掉落下来，我也得去了。三天前我就知道了。难道大夫没有告诉你吗？"

"哟，我从没听到这样荒唐的话。"苏艾装出满不在乎的样子数落她说。"老藤叶同你的病有什么相干？你一向很喜欢那株常春藤，得啦，你这淘气的姑娘。别发傻啦。我倒忘了，大夫今早晨告诉我，你很快康复的机会是——让我想想，他是怎么说的——他说你好的希望是十比一！哟，那几乎跟我们在纽约搭街车或者走过一幢新房子的工地一样，碰到意外的时候很少。现在喝一点儿汤吧。让苏艾继续画图，好卖给编辑先生，换了钱给她的病孩子买点红葡萄酒，也买些猪排填填她自己的馋嘴。"

"你不用再买什么酒啦。"琼珊说，仍然凝视着窗外。"又掉了一片。不，我不要喝汤。只剩四片了。我希望在天黑之前看到最后的藤叶飘落下来。那时候我也该去了。"

"琼珊，亲爱的，"苏艾弯着身子对她说，"你能不能答应我，在我画完之前，别睁开眼睛，别瞧窗外？那些图画我明天得交。我需要光线，不然我早就要把窗帘拉下来了。"

"你不能到另一间屋子里去画吗？"琼珊冷冷地问道。

"我要呆在这儿，跟你在一起。"苏艾说。"而且我不喜

don't want you to keep looking at those silly ivy leaves. "

"Tell me as soon as you have finished,"said Johnsy,
closing her eyes,and lying white and still as a fallen statue,"because I want to see the last one fall. I'm tired of
waiting. I'm tired of thinking. I want to turn loose my
hold on everything,and go sailing down,down,just like
one of those poor,tired leaves. "

"Try to sleep,"said Sue. "I must call Behrman up to
be my model for the old hermit miner. I'll not be gone a
minute. Don't try to move 'til I come back. "

Old Behrman was a painter who lived on the ground
floor beneath them. He was past sixty and had a Michael-
angelo's Moses beard curling down from the head of a
satyr along the body of an imp. Behrman was a failure in
art. Forty years he had wielded the brush without getting
near enough to touch the hem of his Mistress's robe. He
had been always about to paint a masterpiece,but had
never yet begun it. For several years he had painted
nothing except now and then a daub in the line of commerce or advertising. He earned a little by serving as a
model to those young artists in the colony who could not
pay the price of a professional. He drank gin to excess,
and still talked of his coming masterpiece. For the rest he
was a fierce little old man,who scoffed terribly at soft-
ness in any one,and who regarded himself as especial
mastiff-in-waiting to protect the two young artists in the
studio above.

Sue found Behrman smelling strongly of juniper ber-
ries in his dimly lighted den below. In one corner was a
blank canvas on an easel that had been waiting there for
twenty-five years to receive the first line of the masterpiece. She told him of Johnsy's fancy,and how she feared

欢你老盯着那些莫名其妙的藤叶。"

"你一画完就告诉我，"琼珊闭上眼睛说，她脸色惨白，静静地躺着，活像一尊倒坍下来的塑像，"因为我要看那最后的藤叶掉下来。我等得不耐烦了。也想得不耐烦了。我想摆脱一切，像一片可怜的、厌倦的藤叶，悠悠地往下飘，往下飘。"

"你争取睡一会儿。"苏艾说。"我要去叫贝尔曼上来，替我做那个隐居的老矿工的模特儿。我去不了一分钟。在我回来之前，千万别动。"

老贝尔曼是住在楼下底层的画家。他年纪六十开外，有一把像米开朗琪罗的摩西雕像①上的胡子，从萨蒂尔②似的脑袋上顺着小鬼般的身体卷垂下来。贝尔曼在艺术界是个失意的人。他要了四十年的画笔，还是同艺术女神隔有相当距离，连她的长袍的边缘都没有摸到。他老是说就要画一幅杰作，可是始终没有动手。除了偶尔涂抹一些商业画或广告画之外，几年来没有画过什么。他替"艺术区"里那些雇不起职业模特儿的青年艺术家充当模特儿，挣几个小钱。他喝杜松子酒总是过量，老是唠唠叨叨地谈着他未来的杰作。此外，他还是个暴躁的小老头儿，极端瞧不起别人的温情，却认为自己是保护楼上两个青年艺术家的看家凶狗。

苏艾在楼下那间灯光黯淡的小屋子里找到了酒气扑人的贝尔曼。角落里的画架上绷着一幅空白的画布，它在那儿静候杰作的落笔，已经有了二十五个年头。她把琼珊的想法告诉了他，又说她多么担心，唯恐那个虚弱得像枯叶一

---

① 米开朗琪罗（1475—1564）：意大利著名画家、雕塑家、诗人、建筑师。他在罗马教皇朱利二世的墓上雕刻了摩西像。

② 萨蒂尔：希腊神话中半人半兽的森林之神，长着马耳马尾或羊角羊尾。

she would, indeed, light and fragile as a leaf herself, float away, when her slight hold upon the world grew weaker.

Old Behrman, with his red eyes plainly streaming, shouted his contempt and derision for such idiotic imaginings.

"Vass!"he cried. "Is dere people in de world mit der foolishness to die because leafs dey drop off from a confounded vine? I haf not heard of such a thing. No, I will not bose as a model for your fool hermit-dunderhead. Vy do you allow dot silly pusiness to come in der prain of her? Ach, dot poor leetle Miss Yohnsy."

"She is very ill and weak,"said Sue, "and the fever has left her mind morbid and full of strange fancies. Very well, Mr. Behrman, if you do not care to pose for me, you needn't. But I think you are a horrid old—old flibbertigibbet."

"You are just like a woman!"yelled Behrman. "Who said I will not bose? Go on. I come mit you. For half an hour I haf peen trying to say dot I am ready to bose. Gott! dis is not any blace in which one so goot as Miss Yohnsy shall lie sick. Some day I vill baint a masterpiece, and ve shall all go away. Gott! yes."

Johnsy was sleeping when they went upstairs. Sue pulled the shade down to the window-sill, and motioned Behrman into the other room. In there they peered out the window fearfully at the ivy vine. Then they looked at each other for a moment without speaking. A persistent, cold rain was falling, mingled with snow. Behrman, in his old blue shirt, took his seat as the hermit miner on an upturned kettle for a rock.

When Sue awoke from an hour's sleep the next morning she found Johnsy with dull, wide-open eyes star-

般的琼珊抓不住她同世界的微弱牵连，真会撒手去世。

老贝尔曼的充血的眼睛老是迎风流泪，他对这种白痴般的想法大不以为然，连讽带刺地咆哮了一阵子。

"什么话！"他嚷道。"难道世界上竟有这种傻子，因为可恶的藤叶落掉而想死？我活了一辈子也没有听到过这种怪事。不，我没有心思替你当那无聊的隐士模特儿。你怎么能让她脑袋里有这种傻念头呢？唉，可怜的小琼珊小姐。"

"她病得很厉害，很虚弱，"苏艾说，"高烧烧得她疑神疑鬼，满脑袋都是希奇古怪的念头。好吧，贝尔曼先生，既然你不愿意替我当模特儿，我也不勉强了。我认得你这个可恶的老——老贫嘴。"

"你真女人气！"贝尔曼嚷道。"谁说我不愿意？走吧。我跟你一起去。我已经说了半天，愿意替你效劳。天哪！像琼珊小姐那样好的人实在不应该在这种地方害病。总有一天，我要画一幅杰作，那么我们都可以离开这里啦。天哪！是啊。"

他们上楼时，琼珊已经睡着了。苏艾把窗帘拉到窗槛上，做手势让贝尔曼到另一间屋子里去。他们在那儿担心地瞥着窗外的常春藤。接着，他们默默无言地对瞅了一会儿。寒雨夹着雪花下个不停。贝尔曼穿着一件蓝色的旧衬衫，坐在一口翻转过来的权充岩石的铁锅上，扮作隐居的矿工。

第二天早晨，苏艾睡了一个小时醒来的时候，看到琼珊睁着无神的眼睛，凝视着放下来的绿窗帘。

ing at the drawn green shade.

"Pull it up; I want to see," she ordered, in a whisper.

Wearily Sue obeyed.

But, lo! after the beating rain and fierce gusts of wind that had endured through the livelong night, there yet stood out against the brick wall one ivy leaf. It was the last on the vine. Still dark green near its stem, but with its serrated edges tinted with the yellow of dissolution and decay, it hung bravely from a branch some twenty feet above the ground.

"It is the last one," said Johnsy. "I thought it would surely fall during the night. I heard the wind. It will fall to-day, and I shall die at the same time."

"Dear, dear!" said Sue, leaning her worn face down to the pillow, "think of me, if you won't think of yourself. What would I do?"

But Johnsy did not answer. The lonesomest thing in all the world is a soul when it is making ready to go on its mysterious, far journey. The fancy seemed to possess her more strongly as one by one the ties that bound her to friendship and to earth were loosed.

The day wore away, and even through the twilight they could see the lone ivy leaf clinging to its stem against the wall. And then, with the coming of the night the north wind was again loosed, while the rain still beat against the windows and pattered down from the low Dutch eaves.

When it was light enough Johnsy, the merciless, commanded that the shade be raised.

The ivy leaf was still there.

Johnsy lay for a long time looking at it. And then she called to Sue, who was stirring her chicken broth o-

"把窗帘拉上去，我要看。"她用微弱的声音命令着。

苏艾困倦地照着做了。

可是，看哪！经过了漫漫长夜的风吹雨打，仍旧有一片常春藤的叶子贴在墙上。它是藤上最后的一叶了。靠近叶柄的颜色还是深绿的，但那锯齿形的边缘已染上了枯败的黄色，它傲然挂在离地面二十来英尺的一根藤枝上面。

"那是最后的一片叶子。"琼珊说。"我以为昨夜里它一定会掉落的。我听到刮风的声音。它今天会脱落的，同时我也要死了。"

"哎呀，哎呀！"苏艾把她困倦的脸凑到枕边说，"如果你不为自己着想，也得替我想想呀。我可怎么办呢？"

但是琼珊没有回答。一个准备走上神秘遥远的死亡道路的心灵，是全世界最寂寞、最悲凉的了。当她与尘世和友情之间的联系一片片地脱离时，那个玄想似乎更有力地掌握了她。

那一天总算熬了过去。黄昏时，她们看到墙上那片孤零零的藤叶仍旧依附在茎上。随夜晚同来的是北风的怒号，雨点不住地打在窗上，从荷兰式的低屋檐上倾泻下来。

天色刚明的时候，狠心的琼珊又吩咐把窗帘拉上去。

那片常春藤叶仍在墙上。

琼珊躺着对它看了很久。然后她喊苏艾，苏艾正在煤气炉上搅动给琼珊喝的鸡汤。

ver the gas stove.

"I've been a bad girl, Sudie," said Johnsy. "Something has made that last leaf stay there to show me how wicked I was. It is a sin to want to die. You may bring me a little broth now, and some milk with a little port in it, and—no; bring me a hand-mirror first, and then pack some pillows about me, and I will sit up and watch you cook."

An hour later she said:

"Sudie, some day I hope to paint the Bay of Naples."

The doctor came in the afternoon, and Sue had an excuse to go into the hallway as he left.

"Even chances," said the doctor, taking Sue's thin, shaking hand in his. "With good nursing you'll win. And now I must see another case I have downstairs. Behrman, his name is—some kind of an artist, I believe. Pneumonia, too. He is an old, weak man, and the attack is acute. There is no hope for him; but he goes to the hospital today to be made more comfortable."

The next day the doctor said to Sue: "She's out of danger. You've won. Nutrition and care now—that's all."

And that afternoon Sue came to the bed where Johnsy lay, contentedly knitting a very blue and very useless woollen shoulder scarf, and put one arm around her, pillows and all.

"I have something to tell you, white mouse," she said. "Mr. Behrman died of pneumonia to-day in the hospital. He was ill only two days. The janitor found him on the morning of the first day in his room downstairs helpless with pain. His shoes and clothing were wet through

"我真是一个坏姑娘，苏艾，"琼珊说，"冥冥中有什么使那最后的一片叶子不掉下来，启示了我过去是多么邪恶。不想活下去是个罪恶。现在请你拿些汤来，再弄一点掺葡萄酒的牛奶，再——等一下；先拿一面小镜子给我，用枕头替我垫垫高，我要坐起来看你煮东西。"

一小时后，她说：

"苏艾，我希望有朝一日能去那不勒斯海湾写生。"

下午，医生来了，他离去时，苏艾找了个借口，跑到过道上。

"好的希望有了五成。"医生抓住苏艾瘦小的、颤抖的手说。"只要好好护理，你会胜利的。现在我得去楼下看看另一个病人。他姓贝尔曼——据我所知，也是搞艺术的。也是肺炎。他上了年纪，身体虚弱，病势来得很猛。他可没有希望了，不过今天还是要把他送进医院，让他舒服些。"

第二天，医生对苏艾说："她现在脱离危险了。你赢啦。现在只要营养和调理就行啦。"

那天下午，苏艾跑到床边，琼珊靠在那儿，心满意足地在织一条毫无用处的深蓝色肩巾，苏艾连枕头把她一把抱住。

"我有些话要告诉你，小东西。"她说。"贝尔曼先生今天在医院里去世了。他害肺炎，只病了两天。头天早上，看门人在楼下的房间里发现他痛苦得要命。他的鞋子和衣服

and icy cold. They couldn't imagine where he had been on such a dreadful night. And then they found a lantern, still lighted, and a ladder that had been dragged from its place, and some scattered brushes, and a palette with green and yellow colors mixed on it, and—look out the window, dear, at the last ivy leaf on the wall. Didn't you wonder why it never fluttered or moved when the wind blew? Ah, darling, it's Behrman's masterpiece—he painted it there the night that the last leaf fell. "

都湿透了,冰凉冰凉的。他们想不出,在那种凄风苦雨的夜里,他究竟是到什么地方去的。后来,他们找到了一盏还燃着的灯笼,一把从原来地方挪动过的梯子,还有几支散落的画笔,一块调色板,上面和了绿色和黄色的颜料,末了——看看窗外,亲爱的,看看墙上最后的一片叶子。你不是觉得纳闷,它为什么在风中不飘不动吗?啊,亲爱的,那是贝尔曼的杰作——那晚最后的一片叶子掉落时,他画在墙上的。"

Jeff Peters as a
Personal Magnet

JEFF Peters has been engaged in as many schemes for making money as there are recipes for cooking rice in Charleston, S. C.

Best of all I like to hear him tell of his earlier days when he sold liniments and cough cures on street corners, living hand to mouth, heart to heart with the people, throwing heads or tails with fortune for his last coin.

"I struck Fisher Hill, Arkansaw," said he, "in buckskin suit, moccasins, long hair and a thirty-carat diamond ring that I got from an actor in Texarkana. I don't know what he ever did with the pocket knife I swapped him for it.

"I was Dr. Waugh-hoo, the celebrated Indian medicine man. I carried only one best bet just then, and that was Resurrection Bitters. It was made of life-giving plants and herbs accidentally discovered by Ta-qua-la, the beautiful wife of the chief of the Choctaw Nation, while gathering truck to garnish a platter of boiled dog for the annual corn dance.

"Business hadn't been good at the last town, so I only had five dollars. I went to the Fisher Hill druggist and he credited me for a half gross of eight ounce bottles and corks. I had the labels and ingredients in my valise, left over from the last town. Life began to look rosy again after I got in my hotel room with the water running from the tap, and the Resurrection Bitters lining up on the table by the dozen.

催眠术家杰夫·彼得斯

杰夫·彼得斯挣钱的旁门邪道多得像是南卡罗来纳州查尔斯顿煮米饭的方法。

我最爱听他叙说早年的事情，那时候他在街头卖膏药和咳嗽药水，勉强糊口，并跟各种各样的人打交道，拿最后的一枚钱币同命运打赌。

"我到了阿肯色的费希尔山，"他说道，"身穿鹿皮衣，脚登鹿皮靴，头发留得长长的，手上戴着从特克萨卡纳一个演员那里弄来的三十克拉重的金刚钻戒指。我不明白他用戒指换了我的折刀去干什么。

"我当时的身份是著名的印第安巫医沃胡大夫。我只带着一件最好的赌本，那就是用延年益寿的植物和草药浸制的回春药酒。乔克陶族酋长的美貌的妻子塔夸拉为玉米跳舞会①煮狗肉时，想找一些蔬菜搭配，无意中发现了那种草药。

"我在前一站镇上的买卖不很顺手，因此身边只有五块钱。我找到费希尔山的药剂师，向他赊了六打八英两容量的玻璃瓶和软木塞。我的手提箱里还有前一站用剩的标签和原料。我住进旅馆后，就拧开自来水龙头兑好回春药酒，一打一打地排在桌子上，这时候生活仿佛又很美好了。

---

① 印第安人在播种或收获玉米时跳的舞蹈。

"Fake? No, sir. There was two dollars' worth of fluid extract of cinchona and a dime's worth of aniline in that half-gross of bitters. I've gone through towns years afterwards and had folks ask for 'em again.

"I hired a wagon that night and commenced selling the bitters on Main Street. Fisher Hill was a low, malarial town; and a compound hypothetical pneumo-cardiac antiscorbutic tonic was just what I diagnosed the crowd as needing. The bitters started off like sweetbreads-on-toast at a vegetarian dinner. I had sold two dozen at fifty cents apiece when I felt somebody pull my coat tail. I knew what that meant; so I climbed down and sneaked a five-dollar bill into the hand of a man with a German silver star on his lapel.

"'Constable,' says I, 'it's a fine night. '

"'Have you got a city license,' he asks, 'to sell this illegitimate essence of spooju that you flatter by the name of medicine? '

"'I have not. ' says I. 'I didn't know you had a city. If I can find it to-morrow I'll take one out if it's necessary. '

"'I'll have to close you up till you do. ' says the constable.

"I quit selling and went back to the hotel. I was talking to the landlord about it.

"'Oh, you won't stand no show in Fisher Hill, ' says he. 'Dr. Hoskins, the only doctor here, is a brother-in-law of the Mayor, and they won't allow no fake doctors to practice in town. '

"'I don't practice medicine, ' says I, 'I've got a State peddler's license, and I take out a city one wherever they demand it. '

"你说是假药吗？不，先生。那六打药酒里面有值两块钱的金鸡纳皮浸膏和一毛钱的阿尼林。几年以后，我路过那些小镇，人们还问我买呢。

"当晚我就雇了一辆大车，开始在大街上推销药酒。费希尔山是个疟疾流行的卑隰的小镇；据我诊断，镇上的居民正需要一种润肺强心、补血养气的十全大补剂。药酒的销路好得像是吃素的人见到了鱼翅海参。我以每瓶半块钱的价钱卖掉了两打，这时觉得有人在扯我衣服的下摆。我明白那是什么意思；于是我爬下来，把一张五元的钞票偷偷地塞在一个胸襟上佩着德银星章的人的手里。

"'警官，'我说道，'今晚天气不坏。'

"'你推销你称之为药的这种非法假货，'他问道，'可有本市的执照？'

"'没有。'我说。'我不知道你们这里算是城市。明天如果我发现确实有城市的意思，必要的话，我可以领一张。'

"'在你没有领到之前，我得勒令你停业。'警察说。

"我收掉摊子，回到旅馆。我把经过情形告诉了旅馆老板。

"'哦，你这行买卖在费希尔山是吃不开的。'他说。'霍斯金斯大夫是这里唯一的医师，又是镇长的小舅子，他们不允许冒牌郎中在这个镇上行医。'

"'我并没有行医啊，'我说，'我有一张州颁的小贩执照，必要的话，我可以领一张市的执照。'

"I went to the Mayor's office the next morning and they told me he hadn't showed up yet. They didn't know when he'd be down. So Doc Waugh-hoo hunches down a-gain in a hotel chair and lights a jimpson-weed regalia, and waits.

"By and by a young man in a blue necktie slips into the chair next to me and asks the time.

"'Half-past ten,' says I, 'and you are Andy Tucker. I've seen you work. Wasn't it you that put up the Great Cupid Combination package on the Southern States? Let's see, it was a Chilian diamond engagement ring, a wedding ring, a potato masher, a bottle of soothing syrup and Dorothy Vernon—all for fifty cents.'

"Andy was pleased to hear that I remembered him. He was a good street man; and he was more than that——he respected his profession and he was satisfied with 300 per cent. profit. He had plenty of offers to go into the illegitimate drug and garden seed business; but he was never to be tempted off of the straight path.

"I wanted a partner, so Andy and me agreed to go out together. I told him about the situation on Fisher Hill and how finances was low on account of the local mix-ture of politics and jalap. Andy had just got in on the train that morning. He was pretty low himself, and was going to canvass the town for a few dollars to build a new battleship by popular subscription at Eureka Springs. So we went out and sat on the porch and talked it over.

"The next morning at eleven o'clock when I was sit-ting there alone, an Uncle Tom shuffles into the hotel and asked for the doctor to come and see Judge Banks, who, it seems, was the mayor and a mighty sick man.

"第二天早晨,我去到镇长办公室,他们说镇长还没有来,什么时候来可说不准。于是沃胡大夫只好再回到旅馆,在椅子上蜷坐着,点起一支雪茄烟干等着。

"没多久,一个打蓝色领带的年轻人挨挨蹭蹭地坐到我旁边的椅子上,问我有几点钟了。

"'十点半,'我说,'你不是安迪·塔克吗?我见过你玩的把戏。你不是在南方各州推销'丘比特什锦大礼盒'吗?让我想想,那里面有一枚智利钻石订婚戒指,一枚结婚戒指,一个土豆捣碎器,一瓶镇静糖浆和一张多乐西·弗农的照片——一共只卖五毛钱。'

"安迪听说我还记得他,觉得十分高兴。他是一个出色的街头推销员;不仅如此——他还尊重自己的行业,赚到百分之三百的利润就已满足了。人家一再拉他去干非法的贩卖假药的勾当;可是怎么也不能引他离开康庄大道。

"我正需要一个搭档,安迪同我便谈妥了合伙。我向他分析了费希尔山的情况,告诉他由于当地的政治同泻药纠缠在一起,买卖不很顺利。安迪是坐当天早班火车到这里的。他自己手头也不宽裕,打算在镇上募集一些钱,到尤里加喷泉①去造一艘新的兵舰。我们便出去,坐在门廊上从长计议。

"第二天上午十一点钟,当我独自坐着时,一个黑人慢吞吞地走进旅馆,请大夫去瞧瞧班克斯法官,也就是那位镇长,据说他病得很凶。

---

① 尤里加喷泉为阿肯色州西北部的一旅游休养地。

"'I'm no doctor,' says I. 'Why don't you go and get the doctor?'

"'Boss.' says he. 'Doc Hoskin am done gone twenty miles in the country to see some sick persons. He's de only doctor in de town, and Massa Banks am powerful bad off. He sent me to ax you to please, suh, come.'

"'As man to man,' says I, 'I'll go and look him over.' So I put a bottle of Resurrection Bitters in my pocket and goes up on the hill to the mayor's mansion, the finest house in town, with a mansard roof and two cast-iron dogs on the lawn.

"This Mayor Banks was in bed all but his whiskers and feet. He was making internal noises that would have had everybody in San Francisco hiking for the parks. A young man was standing by the bed holding a cup of water.

"'Doc,' says the Mayor, 'I'm awful sick. I'm about to die. Can't you do nothing for me?'

"'Mr. Mayor,' says I, 'I'm not a regular preordained disciple of S. Q. Lapius, I never took a course in a medical college,' says I, 'I've just come as a fellow man to see if I could be of any assistance.'

"'I'm deeply obliged,' says he. 'Doc Waugh-hoo, this is my nephew, Mr. Biddle. He has tried to alleviate my distress, but without success. Oh, Lordy! Ow-ow-ow!!' he sings out.

"I nods at Mr. Biddle and sets down by the bed and feels the mayor's pulse. 'Let me see your liver—your tongue, I mean,' says I. Then I turns up the lids of his eyes and looks close at the pupils of 'em.

"'How long have you been sick?' I asked.

"'I was taken down—ow-ouch—last night,' says the

"'我不是替人瞧病的。'我说。'你干吗不去请那位大夫?'

"'先生,'他说,'霍斯金大夫到二十英里外的乡下地方去替人治病啦。镇上只有他一位大夫,班克斯老爷病得很厉害。他吩咐我来请你,先生。'

"'出于同胞的情谊,'我说,'我不妨去看看他。'我拿起一瓶回春药酒,往口袋里一塞,去到山上的镇长公馆,那是镇上最讲究的房子,斜坡屋顶,门口草坪上有两只铁铸的狗。

"班克斯镇长除了胡子和脚尖之外,全身都摆平在床上。他肚子里发出的响声,如果在旧金山的话,会让人误认为是地震,听了就要夺路往空旷的地方逃跑。一个年轻人拿着一杯水,站在床边。

"'大夫,'镇长说,'我病得很厉害。我快死了。你能不能想想办法救救我?'

"'镇长先生,'我说,'我没有福气做艾斯·库·拉比乌斯①的正式门徒,我从来没有在医科大学里念过书。'我说。'我只不过是以同胞的身份来看看有什么地方可以效劳。'

"'非常感激。'他说。'沃胡大夫,这一位是我的外甥,比德尔先生。他想减轻我的痛苦,可是不行。哦,天哪!哦——哦——哦!'他呻吟起来。

"我招呼了比德尔先生,然后坐在床沿上,试试镇长的脉搏。'让我看看你的肝——我是说舌苔。'我说道。接着,我翻起他的眼睑,仔细看看瞳孔。

"'你病了多久啦?'我问。

"'我这病是——哦——哎呀——昨晚发作的。'镇长

---

① 原文是 S. Q. Lapius。希腊神话中日神之子和医药之神,名为艾斯库拉比乌斯(Aesculapius),作者按照现代英语国家人的姓名把前两个音节换成了缩写字母。

Mayor. 'Gimme something for it,doc,won't you?'

"'Mr. Fiddle,'says I,'raise the window shade a bit, will you?'

"'Biddle,'says the young man. 'Do you feel like you could eat some ham and eggs,Uncle James?'

"'Mr. Mayor,'says I,after laying my ear to his right shoulder blade and listening,'you've got a bad attack of super-inflammation of the right clavicle of the harpsi-chord!'

"'Good Lord!'says he,with a groan. 'Can't you rub something on it,or set it or anything?'

"I picks up my hat and starts for the door.

"'You ain't going, doc?' says the Mayor with a howl. 'You ain't going away and leave me to die with this—superfluity of the clap-boards,are you?'

"'Common humanity, Dr. Whoa-ha,'says Mr. Bid-dle,'ought to prevent your deserting a fellow-human in distress.'

"'Dr. Waugh-hoo,when you get through plowing,' says I. And then I walks back to the bed and throws back my long hair.

"'Mr. Mayor,'says I, 'there is only one hope for you. Drugs will do you no good. But there is another power higher yet,although drugs are high enough,'says I.

"'And what is that?'says he.

"'Scientific demonstrations,'says I. 'The triumph of mind over sarsaparilla. The belief that there is no pain and sickness except what is produced when we ain't feel-ing well. Declare yourself in arrears. Demonstrate.'

"'What is this paraphernalia you speak of,Doc?' says the Mayor. 'You ain't a Socialist,are you?'

说。'给我开点药,大夫,好不好?'

"'飞德尔先生,'我说,'请你把窗帘拉开一点儿,好吗?'

"'比德尔。'年轻人纠正我说。'你不想吃点儿火腿蛋吗,詹姆斯舅舅?'

"我把耳朵贴在他的右肩胛上,听了一会儿后说:'镇长先生,你害的病是非常凶险的喙突右锁骨的超急性炎症!'

"'老天爷!'他呻吟着说。'你能不能在上面抹点儿什么,或者正一正骨,或者想点儿什么别的办法?'

"我拿起帽子,朝门口走去。

"'你不见得要走吧,大夫?'镇长带着哭音说。'你总不见得要离开这儿,让我害着这种——灰秃锁骨的超急性癌症,见死不救吧?'

"'你如果有恻隐之心,哇哈大夫,'比德尔先生开口说,'就不应该眼看一个同胞受苦而撒手不管。'

"'我的名字是沃胡大夫,别像吆喝牲口那样哇哈哇哈的。'我说。接着我回到床边,把我的长头发往后一甩。

"'镇长先生,'我说,'你只有一个希望。药物对你已经起不了作用了。药物的效力固然很大,不过还有一样效力更大的东西。'我说。

"'是什么呀?'他问道。

"'科学的论证。'我说。'意志战胜菝葜①。要相信痛苦和疾病是不存在的,只不过是我们不舒服时的感觉罢了。诚则灵。试试看吧。'

"'你讲的是什么把戏,大夫?'镇长说。'你不是社会主义者吧?'

①　菝葜(sarsaparilla)是百合科植物,根有清血、解毒和发汗作用,可制清凉饮料。镇长听成是"paraphernalia"(用具、配备)。

"'I am speaking,' says I, 'of the great doctrine of psychic financiering—of the enlightened school of long-distance, sub-conscientious treatment of fallacies and meningitis—of that wonderful in-door sport known as personal magnetism.'

"'Can you work it, Doc?' asks the Mayor.

"'I'm one of the Sole Sanhedrims and Ostensible Hooplas of the Inner Pulpit.' says I. 'The lame talk and the blind rubber whenever I make a pass at 'em. I am a medium, a coloratura hypnotist and a spirituous control. It was only through me at the recent seances at Ann Arbor that the late president of the Vinegar Bitters Company could revisit the earth to communicate with his sister Jane. You see me peddling medicine on the streets,' says I, 'to the poor. I don't practice personal magnetism on them. I do not drag it in the dust,' says I, 'because they haven't got the dust.'

"'Will you treat my case?' asks the Mayor.

"'Listen,' says I. 'I've had a good deal of trouble with medical societies everywhere I've been. I don't practice medicine. But, to save your life, I'll give you the psychic treatment if you'll agree as mayor not to push the license question.'

"'Of course I will,' says he. 'And now get to work, Doc, for them pains are coming on again.'

"'My fee will be $250.00, cure guaranteed in two treatments,' says I.

"'All right,' says the Mayor. 'I'll pay it. I guess my life's worth that much.'

"I sat down by the bed and looked him straight in the eye.

"'Now,' says I, 'get your mind off the disease. You

　　"'我讲的是,'我说,'那种叫做催眠术的精神筹资的伟大学说——以远距离、潜意识来治疗谵妄和脑膜炎的启蒙学派——奇妙的室内运动。'

　　"'你能行施那种法术吗,大夫?'镇长问道。

　　"'我是最高长老院的大祭司和内殿法师之一。'我说。'我一施展催眠术,瘸子就能走路,瞎子就能重明。我是灵媒,是花腔催眠术家,是灵魂的主宰。最近在安阿伯①的降神会上,全靠我的法力,已故的酒醋公司经理才能重归世间,同他的妹妹简交谈。你看到我在街上卖药给穷苦人,'我说,'我不在他们身上行施催眠术。我不降格以求,'我说,'因为他们袋中无银。'

　　"'那你肯不肯替我做做呢?'镇长问道。

　　"'听着,'我说,'我不论到什么地方,医药学会总是跟我找麻烦。我并不行医。但是为了救你一命,我可以替你做精神治疗,只要你以镇长的身份保证不追究执照的事。'

　　"'当然可以。'他说。'请你赶快做吧,大夫,因为疼痛又发作了。'

　　"'我的费用是二百五十块钱,治疗两次包好。'我说。

　　"'好吧,'镇长说,'我付。我想我这条命还值二百五十块。'

　　"'现在,'我说,'你不要把心思放在病痛上。你没有生

────────────

　　① 安阿伯:密执安州东南部的城市。

ain't sick. You haven't got a heart or a clavicle or a funny bone or brains or anything. You haven't got any pain. Declare error. Now you feel the pain that you didn't have leaving, don't you?'

"'I do feel some little better, Doc,' says the Mayor, 'darned if I don't. Now state a few lies about my not having this swelling in my left side, and I think I could be propped up and have some sausage and buckwheat cakes.'

"I made a few passes with my hands.

"'Now,' says I, 'the inflammation's gone. The right lobe of the perihelion has subsided. You're getting sleepy. You can't hold your eyes open any longer. For the present the disease is checked. Now, you are asleep.'

"The Mayor shut his eyes slowly and began to snore.

"'You observe, Mr. Tiddle,' says I, 'the wonders of modern science.'

"'Biddle,' says he. 'When will you give uncle the rest of the treatment, Dr. Pooh-pooh?'

"'Waugh-hoo.' says I. I'll come back at eleven tomorrow. When he wakes up give him eight drops of turpentine and three pounds of steak. Good morning.'

"The next morning I went back on time. 'Well, Mr. Riddle,' says I, when he opened the bedroom door, 'and how is uncle this morning?'

"'He seems much better,' says the young man.

"'The Mayor's color and pulse was fine. I gave him another treatment, and he said the last of the pain left him.

"'Now,' says I, 'you'd better stay in bed for a day or two, and you'll be all right. It's a good thing I hap-

病。你根本没有心脏、锁骨、尺骨端、头脑,什么也没有。你没有任何疼痛。否定一切。现在你觉得本来就不存在的疼痛逐渐消失了,是吗?'

"'我确实觉得好了些,大夫,'镇长说,'的确如此。现在请你再撒几句谎,说我左面没有肿胀,我想我就可以跳起来吃些香肠和荞麦饼了。'

"我用手按摩了几下。

"'现在,'我说,'炎症已经好了。近日点的右叶已经消退了。你觉得睡迷迷的了。你的眼睛睁不开了。目前毛病已经止住。现在你睡着了。'

"镇长慢慢闭上眼睛,打起鼾来。

"'铁德尔先生,'我说,'你亲眼看到了现代科学的奇迹。'

"'比德尔,'他说,'其余的治疗你什么时候替舅舅做呀,波波大夫?'

"'沃胡。'我纠正说。'我明天上午十一点钟再来。他醒后,给他吃八滴松节油和三磅肉排。再见。'

"第二天上午我准时到了那里。'好啊,立德尔先生,'他打开卧室房门时,我说,'你舅舅今早晨怎么样?'

"'他仿佛好多啦。'那个年轻人说。

"镇长的气色和脉搏都很好。我再替他做了一次治疗,他说疼痛完全没有了。

"'现在,'我说,'你最好在床上躺一两天,就没事啦。我碰巧到了费希尔山,也是你的运气,镇长先生,'我说,'因

pened to be in Fisher Hill, Mr. Mayor,' says I, 'for all the remedies in the cornucopia that the regular schools of medicine use couldn't have saved you. And now that error has flew and pain proved a perjurer, let's allude to a cheerfuller subject—say the fee of $250. No checks, please, I hate to write my name on the back of a check almost as bad as I do on the front.'

"'I've got the cash here,' says the Mayor, pulling a pocket book from under his pillow.

"He counts out five fifty-dollar notes and holds 'em in his hand.

"'Bring the receipt,' he says to Biddle.

"I signed the receipt and the Mayor handed me the money. I put it in my inside pocket careful.

"'Now do your duty, officer,' says the Mayor, grinning much unlike a sick man.

"Mr. Biddle lays his hand on my arm.

"'You're under arrest, Dr. Waugh-hoo, alias Peters,' says he, 'for practising medicine without authority under the State law.'

"'Who are you?' I asks.

"'I'll tell you who he is,' says the Mayor, sitting up in bed. 'He's a detective employed by the State Medical Society. He's been following you over five counties. He came to me yesterday and we fixed up this scheme to catch you. I guess you won't do any more doctoring around these parts, Mr. Fakir. What was it you said I had, Doc?' the Mayor laughs, 'compound—well it wasn't softening of the brain, I guess, anyway.'

"'A detective,' says I.

"'Correct,' says Biddle. 'I'll have to turn you over to the sheriff.'

为正规医师所用的一切药都救不了你。现在毛病既然好了,疼痛也没有了,不妨让我们来谈谈比较愉快的话题——也就是那二百五十块钱的费用。不要支票,对不起,我不喜欢在反面签署背书,正如不喜欢在正面签发支票一样。'

"'我这儿有现钞。'镇长从枕头底下摸出一只皮夹子,说道。

"他数出五张五十元的钞票,捏在手里。

"'把收据拿来。'他对比德尔说。

"我签了收据,镇长把钱交给了我。我小心翼翼地把它们放在贴身的口袋里。

"'现在你可以执行你的职务啦,警官。'镇长笑嘻嘻地说,一点儿不像是害病的人。

"比德尔先生攥住我的胳臂。

"'你被捕了,沃胡大夫,别名彼得斯,'他说,'罪名是违犯本州法律,无照行医。'

"'你是谁呀?'我问。

"'我告诉你他是谁。'镇长在床上坐起来说。'他是州医药学会雇佣的侦探。他跟踪你,走了五个县。昨天他来找我,我们定下这个计谋来抓你。我想你不能在这一带行医了,骗子先生。你说我害的是什么病呀,大夫?'镇长哈哈大笑说,'灰秃——总之我想不是脑筋失灵吧。'

"'侦探。'我说。

"'不错,'比德尔说,'我得把你移交给司法官。'

"'Let's see you do it,' says I, and I grabs Biddle by the throat and half throws him out the window, but he pulls a gun and sticks it under my chin, and I stand still. Then he puts handcuffs on me, and takes the money out of my pocket.

"'I witness,' says he, 'that they're the same bills that you and I marked, Judge Banks. I'll turn them over to the sheriff when we get to his office, and he'll send you a receipt. They'll have to be used as evidence in the case.'

"'All right, Mr. Biddle,' says the Mayor. 'And now, Doc Waughhoo,' he goes on, 'why don't you demonstrate? Can't you pull the cork out of your magnetism with your teeth and hocus-pocus them handcuffs off?'

"'Come on, officer,' says I, dignified. 'I may as well make the best of it.' And then I turns to old Banks and rattles my chains.

"'Mr. Mayor,' says I, 'the time will come soon when you'll believe that personal magnetism is a success. And you'll be sure that it succeeded in this case, too.'

"And I guess it did.

"When we got nearly to the gate, I says: 'We might meet somebody now, Andy. I reckon you better take 'em off, and—' Hey? Why, of course it was Andy Tucker. That was his scheme; and that's how we got the capital to go into business together."

"'你敢。'我说着突然卡住比德尔的脖子,几乎要把他扔出窗外。但是他掏出一把手枪,抵着我的下巴,我便放老实了,一动不动。他铐住我的手,从我口袋里抄出了那笔钱。

"'我证明,'他说,'这就是你我做过记号的钞票,班克斯法官。我把他押到司法官的办公室时,把这钱交给司法官,由他出一张收据给你。审理本案时,要用它作物证。'

"'没关系,比德尔先生。'镇长说。'现在,沃胡大夫,'他接着说,'你干吗不施展法力呀?你干吗不施出你的催眠术,把手铐催开呀?'

"'走吧,警官。'我大大咧咧地说。'我认啦。'接着我咬牙切齿地转向老班克斯。

"'镇长先生,'我说,'用不了多久,你就会发现催眠术是成功的。你应当知道,在这件事上也是成功的。'

"我想事情确实如此。

"我们走到大门口时,我说:'现在我们也许会碰到什么人,安迪。我想你还是把手铐解掉的好,——'呃?当然啦,比德尔就是安迪·塔克。那是他出的主意;我们就这样搞到了合伙做买卖的本钱。"

While the Auto Waits

PROMPTLY at the beginning of twilight, came again to that quiet corner of that quiet, small park the girl in gray. She sat upon a bench and read a book, for there was yet to come a half hour in which print could be accomplished.

To repeat: Her dress was gray, and plain enough to mask its impeccancy of style and fit. A large-meshed veil imprisoned her turban hat and a face that shone through it with a calm and unconscious beauty. She had come there at the same hour on the day previous, and on the day before that; and there was one who knew it.

The young man who knew it hovered near, relying upon burnt sacrifices to the great joss, Luck. His piety was rewarded, for, in turning a page, her book slipped from her fingers and bounded from the bench a full yard away.

The young man pounced upon it with instant avidity, returning it to its owner with that air that seems to flourish in parks and public places—a compound of gallantry and hope, tempered with respect for the policeman on the beat. In a pleasant voice, he risked an inconsequent remark upon the weather—that introductory topic responsible for so much of the world's unhappiness—and stood poised for a moment, awaiting his fate.

The girl looked him over leisurely; at his ordinary, neat dress and his features distinguished by nothing particular in the way of expression.

"You may sit down, if you like," she said, in a full,

汽车等待的时候

黄昏刚降临,穿灰色衣服的姑娘又来到安静的小公园的安静的角落里。她坐在长椅上看书,白天还有半小时的余晖,可以看清书本上的字。

再说一遍:她的衣服是灰色的,并且朴素得足以掩盖式样和剪裁的完美。一张大网眼的面纱罩住了她的头巾帽和散发着安详恬静的美的脸蛋。昨天同一个时候,她也来到这里,前天也是如此;有一个人了解这个情况。

了解这个情况的年轻人逡巡走近,把希望寄托在幸运之神身上。他的虔诚得到了回报,因为她翻书页的时候,书本从她手里滑了下来,在椅子上一磕,落到足足有一码远的地方。

年轻人迫不及待地扑到书上,带着在公园和公共场所里司空见惯的神情把它还给它的主人,那种神情既殷勤又充满希望,还搀杂了一些对附近那个值班警察的忌惮。他用悦耳的声调冒险说了一句没头没脑的关于天气的话——那种造成了世间多少不幸的开场白——又静静地站了一会儿,等待着他的运气。

姑娘从容不迫地打量了他一下;瞅着他那整洁而平凡的衣服和他那没有什么特殊表情的容貌。

"你高兴的话不妨坐下。"她不慌不忙地说,声调低沉爽

171

deliberate contralto. "Really, I would like to have you do so. The light is too bad for reading. I would prefer to talk."

The vassal of Luck slid upon the seat by her side with complaisance.

"Do you know," he said, speaking the formula with which park chairmen open their meetings, "that you are quite the stunningest girl I have seen in a long time? I had my eye on you yesterday. Didn't know somebody was bowled over by those pretty lamps of yours, did you, honeysuckle?"

"Whoever you are," said the girl, in icy tones, "you must remember that I am a lady. I will excuse the remark you have just made because the mistake was, doubtless, not an unnatural one—in your circle. I asked you to sit down; if the invitation must constitute me your honeysuckle, consider it withdrawn."

"I earnestly beg your pardon," pleaded the young man. His expression of satisfaction had changed to one of penitence and humility. "It was my fault, you know—I mean, there are girls in parks, you know—that is, of course, you don't know, but—"

"Abandon the subject. if you please. Of course I know. Now, tell me about these people passing and crowding, each way, along these paths. Where are they going? Why do they hurry so? Are they happy?"

The young man had promptly abandoned his air of coquetry. His cue was now for a waiting part; he could not guess the rôle he would be expected to play.

"It *is* interesting to watch them," he replied, postulating her mood. "It is the wonderful drama of life. Some are going supper and some to—er—other places. One

朗。"说真的,我倒希望你坐下来。光线太坏了,看书不合适。我宁愿聊聊天。

幸运的侍臣受宠若惊地在她身边坐下。

"你可知道,"他把公园里的主席们宣布开会时的老一套搬出来说,"我很久没有看到像你这样了不起的姑娘啦。昨天我就注意到了你。你可知道,有人被你那双美丽的眼睛迷住啦,小妞儿?"

"不论你是谁,"姑娘冷冰冰地说,"你必须记住我是个上等女人。我可以原谅你刚才说的话,因为这类误会在你的圈子里,毫无疑问,是并不希罕的。我请你坐下来;如果这一请却招来了你的'小妞儿',那就算我没请过。"

"我衷心请你原谅。"年轻人央求说。他的得意神色马上让位于悔罪和卑屈。"是我不对,你明白——我是说,公园里有些姑娘,你明白——那是说,当然啦,你不明白,不过——"

"别谈这种事啦,对不起。我当然明白。现在谈谈在这条小路上来来往往,推推搡搡的人吧。他们去向何方?他们为什么这样匆忙?他们幸福吗?"

年轻人立刻抛开他刚才的调情的神情。现在他只有干等的份儿了;他琢磨不透自己应该扮演什么角色。

"看看他们确实很有意思。"他顺着她的心情说。"这是生活的美妙的戏剧。有的去吃晚饭,有的——呃——到别

wonders what their histories are."

"I do not,"said the girl; "I am not so inquisitive. I come here to sit because here, only, can I be near the great, common, throbbing heart of humanity. My part in life is cast where its beats are never felt. Can you surmise why I spoke to you, Mr. —?"

"Parkenstacker,"supplied the young man. Then he looked eager and hopeful.

"No,"said the girl, holding up a slender finger, and smiling slightly. "You would recognize it immediately. It is impossible to keep one's name out of print. Or even one's portrait. This veil and this hat of my maid furnish me with an *incog*. You should have seen the chauffeur stare at it when he thought I did not see. Candidly, there are five or six names that belong in the holy of holies, and mine, by the accident of birth, is one of them. I spoke to you, Mr. Stackenpot—"

"Parkenstacker,"corrected the young man, modestly.

"—Mr. Parkenstacker, because I wanted to talk, for once, with a natural man—one unspoiled by the despicable gloss of wealth and supposed social superiority. Oh! you do not know how weary I am of it—money, money, money! And of the men who surround me, dancing like little marionettes all cut by the same pattern. I am sick of pleasure, of jewels, of travel, of society, of luxuries of all kinds."

"I always had an idea,"ventured the young man, hesitatingly, "that money must be a pretty good thing."

"A competence is to be desired. But when you have so many millions that—!" She concluded the sentence with a gesture of despair. "It is the monotony of it,"she

的地方去。真猜不透他们的身世是怎么样的。"

"我不去猜,"姑娘说,"我没有那样好奇。我坐在这儿,是因为只有在这儿我才能接近人类伟大的、共同的、搏动的心脏。我在生活中的地位使我永远感不到这种搏动。你猜得出我为什么跟你聊天吗——贵姓?"

"帕肯斯塔格。"年轻人回答说。接着,他急切而期待地盼望她自报姓氏。

"我不能告诉你。"姑娘举起一只纤细的手指,微微一笑说。"一说出来你就知道我的身份了。不让自己的姓名在报刊上出现简直不可能。连照片也是这样。这张面纱和我女仆的帽子掩盖了我的真面目。你应该注意到,我的司机总是在他以为我不留神的时候朝我看。老实说,有五六个显赫的名门望族,我由于出生的关系就属于其中之一。我之所以要跟你说话,斯塔肯帕特先生——"

"帕肯斯塔格。"年轻人谦虚地更正说。

"——帕肯斯塔格先生,是因为我想跟一个普普通通的人谈话,即使一次也好,跟一个没有被可鄙的财富和虚伪的社会地位所玷污的人谈话。哦!你不会知道我是多么厌倦——金钱、金钱、金钱!我还厌倦那些在我周围装模作样的男人,他们活像是一个模子里刻出来的傀儡。欢乐、珠宝、旅行、交际、各式各样的奢华都叫我腻味透顶。"

"我始终有一个想法,"年轻人吞吞吐吐地试探说,"金钱准是一样很好的东西。"

"金钱只要够你过富裕的生活就行啦。可是当你有了几百万、几百万的时候——"她做了个表示无奈的手势,结束了这句话。"叫人生厌的是那种单调,"她接下去说,"乘

continued, "that palls. Drives, dinners, theatres, balls, suppers, with the gilding of superfluous wealth over it all. Sometimes the very tinkle of the ice in my champagne glass nearly drives me mad."

Mr. Parkenstacker looked ingenuously interested.

"I have always liked," he said, "to read and hear about the ways of wealthy and fashionable folks. I suppose I am a bit of a snob. But I like to have my information accurate. Now, I had formed the opinion that champagne is cooled in the bottle and not by placing ice in the glass."

The girl gave a musical laugh of genuine amusement.

"You should know," she explained, in an indulgent tone, "that we of the non-useful class depend for our amusement upon departure from precedent. Just now it is a fad to put ice in champagne. The idea was originated by a visiting Prince of Tartary while dining at the Waldorf. It will soon give way to some other whim. Just as at a dinner party this week on Madison Avenue a green kid glove was laid by the plate of each guest to be put on and used while eating olives."

"I see," admitted the young man, humbly. "These special diversions of the inner circle do not become familiar to the common public."

"Sometimes," continued the girl, acknowledging his confession of error by a slight bow, "I have thought that if I ever should love a man it would be one of lowly station. One who is a worker and not a drone. But, doubtless, the claims of caste and wealth will prove stronger than my inclination. Just now I am besieged by two. One is a Grand Duke of a German principality. I think he

车兜风、午宴、看戏、舞会、晚宴，以及这一切像镀金似地蒙在外面的过剩的财富。有时候，我的香槟酒杯里冰块的叮当声几乎要使我发疯。"

帕肯斯塔格先生坦率地显出很感兴趣的样子。

"我有这么一种脾气，"他说，"就是喜欢看书报上写的，或者听人家讲的关于富有的时髦人物的生活方式。我想我有点儿虚荣。不过我喜欢了解得彻底一些。我一向有一个概念，认为香槟酒是连瓶冰镇，而不是把冰搁在酒杯里的。"

姑娘发出一连串银铃般的，觉得有趣的笑声。

"你应当知道，"她带着原谅的口吻说，"我们这种吃饱饭没事干的人就靠标新立异来找消遣。目前流行的花样是把冰块搁在香槟酒里。这个办法是一位鞑靼王子在沃尔多夫大饭店吃饭时发明的。不用多久它就会让位给别的怪念头了。正如在本星期麦迪逊大街的一次宴会上，每位客人的盘子旁边都放了一只绿色羊皮手套，以便吃橄榄的时候戴用。

"我明白啦。"年轻人谦虚地承认说。"小圈子里的这些特别花样，普通人是不熟悉的。"

"有时候，"姑娘略微欠身，接受了他的认错，"我这样想，假如我有一天爱上一个人的话，那个人一定是地位很低的。一个劳动的人，而不是不干活的懒汉。不过，毫无疑问，对于阶级和财富的考虑可能压倒我原来的意图。目前就有两个人在追求我。一个是某个日耳曼公国的大公爵。

has, or has had, a wife, somewhere, driven mad by his intemperance and cruelty. The other is an English Marquis, so cold and mercenary that I even prefer the diabolism of the Duke. What is it that impels me to tell you these things, Mr. Packenstacker?"

"Parkenstacker," breathed the young man. "Indeed, you cannot know how much I appreciate your confidences."

The girl contemplated him with a calm, impersonal regard that befitted the difference in their stations.

"What is your line of business, Mr. Parkenstacker?" she asked.

"A very humble one. But I hope to rise in the world. Were you really in earnest when you said that you could love a man of lowly position?"

"Indeed I was. But I said 'might'. There is the Grand Duke and the Marquis, you know. Yes; no calling could be too humble were the man what I would wish him to be."

"I work." declared Mr. Parkenstacker, "in a restaurant."

The girl shrank slightly.

"Not as a waiter?" she said, a little imploringly. "Labor is noble. but—personal attendance, you know—valets and —"

"I am not a waiter. I am cashier in"—on the street they faced that bounded the opposite side of the park was the brilliant electric sign "RESTAURANT"—"I am cashier in that restaurant you see there."

The girl consulted a tiny watch set in a bracelet of rich design upon her left wrist, and rose, hurriedly. She thrust her book into a glittering reticule suspended from

178

我猜想他现在有,或者以前有过一个妻子,被他的放纵和残忍逼得发了疯。另一个是英国侯爵,他是那样地冷酷和惟利是图,以至相比之下,我倒宁愿选择那个魔鬼似的公爵了。我怎么会把这些都告诉你的啊,帕肯斯塔格先生?"

"帕肯斯塔格。"年轻人倒抽了一口气说。"说真的,你想象不出你这般推心置腹使我感到有多么荣幸。"

姑娘无动于衷地看看他,那种漠然的眼色正适合他们之间地位悬殊的状况。

"你是干哪一行的,帕肯斯塔格先生"她问道。

"很低微。但是我希望在社会上混出一个模样来。你刚才说你可能爱上一个地位卑贱的人,这话可当真?"

"自然当真。不过我刚才说的是'有可能'。还有大公爵和侯爵在呢,你明白。是啊,假如一个男人合我的心意,职业低微也不是太大的障碍。"

"我是,"帕肯斯塔格宣布说,"在饭馆里干活的。"

姑娘稍稍一震。

"不是侍者吧?"姑娘略微带着央求的口气说。"劳动是高尚的,不过——服侍别人,你明白——仆从和——"

"我不是侍者。我是出纳员,就在"——他们面前正对着公园的街上有一块耀眼的"饭店"灯光招牌——"你看到那家饭馆吗,我就在里面当出纳员。"

姑娘看看左腕上镶在式样华丽的手镯上的小表,急忙站了起来。她把书塞进一个吊在腰际的闪闪发亮的手提袋

her waist, for which, however, the book was too large.

"Why are you not at work?" she asked.

"I am on the night turn," said the young man; "it is yet an hour before my period begins. May I not hope to see you again?"

"I do not know. Perhaps—but the whim may not seize me again. I must go quickly now. There is a dinner, and a box at the play—and, oh! the same old round. Perhaps you noticed an automobile at the upper corner of the park as you came. One with a white body."

"And red running gear?" asked the young man, knitting his brows reflectively.

"Yes. I always come in that. Pierre waits for me there. He supposes me to be shopping in the department store across the square. Conceive of the bondage of the life wherein we must deceive even our chauffeurs. Goodnight."

"But it is dark now." said Mr. Parkenstacker, "and the park is full of rude men. May I not walk—?"

"If you have the slightest regard for my wishes," said the girl, firmly, "you will remain at this bench for ten minutes after I have left. I do not mean to accuse you, but you are probably aware that autos generally bear the monogram of their owner. Again, goodnight."

Swift and stately she moved away through the dusk. The young man watched her graceful form as she reached the pavement at the park's edge, and turned up along it toward the corner where stood the automobile. Then he treacherously and unhesitatingly began to dodge and skim among the park trees and shrubbery in a course parallel to her route, keeping her well in sight.

When she reached the corner she turned her head to

里,可是书比手提袋大多了。

"你怎么不上班呢?"她问道。

"我值夜班,"年轻人说,"再过一小时我才上班。我可不可以跟你再会面?"

"很难说。也许——不过我可能不再发这种奇想了。现在我得赶快走啦。还有一个宴会,之后上剧院——再之后,哦! 总是老一套。你来的时候也许注意到公园前头的拐角上有一辆汽车吧。一辆白色车身的。"

"红轮子的那辆吗?"年轻人皱着眉头沉思地说。

"是的。我总是乘那辆车子。皮埃尔在那里等我。他以为我在广场对面的百货公司里买东西。想想看,这种生活该有多么狭隘,甚至对自己的司机都要隐瞒。再见。"

"现在天黑啦,"帕肯斯塔格先生说,"公园里都是一些粗鲁的人。我可不可以陪你——"

"假如你尊重我的愿望,"姑娘坚决地说,"我希望你等我离开之后,在椅子上坐十分钟再走。我并不是说你有什么企图,不过你也许知道汽车上一般都有主人姓氏的字母装饰。再见吧。"

她在薄暮中迅疾而端庄地走开了。年轻人看着她那优美的身形走到公园边上的人行道,然后在人行道上朝汽车停着的拐角走去。接着,他不怀好意,毫不犹豫地借着公园里树木的掩护,沿着同她平行的路线,一直牢牢地盯着她。

她走到拐角处,扭过头来朝汽车瞥了一眼,然后经过汽

glance at the motor car, and then passed it, continuing on across the street. Sheltered behind a convenient standing cab, the young man followed her movements closely with his eyes. Passing down the sidewalk of the street opposite the park, she entered the restaurant with the blazing sign. The place was one of those frankly glaring establishments, all white paint and glass, where one may dine cheaply and conspicuously. The girl penetrated the restaurant to some retreat at its rear, whence she quickly emerged without her hat and veil.

The cashier's desk was well to the front. A red-haired girl on the stool climbed down, glancing pointedly at the clock as she did so. The girl in gray mounted in her place.

The young man thrust his hands into his pockets and walked slowly back along the sidewalk. At the corner his foot struck a small, paper-covered volume lying there, sending it sliding to the edge of the turf. By its picturesque cover he recognized it as the book the girl had been reading. He picked it up carelessly, and saw that its title was "New Arabian Nights", the author being of the name of Stevenson. He dropped it again upon the grass, and lounged, irresolute, for a minute. Then he stepped into the automobile, reclined upon the cushions, and said two words to the chauffeur:

"Club, Henry."

车旁边,继续向对街走去。年轻人躲在一辆停着的马车背后,密切注意她的行动。她走上公园对面马路的人行道,进了那家有耀眼的灯光招牌的饭馆。那家饭馆全是由白漆和玻璃装修的,一览无遗,人们可以没遮没拦地在那里吃价钱便宜的饭菜。姑娘走进饭馆后部一个比较隐蔽的地方,再出来时,帽子和面纱已经取下来了。

出纳员的柜台在前面。凳子上一个红头发的姑娘爬了下来,一面爬,一面露骨地瞅瞅挂钟。穿灰色衣服的姑娘登上了她的座位。

年轻人两手往口袋里一插,在人行道上慢慢地往回走。在拐角上,他脚下碰到一本小小的、纸面的书,把它踢到了草皮边上。那张花花绿绿的封面让他认出这就是那姑娘刚才看的书。他漫不经心地捡了起来,看到书名是《新天方夜谭》,作者是斯蒂文森①。他仍旧把它扔在草地上,迟疑地逗留了片刻。然后,他跨进那辆在等着的汽车,舒舒服服地往座垫上一靠,简单地对司机说:

"俱乐部,昂利。"

---

① 斯蒂文森(1850—1894):英国作家,《新天方夜谭》是一部带有异国情调的惊险浪漫故事集,其中刻意追求新奇和刺激,脱离了现实。

"Next to Reading Matter"

HE compelled my interest as he stepped from the ferry at Desbrosses Street. He had the air of being familiar with hemispheres and worlds, and of entering New York as the lord of a demesne who revisited it after years of absence. But I thought that, with all his air, he had never before set foot on the slippery cobblestones of the City of Too Many Caliphs.

He wore loose clothes of strange bluish drab color, and a conservative, round Panama hat without the cock-a-loop indentations and cants with which Northern fanciers disfigure the tropic head-gear. Moreover, he was the homeliest man I have ever seen. His ugliness was less repellent than startling—arising from a sort of Lincolnian ruggedness and irregularity of feature that spellbound you with wonder and dismay. So may have looked afrites of the shapes metamorphosed from the vapor of the fisherman's vase. As he afterward told me, his name was Judson Tate; and he may as well be called so at once. He wore his green silk tie through a topaz ring; and he carried a cane made of the vertebrae of a shark.

Judson Tate accosted me with some large and casual inquiries about the city's streets and hotels, in the manner of one who had but for the moment forgotten the trifling details. I could think of no reason for dispraising my own quiet hotel in the downtown district; so the mid-morning of the night found us already victualed and drinked (at my expense), and ready to be chaired and tobaccoed in a quiet corner of the lobby.

"醉 翁 之 意"

　　他从德斯布罗萨斯街的渡口出来时,使我不由得对他发生了兴趣。看他那神气,是个见多识广,四海为家的人;来到纽约的样子,又像是一个暌违多年,重新回到自己领地来的领主。尽管他露出这种神情,我却断定他以前从未踩上过这个满是哈里发①的城市的滑溜的圆石铺的街道。

　　他穿着一套宽大的、蓝中带褐、颜色古怪的衣服,戴着一顶老式的、圆圆的巴拿马草帽,不像北方的时髦人物那样,在帽帮上捏出花哨的凹塘,斜戴成一个角度。此外,他那出奇的丑陋不但使人厌恶,而且使人吃惊——他那副林肯式的愁眉蹙额的模样和不端正的五官,简直会使你诧异和害怕得目瞪口呆。渔夫捞到的瓶子里蹿出的一股妖气变成的怪物,恐怕也不过如此②。后来他告诉我,他名叫贾德森·塔特;为了方便起见,我们从现在起就用这个名字来称呼他。他的绿色绸领带用黄玉环扣住,手里握着一支鲨鱼脊骨做的手杖。

　　贾德森·塔特招呼了我,仿佛旧地重游记不清一些无关紧要的细节似的,大大咧咧地向我打听本市街道和旅馆的一般情况。我觉得没有理由贬低我自己下榻的商业区那家清静的旅馆;于是,到了下半夜,我们已经吃了饭,喝了酒(是我付的账),就打算在那家旅馆的休息室里找一个清静的角落坐下来抽烟了。

---

　　①　哈里发:伊斯兰教国家政教合一的领袖称号。
　　②　这里指《天方夜谭》中的故事。

There was something on Judson Tate's mind, and such as it was, he tried to convey it to me. Already he had accepted me as his friend; and when I looked at his great, snuff-brown first-mate's hand, with which he brought emphasis to his periods, within six inches of my nose, I wondered if, by any chance, he was as sudden in conceiving enmity against strangers.

When this man began to talk I perceived in him a certain power. His voice was a persuasive instrument, upon which he played with a somewhat specious but effective art. He did not try to make you forget his ugliness; he flaunted it in your face and made it part of the charm of his speech. Shutting your eyes, you would have trailed after this rat-catcher's pipes at least to the walls of Hamelin. Beyond that you would have had to be more childish to follow. But let him play his own tune to the words set down, so that if all is too dull, the art of music may bear the blame.

"Women," said Judson Tate, "are mysterious creatures."

My spirits sank. I was not there to listen to such a world-old hypothesis—to such a time-worn, long-ago-refuted, bald, feeble, illogical, vicious, patent sophistry—to an ancient, baseless, wearisome, ragged, unfounded, insidious falsehood originated by women themselves, and by them insinuated, foisted, thrust, spread, and ingeniously promulgated into the ears of mankind by underhanded, secret, and deceptive methods, for the purpose of augmenting, furthering, and reinforcing their own charms and designs.

"Oh, I don't know!" said I, vernacularly.

"Have you ever heard of Oratama?" he asked.

　　贾德森·塔特仿佛有什么话要讲给我听。他已经把我当做朋友了；他每说完一句话，便把那只给鼻烟染黄的、像轮船大副一般粗大的手在我鼻子前面不到六英寸的地方晃着。我不由地想起，他把陌生人当做敌人时是不是也这么突兀。

　　我发觉这个人说话时身上散发出一种力量。他的声音像是动人的乐器，被他用华彩出色的手法弹奏着。他并不想让你忘却他的丑陋；反而在你面前炫示，并且使之成为他言语魅力的一部分。如果你闭上眼睛，至少会跟着这个捕鼠人的笛声走到哈默尔恩的城墙边。你不至于稚气得再往前走。不过让他替他的言词谱上音乐吧，如果不够味，那该由音乐负责。

　　"女人，"贾德森·塔特说，"是神秘的。"

　　我的心一沉。我可不愿意听这种老生常谈——不愿意听这种陈腐浅薄，枯燥乏味，不合逻辑，不能自圆其说，早就给驳倒的诡辩——这是女人自己创造出来的古老，无聊，毫无根据，不着边际，残缺而狡猾的谎言；这是她们为了证明、促进和加强她们自己的魅力和谋算而采取的卑劣、秘密和欺诈的方法，从而暗示，蒙混，灌输，传播和聪明地散布给人们听的。

　　"哦，原来如此！"我说的是大白话。

　　"你有没有听说过奥拉塔马？"他问道。

"Possibly,"I answered. "I seem to recall a toe dancer—or a suburban addition—or was it a perfume? —of some such name. "

"It is a town,"said Judson Tate,"on the coast of a foreign country of which you know nothing and could understand less. It is a country governed by a dictator and controlled by revolutions and insubordination. It was there that a great life-drama was played, with Judson Tate,the homeliest man in America,and Fergus McMahan,the handsomest adventurer in history or fiction,and Señorita Anabela Zamora,the beautiful daughter of the alcalde of Oratama,as chief actors. And,another thing— nowhere else on the globe except in the Department of Treinta-y-Tres in Uruguay does the *chuchula* plant grow. The products of the country I speak of are valuable woods,dye-stuffs,gold,rubber,ivory,and cocoa. "

"I was not aware,"said I,"that South America produced any ivory. "

"There you are twice mistaken,"said Judson Tate, distributing the words over at least an octave of his wonderful voice. "I did not say that the country I spoke of was in South America—I must be careful,my dear man;I have been in politics there, you know. But, even so—I have played chess against its president with a set carved from the nasal bones of the tapir—one of our native specimens of the order of *perissodactyle ungulates* inhabiting the Cordilleras—which was as pretty ivory as you would care to see.

"But it was of romance and adventure and the ways of women that I was going to tell you, and not of zoölogical animals.

"For fifteen years I was the ruling power behind old

"可能听说过。"我回答说。"我印象中仿佛记得那是一个芭蕾舞演员——或者是一个郊区——或者是一种香水的名字?"

"那是外国海岸上的一个小镇,"贾德森·塔特说,"那个国家的情况,你一点儿也不知道,也不可能了解。它由一个独裁者统治着,经常发生革命和叛乱。一出伟大的生活戏剧就是在那里演出的,主角是美国最丑的人贾德森·塔特,还有无论在历史或小说中都算是最英俊的冒险家弗格斯·麦克马汉,以及奥拉塔马镇镇长的美貌女儿安娜贝拉·萨莫拉。还有一件事应该提一提——除了乌拉圭三十三人省①以外,世界上任何别的地方都没有一种叫楚楚拉的植物。我刚才提到的那个国家的产品有贵重木料、染料、黄金、橡胶、象牙和可可。"

"我一向以为南美洲是不产象牙的呢。"我说。

"那你就错上加错了。"贾德森·塔特说。他那美妙动人的声音抑扬顿挫,至少有八个音度宽。"我并没说我所谈的国家在南美洲呀——我必须谨慎,亲爱的朋友;要知道,我在那里是搞过政治的。虽然如此,我跟那个国家的总统下过棋,棋子是用貘的鼻骨雕刻成的——貘是安第斯山区的一种奇蹄类动物——看起来同上好的象牙一模一样。

"我要告诉你的不是动物,而是浪漫史和冒险,以及女人的气质。

"十五年来,我一直是那个共和国至高无上的独裁者老

---

① 三十三人省:乌拉圭东部省名及省会名。1825 年,以拉瓦列哈为首的三十三名乌拉圭爱国者在乌拉圭河岸阿格拉西亚达登陆,开始了反巴西统治的武装斗争,后人遂将该地命名为"三十三人"。

Sancho Benavides, the Royal High Thumbscrew of the
republic. You've seen his picture in the papers—a mushy
black man with whiskers like the notes on a Swiss music-
box cylinder, and a scroll in his right hand like the ones
they write births on in the family Bible. Well, that choc-
olate potentate used to be the biggest item of interest anywhere between the color line and the parallels of lati-
tude. It was three throws, horses, whether he was to wind
up in the Hall of Fame or the Bureau of Combustibles.
He'd have been sure called the Roosevelt of the Southern
Continent if it hadn't been that Grover Cleveland was
President at the time. He'd hold office a couple of terms,
then he'd sit out for a hand—always after appointing his
own successor for the interims.

"But it was not Benavides, the Liberator, who was
making all this fame for himself. Not him. It was Judson
Tate. Benavides was only the chip over the bug. I gave
him the tip when to declare war and increase import du-
ties and wear his state trousers. But that wasn't what I
wanted to tell you. How did I get to be it? I'll tell you.
Because I'm the most gifted talker that ever made vocal
sounds since Adam first opened his eyes, pushed aside the
smelling-salts, and asked: 'Where am I?'

"As you observe, I am about the ugliest man you ever saw outside the gallery of photographs of the New
England early Christian Scientists. So, at an early age, I
perceived that what I lacked in looks I must make up in
eloquence. That I've done. I get what I go after. As the
back-stop and still small voice of old Benavides I made
all the great historical powers-behind-the-throne, such as
Talleyrand, Mrs. de Pompadour, and Loeb, look as small
as the minority report of a Duma. I could talk nations in-

190

桑乔·贝纳维德斯背后的统治力量。你在报上见过他的相片——一个窝囊的黑家伙，脸上的胡子像是瑞士音乐盒圆筒上的钢丝，右手握着一卷像是记家谱的《圣经》扉页那样的纸头。这个巧克力色的统治者一向是种族分界线和纬线之间最惹人注意的人物。很难预料他的结局是登上群英殿呢，还是身败名裂。当时，如果不是格罗弗·克利夫兰①在做总统的话，他一定会被称作是南方大陆的罗斯福。他总是当一两任总统，指定了暂时继任人选之后，再退休一个时期。

"但是替'解放者'贝纳维德斯赢得这些声誉的并不是他自己。不是他，而是贾德森·塔特。贝纳维德斯只不过是个傀儡。我总是指点他，什么时候该宣战，什么时候该提高进口税，什么时候该穿大礼服。但是我要讲给你听的并不是这种事情。我怎么会成为有力人物的呢？我告诉你吧。自从亚当睁开眼睛，推开嗅盐瓶，问道：'我怎么啦'以来，能发出声音的人中间，要数我最出色。

"你也看到，除了新英格兰早期主张信仰疗法的基督徒的相片以外，我可以算是你生平碰见的最丑的人。因此，我很年轻时便知道必须用口才来弥补相貌的不足。我做到了这一点。我要的东西总能到手。作为在老贝纳维德斯背后出主意的人，我把历史上所有伟大的幕后人物，诸如塔利兰、庞巴杜夫人和洛布②，都比得像俄国杜马中少数派的提案了。我用三寸不烂之舌可以说得国家负债或者不负债，

① 克利夫兰(1837—1908)：美国第二十二任和第二十四任总统，民主党人。

② 洛布(1866—1937)：美国商人，西奥多·罗斯福任纽约州长与总统时的私人秘书。

to or out of debt,harangue armies to sleep in the battle-
field, reduce insurrections, inflammations, taxes, appro-
priations or surpluses with a few words,and call up the
dogs of war or the dove of peace with the same bird-like
whistle. Beauty and epaulettes and curly moustaches and
Grecian profiles in other men were never in my way.
When people first look at me they shudder. Unless they
are in the last stages of *angina pectoris* they are mine in
ten minutes after I begin to talk. Woman and men—I win
'em as they come. Now, you wouldn't think women would
fancy a man with a face like mine, would you?"

"Oh, yes, Mr. Tate," said I. "History is bright and
fiction dull with homely men who have charmed women.
There seems—"

"Pardon me," interrupted Judson Tate, "but you
don't quite understand. You have yet to hear my story.

"Fergus McMahan was a friend of mine in the capital. For a handsome man I'll admit he was the duty-free
merchandise. He had blond curls and laughing blue eyes
and was featured regular. They said he was a ringer for
the statue they call Herr Mees, the god of speech and eloquence resting in some museum in Rome. Some German
anarchist, I suppose. They are always resting and talking.

"But Fergus was no talker. He was brought up with
the idea that to be beautiful was to make good. His conversation was about as edifying as listening to a leak
dropping in a tin dish-pan at the head of the bed when
you want to go to sleep. But he and me got to be
friends—maybe because we was so opposite, don't you
think? Looking at the Hallowe'en mask that I call my
face when I'm shaving seemed to give Fergus pleasure;
and I'm sure that whenever I heard the feeble output of

使军队在战场上沉睡,用寥寥数语来减少暴动、骚乱、税收、拨款或者盈余,用鸟鸣一般的唿哨唤来战争之犬或者和平之鸽。别人身上的俊美、肩章、拳曲的胡须和希腊式的面相同我是无缘的。人家一看到我就要打寒战。可是我一开口说话,不出十分钟,听的人就被我迷住了,除非他们害了晚期心绞痛。不论男女,只要碰到我,无不被我迷住。呃,你不会认为女人会爱上像我这种面相的人吧?"

"哦,不,塔特先生。"我说。"迷住女人的丑男子常常替历史增添光彩,使小说黯然失色。我觉得——"

"对不起。"贾德森·塔特打断了我的话。"你还不明白我的意思。你先请听我的故事。"

"弗格斯·麦克马汉是我在京都的一个朋友。拿俊美来说,我承认他是货真价实的。他五官端正,有着金黄色的鬈发和笑吟吟的蓝眼睛。人们说他活像那个叫做赫耳·墨斯[①]的塑像,就是摆在罗马博物馆里的语言与口才之神。我想那大概是一个德国的无政府主义者。那种人老是装腔作势,说个没完。

"不过弗格斯没有口才。他从小就形成了一个观念,认为只要长得漂亮,一辈子就受用不尽。听他谈话,就好比你想睡觉时听到了水滴落到床头的一个铁皮碟子上的声音一样。他和我却交上了朋友——也许是因为我们如此不同吧,你不觉得吗?我刮胡子时,弗格斯看看我那张像是在万圣节前夜戴的面具的怪脸,似乎就觉得高兴;当我听到他那

---

①　赫耳墨斯(Hermes)是希腊神话中商业、演说、竞技之神,作者在这里把原文拆开,成了德文中的"墨斯先生"(Herr Mees),因此下文有"德国无政府主义者"之说。

throat noises that he called conversation I felt contented to be a gargoyle with a silver tongue.

"One time I found it necessary to go down to this coast town of Oratama to straighten out a lot of political unrest and chop off a few heads in the customs and military departments. Fergus, who owned the ice and sulphur-match concessions of the republic, says he'll keep me company.

"So, in a jangle of mule-train bells, we gallops into Oratama, and the town belonged to us as much as Long Island Sound doesn't belong to Japan when T. R. is at Oyster Bay. I say us; but I mean me. Everybody for four nations, two oceans, one bay and isthmus, and five archipelagoes around had heard of Judson Tate. Gentleman adventurer, they called me. I had been written up in five columns of the yellow journals, 40,000 words (with marginal decorations) in a monthly magazine, and a stickful on the twelfth page of the *New York Times*. If the beauty of Fergus McMahan gained any part of our reception in Oratama, I'll eat the price-tag in my Panama. It was me that they hung out paper flowers and palm branches for. I am not a jealous man; I am stating facts. The people were Nebuchadnezzars; they bit the grass before me; there was no dust in the town for them to bite. They bowed down to Judson Tate. They knew that I was the power behind Sancho Benavides. A word from me was more to them than a whole deckle-edged library from East Aurora in sectional bookcases was from anybody else. And yet there are people who spend hours fixing their faces—rubbing in cold cream and massaging the muscles (always toward the eyes) and taking in the slack with tincture of benzoin and electrolyzing moles—to

自称为谈话的微弱的喉音时,我觉得作为一个银嗓子的丑八怪也可以心满意足了。

"有一次,我不得不到奥拉塔马这个滨海小镇来解决一些政治动乱。在海关和军事部门砍掉几颗脑袋。弗格斯,他掌握着这个共和国的冰和硫磺火柴的专卖权,说是愿意陪我跑一趟。

"在骡帮的铃铛声中,我们长驱直入奥拉塔马,这个小镇便属于我们了;正如西奥多·罗斯福在奥伊斯特湾①时,长岛海峡不属于日本人一样。我说的虽然是'我们',事实上是指'我'。只要是到过四个国家,两个海洋,一个海湾和地峡,以及五个群岛的人,都听到过贾德森·塔特的大名。人们管我叫绅士冒险家。黄色报纸用了五栏,一个月刊用了四万字(包括花边装饰),《纽约时报》用第十二版的全部篇幅来报导我的消息。如果说我们在奥拉塔马受到的欢迎部分原因是由于弗格斯·麦克马汉的俊美,我就可以把我那顶巴拿马草帽里的标签吃下去。他们张灯结彩是为了我。我不是爱妒忌的人;我说的是事实。镇上的人都是尼布甲尼撒②;他们在我面前拜倒草地;因为这个镇里没有尘埃可供他们拜倒。他们向贾德森·塔特顶礼膜拜。他们知道我是桑乔·贝纳维德斯背后的主宰。对他们来说,我的一句话比任何别人的话更像是东奥罗拉图书馆书架上的全部毛边书籍。居然有人把时间花在美容上——抹冷霜,按摩面部(顺眼睛内角按摩),用安息香酊防止皮肤松弛,用电

---

① 奥伊斯特湾:美国长岛北部的村落,西奥多·罗斯福的家乡。
② 尼布甲尼撒(公元前605—公元前562):巴比伦王,《圣经·旧约·但以理书》第4章第29至33节有尼布甲尼撒"吃草如牛"之语。

what end? Looking handsome. Oh, what a mistake! It's the larynx that the beauty doctors ought to work on. It's words more than warts, talk more than talcum, palaver more than power, blarney more than bloom that counts—the phonograph instead of the photograph. But I was going to tell you.

"The local Astors put me and Fergus up at the Centipede Club, a frame building built on posts sunk in the surf. The tide's only nine inches. The Little Big High Low Jack-in-the-game of the town came around and kowtowed. Oh, it wasn't to Herr Mees. They had heard about Judson Tate.

"One afternoon me and Fergus McMahan was sitting on the seaward gallery of the Centipede, drinking iced rum and talking.

"'Judson,' says Fergus, 'there's an angel in Oratama.'

"'So long,' says I, 'as it ain't Gabriel, why talk as if you had heard a trump blow?'

"'It's the Señorita Anabela Zamora,' says Fergus. 'She's—she's—she's as lovely as—as hell!'

"'Bravo!' says I, laughing heartily. 'You have a true lover's eloquence to paint the beauties of your inamorata. You remind me,' says I, 'of Faust's wooing of Marguerite —that is, if he wooed her after he went down the trap-door of the stage.'

"'Judson,' says Fergus, 'you know you are as beautiless as a rhinoceros. You can't have any interest in women. I'm awfully gone on Miss Anabela. And that's why I'm telling you.'

"'Oh, *seguramente*,' says I. 'I know I have a front elevation like an Aztec god that guards a buried treasure

疗来除黑痣——为了什么目的？要漂亮。哦，真是大错特错！美容师应该注意的是喉咙。起作用的不是赘疣而是言语，不是爽身粉而是谈吐，不是香粉而是聊天，不是花颜玉容而是甘言巧语——不是照片而是留声机。闲话少说，还是谈正经的吧。

"当地头面人物把我的弗格斯安顿在蜈蚣俱乐部里，那是一座建筑在海边桩子上的木头房子。涨潮时海水和房子地板相距只有九英寸。镇里的大小官员、诸色人等都来致敬。哦，并不是向赫耳·墨斯致敬。他们早听到贾德森·塔特的名声了。

"一天下午，我和弗格斯·麦克马汉坐在蜈蚣旅馆朝海的回廊里，一面喝冰甘蔗酒，一面聊天。

"'贾德森，'弗格斯说道，'奥拉塔马有一个天使。'

"'只要这个天使不是加百列，'我说，'你谈话的神情为什么像是听到了最后审判的号角声时那样紧张？'

"'是安娜贝拉·萨莫拉小姐。'弗格斯说。'她——她——她美得——没治！'

"'呵呵！'我哈哈大笑说。'听你形容你情人的口吻倒真像是一个情种儿。你叫我想起了浮士德追求玛格丽特的事——就是说，假如他进了舞台的活板底下之后仍旧追求她的话。'

"'贾德森，'弗格斯说，'你知道你自己像犀牛一般丑。你不可能对女人发生兴趣。我却发疯般地迷上了安娜贝拉小姐。因此我才讲给你听。'

"'哦，当然啦。'我说。'我知道我自己的面孔像是尤卡坦杰斐逊县那个守着根本不存在的窖藏的印第安阿兹特克

197

that never did exist in Jefferson County, Yucatan. But there are compensations. For instance, I am It in this country as far as the eye can reach, and then a few perches and poles. And again.'says I, 'when I engage people in a set-to of oral, vocal, and laryngeal utterances, I do not usually confine my side of the argument to what may be likened to a cheap phonographic reproduction of the ravings of a jellyfish.'

"'Oh, I know,'says Fergus, amiable, 'that I'm not handy at small talk. Or large, either. That's why I'm telling you. I want you to help me.'

"'How can I do it?'I asked.

"'I have subsidized,'says Fergus, 'the services of Señorita Anabela's duenna, whose name is Francesca. You have a reputation in this country, Judson,'says Fergus, 'of being a great man and a hero.'

"'I have,'says I. 'And I deserve it.'

"'And I,'says Fergus, 'am the best-looking man between the arctic circle and antarctic ice pack.'

"'With limitations,'says I, 'as to physiognomy and geography. I freely concede you to be.'

"'Between the two of us,'says Fergus, 'we ought to land the Señorita Anabela Zamora. The lady, as you know, is of an old Spanish family, and further than looking at her driving in the family *carruaje* of afternoons around the plaza, or catching a glimpse of her through a barred window of evenings, she is as unapproachable as a star.'

"'Land her for which one of us?'says I.

"'For me, of course,'says Fergus. 'You've never seen her. Now, I've had Francesca point me out to her as being you on several occasions. When she sees me on the

偶像。不过有补偿的办法。比如说,在这个国家里抬眼望到的地方,以及更远的地方,我都是至高无上的人物。此外,当我和人们用口音、声音、喉音争论的时候,我说的话并不限于那种低劣的留声机式的胡言乱语。'

"'哦,'弗格斯亲切地说,'我知道不论闲扯淡或者谈正经,我都不成。因此我才请教你。我要你帮我忙。'

"'我怎么帮忙呢?'我问道。

"'我已经买通了安娜贝拉小姐的陪媪,'弗格斯说,'她名叫弗朗西斯卡。贾德森,你在这个国家里博得了大人物和英雄的名声。'

"'正是,'我说,'我是当之无愧的。'

"'而我呢,'弗格斯说,'我是北极和南极之间最漂亮的人。'

"'如果只限于相貌和地理,'我说,'我完全同意你的说法。'

"'你我两人,'弗格斯说,'我们应该能把安娜贝拉·萨莫拉小姐弄到手。你知道,这位小姐出身于一个古老的西班牙家族,除了看她坐着马车在广场周围兜圈子,或者傍晚在栅栏窗外瞥见她一眼之外,她简直像是星星那样高不可攀。'

"'替我们中间哪一个去弄呀?'我问道。

"'当然是替我。'弗格斯说。'你从来没有见过她。我吩咐弗朗西斯卡把我当做你,已经指点给安娜贝拉看过好

plaza, she thinks she's looking at Don Judson Tate, the greatest hero, statesman, and romantic figure in the country. With your reputation and my looks combined in one man, how can she resist him? She's heard all about your thrilling history, of course. And she's seen me. Can any woman want more? 'asks Fergus McMahan.

"'Can she do with less?' I ask. 'How can we separate our mutual attractions, and how shall we apportion the proceeds?'

"Then Fergus tells me his scheme.

"The house of the alcalde, Don Luis Zamora, he says, has a *patio*, of course—a kind of inner courtyard opening from the street. In an angle of it is his daughter's window—as dark a place as you could find. And what do you think he wants me to do? Why, knowing my freedom, charm, and skilfulness of tongue, he proposes that I go into the *patio* at midnight, when the hobgoblin face of me cannot be seen, and make love to her for him—for the pretty man that she has just seen on the plaza, thinking him to be Don Judson Tate.

"Why shouldn't I do it for him—for my friend, Fergus McMahan? For him to ask me was a compliment—an acknowledgment of his own shortcomings.

"'You little, lily-white, fine-haired, highly polished piece of dumb sculpture,' says I, 'I'll help you. Make your arrangements and get me in the dark outside her window and my stream of conversation opened up with the moonlight tremolo stop turned on, and she's yours.'

"'Keep your face hid, Jud,' says Fergus. 'For heaven's sake, keep your face hid. I'm a friend of yours in all kinds of sentiment, but this is a business deal. If I could talk I wouldn't ask you. But seeing me and listening

几次了。她在广场上看见我的时候,以为看到的是全国最伟大的英雄、政治家和浪漫人物堂贾德森·塔特呢。把你的声名和我的面貌合在一个人身上,她是无法抗拒的。她当然听到过你那惊人的经历,又见到过我。一个女人还能有什么别的企求?'弗格斯·麦克马汉说。

"'她的要求不能降低点儿吗?'我问道。'我们怎样各显身手,怎样分摊成果呢?'

"弗格斯把他的计划告诉了我。

"他说,镇长堂路易斯·萨莫拉的房子有一个院子——通向街道的院子。院内一角是他女儿房间的窗口——那地方黑得不能再黑了。你猜他要我怎么办? 他知道我口才流利,有魅力,有技巧,让我半夜到院子里去,那时候我这张鬼脸看不清了,然后代他向萨莫拉小姐求爱——代她在广场上照过面的,以为是堂贾德森·塔特的美男子求爱。

"我为什么不替他,替我的朋友弗格斯·麦克马汉效劳呢? 他来请求我就是看得起我——承认了他自己的弱点。

"'你这个白百合一般的,金头发,精打细磨的,不会开口的小木头,'我说,'我可以帮你忙。你去安排好,晚上带我到她窗外,在月光颤音的伴奏下,我滔滔不绝地谈起来,她就是你的了。'

"'把你的脸遮住,贾德。'弗格斯说。'千万把你的脸遮严实。讲到感情,你我是生死之交,但是这件事非同小可。我自己能说话也不会请你去。如今看到我的面孔,听到你

to you I don't see why she can't be landed.'

"'By you?'says I.

"'By me.'says Fergus.

"Well, Fergus and the duenna, Francesca, attended to the details. And one night they fetched me a long black cloak with a high collar, and led me to the house at midnight. I stood by the window in the *patio* until I heard a voice as soft and sweet as an angel's whisper on the other side of the bars. I could see only a faint, white-clad shape inside; and, true to Fergus, I pulled the collar of my cloak high up, for it was July in the wet season, and the nights were chilly. And, smothering a laugh as I thought of the tongue-tied Fergus, I began to talk.

"Well, sir, I talked an hour at the Señorita Anabela. I say 'at' because it was not 'with'. Now and then she would say: 'Oh, Señor,' or 'Now, ain't you foolin'?' or 'I know you don't mean that,' and such things as women will when they are being rightly courted. Both of us knew English and Spanish; so in two languages I tried to win the heart of the lady for my friend Fergus. But for the bars to the window I could have done it in one. At the end of the hour she dismissed me and gave me a big, red rose. I handed it over to Fergus when I got home.

"For three weeks every third or fourth night I impersonated my friend in the *patio* at the window of Señorita Anabela. At last she admitted that her heart was mine, and spoke of having seen me every afternoon when she drove in the plaza. It was Fergus she had seen, of course. But it was my talk that won her. Suppose Fergus had gone there and tried to make a hit in the dark with his beauty all invisible, and not a word to say for himself!

的说话,我想她非给弄到手不可了。'

"'到你的手?'我问道。

"'我的。'弗格斯说。

"嗯,弗格斯和陪媪弗朗西斯卡安排好了细节。一天晚上,他们替我准备好一件高领子的黑色长披风,半夜把我领到那座房子那里。我站在院子里窗口下面,终于听到栅栏那边有一种天使般又柔和又甜蜜的声音。我依稀看到里面有一个穿白衣服的人影;我把披风领子翻了上来,一方面是忠于弗格斯,一方面是因为那时正当七月潮湿的季节,夜晚寒意袭人。我想到结结巴巴的弗格斯,几乎笑出声来,接着我开始说话了。

"嗯,先生,我对安娜贝拉小姐说了一小时话。我说'对她',因为根本没有'同她'说话。她只是偶尔说一句:'哦,先生,'或者'呀,你不是骗人吧?'或者'我知道你不是那个意思',以及诸如此类的,女人被追求得恰到好处时所说的话。我们两人都懂得英语和西班牙语;于是我运用这两种语言替我的朋友弗格斯去赢得这位小姐的心。如果窗口没有栅栏,我用一种语言就行了。一小时之后,她打发我走,并且给了我一朵大大的红玫瑰花。我回来后把它转交给了弗格斯。

"每隔三四个晚上,我就代我的朋友到安娜贝拉小姐的窗子下面去一次,这样持续了三星期之久。最后,她承认她的心已经属于我了,还说每天下午驾车去广场的时候都看到了我。她见到的当然是弗格斯。但是赢得她心的是我的谈话。试想,如果弗格斯自己跑去呆在黑暗里,他的俊美一点儿也看不见,他一句话也不说,哪能有什么成就!

"On the last night she promised to be mine—that is, Fergus's. And she put her hand between the bars for me to kiss. I bestowed the kiss and took the news to Fergus.

"'You might have left that for me to do,' says he.

"'That'll be your job hereafter,' says I. 'Keep on doing that and don't try to talk. Maybe after she thinks she's in love she won't notice the difference between real conversation and the inarticulate sort of droning that you give forth.'

"Now, I had never seen Señorita Anabela. So, the next day Fergus asks me to walk with him through the plaza and view the daily promenade and exhibition of Oratama society, a sight that had no interest for me. But I went; and children and dogs took to the banana groves and mangrove swamps as soon as they had a look at my face.

"'Here she comes,' said Fergus, twirling his moustache —'the one in white, in the open carriage with the black horse.'

"I looked and felt the ground rock under my feet. For Señorita Anabela Zamora was the most beautiful woman in the world, and the only one from that moment on, so far as Judson Tate was concerned. I saw at a glance that I must be hers and she mine forever. I thought of my face and nearly fainted; and then I thought of my other talents and stood upright again. And I had been wooing her for three weeks for another man!

"As Señorita Anabela's carriage rolled slowly past, she gave Fergus a long, soft glance from the corners of her night-black eyes, a glance that would have sent Judson Tate up into heaven in a rubber-tired chariot. But she never looked at me. And that handsome man only ruffles

"最后一晚,她答应跟我结婚了——那是说,跟弗格斯。她把手从栅栏里伸出来让我亲吻。我给了她一吻,并且把这消息告诉了弗格斯。

"'那件事应该留给我来做。'他说。

"'那将是你以后的工作。'我说。'一天到晚别说话,光是吻她。以后等她认为已经爱上你时,她也许就辨不出真正的谈话和你发出的嗫嚅之间的区别了。'

"且说,我从来没有清楚地见过安娜贝拉小姐。第二天,弗格斯邀我一起去广场上,看看我不感兴趣的奥拉塔马交际界人物的行列。我去了;小孩儿和狗一看到我的脸都往香蕉林和红树沼地上逃。

"'她来啦,'弗格斯捻着胡子说,'穿白衣服,坐着黑马拉的敞篷车。'

"我一看,觉得脚底下的地皮都在晃动。因为对贾德森·塔特来说,安娜贝拉·萨莫拉小姐是世界上最美的女人,并且从那一刻起,是唯一最美的女人。我一眼就明白我必须永远属于她,而她也必须永远属于我。我想起自己的脸,几乎晕倒;紧接着我又想起我其他方面的才能,又站稳了脚跟。何况我曾经代替一个男人追求了她有三星期之久呢!

"安娜贝拉小姐缓缓驶过时,她用那乌黑的眼睛温柔地、久久地瞟了弗格斯一下,那个眼色足以使贾德森·塔特魂魄飞扬,仿佛坐着胶轮车似地直上天堂。但是她没有看我。而那个美男子只是在我身边拢拢他的鬈发,像浪子似

his curls and smirks and prances like a lady-killer at my side.

"'What do you think of her, Judson?' asks Fergus, with an air.

"'This much.' says I. 'She is to be Mrs. Judson Tate. I am no man to play tricks on a friend. So take your warning.'

"I thought Fergus would die laughing.

"'Well, well, well,' said he, 'you old dough-face! Struck too. are you? That's great! But you're too late. Francesca tells me that Anabela talks of nothing but me, day and night. Of course, I'm awfully obliged to you for making that chin-music to her of evenings. But, do you know, I've an idea that I could have done it as well myself.'

"'Mrs. Judson Tate,' says I. 'Don't forget the name. You've had the use of my tongue to go with your good looks, my boy. You can't lend me your looks; but hereafter my tongue is my own. Keep your mind on the name that's to be on the visiting cards two inches by three and a half—"Mrs. Judson Tate."That's all.'

"'All right,' says Fergus, laughing again. ' I've talked with her father, the alcalde, and he's willing. He's to give a *baile* to-morrow evening in his new warehouse. If you were a dancing man, Jud, I'd expect you around to meet the future Mrs. McMahan.'

"But on the next evening, when the music was playing loudest at the Alcalde Zamora's *baile*, into the room steps Judson Tate in new white linen clothes as if he were the biggest man in the whole nation, which he was.

"Some of the musicians jumped off the key when they saw my face, and one or two of the timidest

地嬉笑着昂首阔步。

"'你看她怎么样,贾德森?'弗格斯得意洋洋地问道。

"'就是这样。'我说。'她将成为贾德森·塔特夫人。我一向不做对不起朋友的事。所以言明在先。'

"我觉得弗格斯简直要笑破肚皮。

"'呵,呵,呵,'他说,'你这个丑八怪!你也给迷住了,是吗?好极啦!不过你太迟啦。弗朗西斯卡告诉我,安娜贝拉日日夜夜不谈别的,光谈我。当然,你晚上同她谈话,我非常领你的情。不过你要明白,我觉得我自己去的话也会成功的。'

"'贾德森·塔特夫人。'我说。'别忘掉这个称呼。你利用我的舌头来配合你的漂亮,老弟。你不可能把你的漂亮借给我;但是今后我的舌头是我自己的了。记住"贾德森·塔特夫人",这个称呼将印在两英寸阔,三英寸半长的名片上。就是这么一回事。'

"'好吧。'弗格斯说着又笑了。'我跟她的镇长爸爸讲过,他表示同意。明天晚上,他要在他的新仓库里举行招待舞会。如果你会跳舞,贾德,我希望你也去见见未来的麦克马汉夫人。'

"第二天傍晚,在萨莫拉镇长举行的舞会上,当音乐奏得最响亮的时候,贾德森·塔特走了进去。他穿着一套新麻布衣服,神情像是全国最伟大的人物,事实上也是如此。

"有几个乐师见到我的脸,演奏的乐曲马上走了调。一

señoritas let out a screech or two. But up prances the alcalde and almost wipes the dust off my shoes with his forehead. No mere good looks could have won me that sensational entrance.

"'I hear much, Señor Zamora,' says I, 'of the charm of your daughter. It would give me great pleasure to be presented to her.'

"There were about six dozen willow rocking-chairs, with pink tidies tied on to them, arranged against the walls. In one of them sat Señorita Anabela in white Swiss and red slippers, with pearls and fireflies in her hair. Fergus was at the other end of the room trying to break away from two maroons and a claybank girl.

"The alcalde leads me up to Anabela and presents me. When she took the first look at my face she dropped her fan and nearly turned her chair over from the shock. But I'm used to that.

"I sat down by her and began to talk. When she heard me speak she jumped, and her eyes got as big as alligator pears. She couldn't strike a balance between the tones of my voice and the face I carried. But I kept on talking in the key of C, which is the ladies' key; and presently she sat still in her chair and a dreamy look came into her eyes. She was coming my way. She knew of Judson Tate, and what a big man he was, and the big things he had done; and that was in my favor. But, of course, it was some shock to her to find out that I was not the pretty man that had been pointed out to her as the great Judson. And then I took the Spanish language, which is better than English for certain purposes, and played on it like a harp of a thousand strings. I ranged from the second G below the staff up to F-sharp above it. I set my

208

两个最胆小的小姐禁不住尖叫起来。但是镇长忙不迭地跑过来,一躬到地,几乎用他的额头擦去了我鞋子上的灰尘。光靠面孔漂亮是不会引起这么惊人的注意的。

"'萨莫拉先生,'我说,'我久闻你女儿的美貌。我很希望有幸见见她。'

"约莫有六打粉红色布套的柳条椅靠墙放着。安娜贝拉小姐坐在一张摇椅上,她穿着白棉布衣服和红便鞋,头发上缀着珠子和萤火虫。弗格斯在屋子的另一头,正想摆脱两个咖啡色,一个巧克力色的女郎的纠缠。

"镇长把我领到安娜贝拉面前,作了介绍。她一眼看到我的脸,大吃一惊,手里的扇子掉了下来,摇椅几乎翻了身。我倒是习惯于这种情形的。

"我在她身边坐下,开始谈话。她听到我的声音不禁一怔,眼睛睁得像鳄梨一般大。她简直无法把我的声音和我的面相配合起来。不过我继续不断地用 C 调谈着话,那是对女人用的调子;没多久她便安安静静地坐在椅子上,眼睛里露出一种恍惚的样子。她慢慢地入彀了。她听说过有关贾德森·塔特的事情,听说过他是一个多么伟大的人物,干过许多伟大的事业;那对我是有利的。但是,当她发觉伟大的贾德森并不是人家指点给她看的那个美男子时,自然不免有些震惊。接着,我改说西班牙语,在某种情况下,它比英语好,我把它当做一个有千万根弦的竖琴那样运用自如,从降 G 调一直到 F 高半音。我用我的声音来体现诗歌、艺

voice to poetry, art, romance, flowers, and moonlight. I
repeated some of the verses that I had murmured to her
in the dark at her window; and I knew from a sudden
soft sparkle in her eye that she recognized in my voice
the tones of her midnight mysterious wooer.

"Anyhow, I had Fergus McMahan going. Oh, the vocal is the true art—no doubt about that. Handsome is as
handsome palavers. That's the renovated proverb.

"I took Señorita Anabela for a walk in the lemon
grove while Fergus, disfiguring himself with an ugly
frown, was waltzing with the claybank girl. Before we
returned I had permission to come to her window in the
patio the next evening at midnight and talk some more.

"Oh, it was easy enough. In two weeks Anabela was
engaged to me, and Fergus was out. He took it calm, for a
handsome man, and told me he wasn't going to give in.

"'Talk may be all right in its place, Judson,' he says
to me, 'although I've never thought it worth cultivating.
But,' says he, 'to expect mere words to back up success-
fully a face like yours in a lady's good graces is like ex-
pecting a man to make a square meal on the ringing of a
dinner-bell. '

"But I haven't begun on the story I was going to tell
you yet.

"One day I took a long ride in the hot sunshine, and
then took a bath in the cold waters of a lagoon on the
edge of the town before I'd cooled off.

"That evening after dark I called at the alcalde's to
see Anabela. I was calling regular every evening then,
and we were to be married in a month. She was looking
like a bulbul, a gazelle, and a tea-rose, and her eyes were
as soft and bright as two quarts of cream skimmed off

术、传奇、花朵和月光。我还把我晚上在她窗前念给她的诗背了几句；她的眼睛突然闪出柔和的光亮，我知道她已经辨出了半夜里向她求爱的那个神秘人的声音。

"总之，我把弗格斯·麦克马汉挤垮了。啊，口才是货真价实的艺术——那是不容置疑的。言语漂亮，才是漂亮。这句谚语应当改成这样①。

"我和安娜贝拉小姐在柠檬林子里散了一会儿步，'弗格斯正愁眉苦脸地在同那个巧克力色的姑娘跳华尔兹。我们回去之前，她同意我第二天半夜到院子里去，在她窗下再谈谈话。

"呃，经过非常顺利。不出两星期，安娜贝拉和我订了婚，弗格斯完了。作为一个漂亮的人，他处之泰然，并且对我说他不准备放弃。

"'口才本身很起作用，贾德森，'他对我说，'尽管我以前从没有想到要培养它。但是凭你的尊容，指望用一些话语来博得女人的欢心，那简直是画饼充饥了。'

"我还没有讲到故事的正文呢。

"一天，我在火热的阳光底下骑马骑了好久，没等到凉爽下来，就在镇边的礁湖里洗了一个冷水澡。

"天黑之后，我去镇长家看安娜贝拉。那时候，我每天傍晚都去看她，我们打算一个月后结婚。她仿佛是一只夜莺，一头羚羊，一朵庚申蔷薇，她的眼睛又明亮又柔和，活像银河②上撇下来的两夸脱奶油。她看到我那丑陋的相貌

---

① 英文有"行为漂亮，才是漂亮"一成语。
② "银河"的原文是"牛奶路"（Milky Way）。

from the Milky Way. She looked at my rugged features without any expression of fear or repugnance. Indeed, I fancied that I saw a look of deep admiration and affection, such as she had cast at Fergus on the plaza.

"I sat down, and opened my mouth to tell Anabela what she loved to hear—that she was a trust, monopolizing all the loveliness of earth. I opened my mouth, and instead of the usual vibrating words of love and compliment, there came forth a faint wheeze such as a baby with croup might emit. Not a word—not a syllable—not an intelligible sound. I had caught cold in my laryngeal regions when I took my injudicious bath.

"For two hours I sat trying to entertain Anabela. She talked a certain amount, but it was perfunctory and diluted. The nearest approach I made to speech was to formulate a sound like a clam trying to sing 'A Life on the Ocean Wave' at low tide. It seemed that Anabela's eyes did not rest upon me as often as usual. I had nothing with which to charm her ears. We looked at pictures and she played the guitar occasionally, very badly. When I left, her parting manner seemed cool—or at least thoughtful.

"This happened for five evenings consecutively.

"On the sixth day she ran away with Fergus McMahan.

"It was known that they fled in a sailing yacht bound for Belize. I was only eight hours behind them in a small steam launch belonging to the Revenue Department.

"Before I sailed, I rushed into the *botica* of old Manuel Iquito, a half-breed Indian druggist. I could not speak, but I pointed to my throat and made a sound like escaping steam. He began to yawn. In an hour, according

时,并没有害怕或厌恶的样子。老实说,我觉得我看到的是无限的柔情蜜意,正像她在广场上望着弗格斯时那样。

"我坐下来,开始讲一些安娜贝拉爱听的话——我说她是一个托拉斯,把全世界的美丽都垄断了。我张开嘴巴,发出来的不是往常那种打动心弦的爱慕和奉承的话语,却是像害喉炎的娃娃发出的微弱的嘶嘶声。我说不出一个字,一个音节,一声清晰的声音。我洗澡不小心,着凉倒了嗓子。

"我坐了两个小时,想给安娜贝拉提供一些消遣。她也说了一些话,不过显得虚与委蛇,淡而无味。我想竭力达到的算是话语的声音,只是退潮时分蛤蜊所唱的那种'海洋里的生活'。安娜贝拉的眼睛仿佛也不像平时那样频频地望着我了。我没有办法来诱惑她的耳朵。我们看了一些画,她偶尔弹弹吉他,弹得非常坏。我离去时,她的态度很冷漠——至少可以说是心不在焉。

"这种情况持续了五个晚上。

"第六天,她跟弗格斯·麦克马汉跑了。

"据说他们是乘游艇逃到贝里塞去的,他们离开了已有八小时。我乘了税务署的一条小汽艇赶去。

"我上船之前,先到老曼努埃尔·伊基托,一个印第安混血药剂师的药房里去。我说不出话,只好指指喉咙,发出一种管子漏气似的声音。他打起呵欠来。根据当地的习

213

to the customs of the country, I would have been waited
on. I reached across the counter, seized him by the
throat, and pointed again to my own. He yawned once
more, and thrust into my hand a small bottle containing a
black liquid.

"'Take one small spoonful every two hours ,' says
he.

"I threw him a dollar and skinned for the steamer.

"I steamed into the harbor at Belize thirteen seconds
behind the yacht that Anabela and Fergus were on. They
started for the shore in a dory just as my skiff was low-
ered over the side. I tried to order my sailormen to row
faster, but the sounds died in my larynx before they came
to the light. Then I thought of old Iquito's medicine, and
I got out his bottle and took a swallow of it.

"The two boats landed at the same moment. I
walked straight up to Anabela and Fergus. Her eyes rested upon me for an instant; then she turned them, full of
feeling and confidence, upon Fergus. I knew I could not
speak, but I was desperate. In speech lay my only hope. I
could not stand beside Fergus and challenge comparison
in the way of beauty. Purely involuntarily, my larynx and
epiglottis attempted to reproduce the sounds that my
mind was calling upon my vocal organs to send forth.

"To my intense surprise and delight the words rolled
forth beautifully clear, resonant, exquisitely modulated,
full of power, expression, and long-repressed emotion.

"'Señorita Anabela,' says I, 'may I speak with you
aside for a moment?'

"You don't want details about that, do you?
Thanks. The old eloquence had come back all right. I led
her under a cocoanut palm and put my old verbal spell on

惯,他要过一小时才理会我。我隔着柜台探过身去,抓住他的喉咙,再指指我自己的喉咙。他又打了一呵欠,把一个盛着黑色药水的小瓶放在我手里。

"'每隔两小时吃一小匙。'他说。

"我扔下一块钱,赶到汽艇上。

"我在安娜贝拉和弗格斯的游艇后面赶到了贝里塞港口,只比他们迟了十三秒。我船上的舢板放下去时,他们的舢板刚向岸边划去。我想吩咐水手们划得快些,可声音还没有发出就在喉头消失了。我记起了老伊基托的药水,连忙掏出瓶子喝了一口。

"两条舢板同时到岸。我笔直地走到安娜贝拉和弗格斯面前。她的眼光在我身上停留了一会儿;接着便掉过头去,充满感情和自信地望着弗格斯。我知道自己说不出话,但是也顾不得了。我全部的希望都寄托在话语上面。在美貌方面,我是不能站在弗格斯身边同他相比的。我的喉咙和会厌软骨纯粹出于自动,要发出我心里想说的话。

"使我大吃一惊、喜出望外的是,我的话语滔滔不绝地说了出来,非常清晰、响亮、圆润,充满了力量和压抑已久的感情。

"'安娜贝拉小姐,'我说,'我可不可以单独同你谈一会儿?'

"你不见得想听那件事的细节了吧?多谢。我原有的口才又回来了。我带她到一株椰子树下,把以前的言语魅力又加在她身上。

her again.

"'Judson,'says she,'when you are talking to me I can hear nothing else—I can see nothing else—there is nothing and nobody else in the world for me.'

"Well, that's about all of the story. Anabela went back to Oratama in the steamer with me. I never heard what became of Fergus. I never saw him any more. Anabela is now Mrs. Judson Tate. Has my story bored you much?"

"No,"said I. "I am always interested in psychological studies. A human heart—and especially a woman's—is a wonderful thing to contemplate."

"It is,"said Judson Tate. "And so are the trachea and the bronchial tubes of man. And the larynx,too. Did you ever make a study of the windpipe?"

"Never,"said I. "But I have taken much pleasure in your story. May I ask after Mrs. Tate,and inquire of her present health and whereabouts?"

"Oh,sure,"said Judson Tate. "We are living in Bergen Avenue,Jersey City. The climate down in Oratama didn't suit Mrs. T. I don't suppose you ever dissected the arytenoid cartilages of the epiglottis,did you?"

"Why,no,"said I,"I am no surgeon."

"Pardon me," said Judson Tate, "but every man should know enough of anatomy and therapeutics to safeguard his own health. A sudden cold may set up capillary bronchitis or inflammation of the pulmonary vesicles,which may result in a serious affection of the vocal organs."

"Perhaps so,"said I,with some impatience;"but that is neither here nor there. Speaking of the strange manifestations of the affection of women. I—"

"'贾德森,'她说,'你同我说话的时候,我别的都听不见了——都看不到了——世界上任何事情、任何人都不在我眼里了。'

"嗯,故事到这里差不多完了。安娜贝拉随我乘了汽艇回到奥拉塔马。我再没有听到弗格斯的消息,再也没有见到他。安娜贝拉成了现在的贾德森·塔特夫人。我的故事是不是使你厌烦?"

"不。"我说。"我一向对心理研究很感兴趣。人的心——尤其是女人的心——真是值得研究的奇妙的东西。"

"不错。"贾德森·塔特说。"人的气管和支气管也是如此。还有喉咙。你有没有研究过气管?"

"从来没有,你的故事使我很感兴趣。我可不可以问候塔特夫人,她目前身体可好,在什么地方?"

"哦,当然。"贾德森·塔特说。"我们住在泽西城伯根路。奥拉塔马的天气对塔特太太并不合适。我想你从来没有解剖过会厌杓状软骨,是吗?"

"没有,"我说,"我不是外科医生。"

"对不起,"贾德森·塔特说,"但是每一个人都应该懂得足够的解剖学和治疗学,以便保护自己的健康。突然着凉可能会引起支气管炎或者肺气胞炎症,从而严重地影响发音器官。"

"也许是这样,"我有点不耐烦地说,"不过这话跟我们刚才谈的毫不相干。说到女人感情的奇特,我——"

"Yes, yes," interrupted Judson Tate, "they have peculiar ways. But, as I was going to tell you: when I went back to Oratama I found out from Manuel Iquito what was in that mixture he gave me for my lost voice. I told you how quick it cured me. He made that stuff from the *chuchula* plant. Now, look here."

Judson Tate drew an oblong white pasteboard box from his pocket.

"For any cough," he said, "or cold, or hoarseness, or bronchial affection whatsoever, I have here the greatest remedy in the world. You see the formula printed on the box. Each tablet contains licorice, 2 grains; balsam tolu, 1/10 grain; oil of anise, 1/20 minim; oil of tar, 1/60 minim; oleo-resin of cubebs, 1/60 minim; fluid extract of *chuchula*, 1/10 minim.

"I am in New York," went on Judson Tate, "for the purpose of organizing a company to market the greatest remedy for throat affections ever discovered. At present I am introducing the lozenges in a small way. I have here a box containing four dozen, which I am selling for the small sum of fifty cents. If you are suffering—"

I got up and went away without a word. I walked slowly up to the little park near my hotel, leaving Judson Tate alone with his conscience. My feelings were lacerated. He had poured gently upon me a story that I might have used. There was a little of the breath of life in it, and some of the synthetic atmosphere that passes, when cunningly tinkered, in the marts. And, at the last it had proven to be a commercial pill, deftly coated with the sugar of fiction. The worst of it was that I could not offer it for sale. Advertising departments and counting-

　　"是啊,是啊,"贾德森·塔特插嘴说,"她们的确特别。不过我要告诉你的是:我回到奥拉塔马以后,从老曼努埃尔·伊基托那里打听到了他替我医治失音的药水里有着什么成分。我告诉过你,它的效力有多么快。他的药水是用楚楚拉植物做的。嗨,你瞧。"

　　贾德森·塔特从口袋里掏出一个椭圆形的白色纸盒。

　　"这是世界第一良药,"他说,"专治咳嗽、感冒、失音或者气管炎症。盒子上印有成分仿单。每片内含甘草 2 喱,妥鲁香胶 1/10 喱,大茴香油 1/20 量滴,松馏油 1/60 量滴,荜澄茄油树脂 1/60 量滴,楚楚拉浸膏 1/10 量滴。

　　"我来纽约,"贾德森·塔特接着说,"是想组织一家公司,经售这种空前伟大的喉症药品。目前我只是小规模地在推销。我这里有一盒四打装的喉片,只卖五毛钱。假如你害——"

　　我站起身,一声不响地走开了。我慢慢逛到旅馆附近的小公园,让贾德森·塔特心安理得地独自呆着。我心里很不痛快。他慢慢地向我灌输了一个我可能利用的故事。那里面有一丝生活的气息,还有一些结构,如果处理得当,是可以出笼的。结果它却证明是一颗包着糖衣的商业药

rooms look down upon me. And it would never do for the literary. Therefore I sat upon a bench with other disappointed ones until my eyelids drooped.

I went to my room, and, as my custom is, read for an hour stories in my favorite magazines. This was to get my mind back to art again.

And as I read each story, I threw the magazines sadly and hopelessly, one by one, upon the floor. Each author, without one exception to bring balm to my heart, wrote liltingly and sprightly a story of some particular make of motor-car that seemed to control the sparking plug of his genius.

And when the last one was hurled from me I took heart.

"If readers can swallow so many proprietary automobiles," I said to myself, "they ought not to strain at one of Tate's Compound Magic Chuchula Bronchial Lozenges."

And so if you see this story in print you will understand that business is business, and that if Arts gets very far ahead of Commerce, she will have to get up and hustle.

I may as well add, to make a clean job of it, that you can't buy the *chuchula* plant in the drug stores.

丸。最糟的是我不能抛售它。广告部和会计室会看不起我的。并且它根本够不上文学作品的条件。因此,我同别的失意的人们一起坐在公园的椅子上,眼皮逐渐耷拉下来。

我回到自己的房间,照例看了一小时我喜欢的杂志上的故事。这是为了让我的心思重新回到艺术上去。

我看了一篇故事,就伤心地把杂志一本本地扔在地上。每一位作家毫无例外地都不能安慰我的心灵,只是轻快活泼地写着某种特殊牌子的汽车的故事,仿佛因而抑制了自己的天才的火花塞。

当我扔开最后一本杂志的时候,我打起精神来了。

"如果读者受得了这许多汽车,"我暗忖着,当然也受得了塔特的奇效楚楚拉气管炎复方含片。"

假如你看到这篇故事发表的话,你明白生意总是生意,如果艺术远远地跑在商业前面,商业是会急起直追的。

为了善始善终起见,我不妨再加上一句:楚楚拉这种草药在药房里是买不到的。

A Double-dyed Deceiver

THE trouble began in Laredo. It was the Llano Kid's
fault, for he should have confined his habit of mans-
laughter to Mexicans. But the Kid was past twenty; and
to have only Mexicans to one's credit at twenty is to
blush unseen on the Rio Grande border.

It happened in old Justo Valdo's gambling house.
There was a poker game at which sat players who were
not all friends, as happens often where men ride in from
afar to shoot Folly as she gallops. There was a row over
so small a matter as a pair of queens; and when the
smoke had cleared away it was found that the Kid had
committed an indiscretion, and his adversary had been
guilty of a blunder. For, the unfortunate combatant, instead of being a Greaser, was a high-blooded youth from
the cow ranches, of about the Kid's own age and pos-
sessed of friends and champions. His blunder in missing
the Kid's right ear only a sixteenth of an inch when he
pulled his gun did not lessen the indiscretion of the better
marksman.

The Kid, not being equipped with a retinue, nor
bountifully supplied with personal admirers and support-
ers—on account of a rather umbrageous reputation, even
for the border—considered it not incompatible with his
indisputable gameness to perform that judicious traction-
al act known as "pulling his freight".

Quickly the avengers gathered and sought him.
Three of them overtook him within a rod of the station.
The Kid turned and showed his teeth in that brilliant but

双 料 骗 子

乱子出在拉雷多。这件事要怪小利亚诺,因为他应该把杀人的对象仅限于墨西哥人。但是小利亚诺已经二十出头了;在格朗德河边境上,年过二十的人只有杀墨西哥人的纪录未免有点儿寒碜。

事情发生在老胡斯托·伐尔多斯的赌场里。当时有一场扑克牌戏,玩牌的人大多素昧平生。人们打老远的地方骑马来碰碰运气,互不相识也是常有的事。后来却为了一对皇后这样的小事吵了起来;硝烟消散之后,发现小利亚诺闯了祸,他的对手也犯了大错。那个不幸的家伙并不是墨西哥人,而是一个来自牧牛场的出身很好的青年,年纪同小利亚诺相仿,有着一批支持他的朋友。他的过错在于开枪时,子弹擦过小利亚诺右耳十六分之一英寸的地方,没打中;这一失误并没有减少那个更高明的枪手的莽撞。

小利亚诺没有随从,也没有许多钦佩他和支持他的人——因为即使在边境上,他的脾气也算是出名的暴躁——他觉得采取那个"走为上策"的审慎行动,同他那无可争辩的倔强性格并不矛盾。

复仇的人迅速集结追踪而来。有三个人在火车站附近赶上了小利亚诺。他转过身,露出了他通常在采取横蛮和

mirthless smile that usually preceded his deeds of inso-
lence and violence, and his pursuers fell back without
making it necessary for him even to reach for his weap-
on.

But in this affair the Kid had not felt the grim thirst
for encounter that usually urged him on to battle. It had
been a purely chance row, born of the cards and certain
epithets impossible for a gentleman to brook that had
passed between the two. The Kid had rather liked the
slim, haughty, brown-faced young chap whom his bullet
had cut off in the first pride of manhood. And now he
wanted no more blood. He wanted to get away and have
a good long sleep somewhere in the sun on the mesquite
grass with his handkerchief over his face. Even a Mexican might have crossed his path in safety while he was in
this mood.

The Kid openly boarded the north-bound passenger
train that departed five minutes later. But at Webb, a few
miles out, where it was flagged to take on a traveller, he
abandoned that manner of escape. There were telegraph
stations ahead; and the Kid looked askance at electricity
and steam. Saddle and spur were his rocks of safety.

The man whom he had shot was a stranger to him.
But the Kid knew that he was of the Coralitos outfit
from Hidalgo; and that the punchers from that ranch
were more relentless and vengeful than Kentucky feud-
ists when wrong or harm was done to one of them. So,
with the wisdom that has characterized many great fight-
ers, the Kid decided to pile up as many leagues as possible
of chaparral and pear between himself and the retalia-
tion of the Coralitos bunch.

Near the station was a store; and near the store, scat-

暴力手段前的不怀好意的狞笑。追他的人甚至没等他伸手拔枪，便退了回去。

当初，小利亚诺并不像平时那样好勇斗狠，存心找人拼命。那纯粹是一场偶然的口角，由于两人玩牌时某些使人按捺不住的粗话引起的。小利亚诺还相当喜欢那个被他枪杀的瘦长、傲慢、褐色脸膛、刚成年的小伙子。目前他不希望再发生什么流血事件。他想避开，找块牧豆草地，在太阳底下用手帕盖住脸，好好睡一大觉。他有这种情绪的时候，即使墨西哥人碰到他也是安全的。

小利亚诺大模大样地搭上北行的客车，五分钟后便出站了。可是列车行驶了不久，到了韦布，便接到讯号，临时停下来让一个旅客上车，这使小利亚诺放弃了搭车逃跑的办法。前面还有不少电报局；小利亚诺看到电气和蒸汽之类的玩意儿就恼火。马鞍和马刺才是安全的保证。

小利亚诺并不认识那个被他枪杀的人，只不过知道他是伊达尔戈的科拉里托斯牛队的；那个牧场里的人，如果有一个吃了亏，就比肯塔基的冤冤相报的人更残酷，更爱寻仇。因此，小利亚诺以大勇者的大智决定尽可能远离科拉里托斯那帮人的报复。

车站附近有一家店铺；店铺附近的牧豆树和榆树间有

tered among the mesquite and elms, stood the saddled horses of the customers. Most of them waited, half a-sleep, with sagging limbs and drooping heads. But one, a long-legged roan with a curved neck, snorted and pawed the turf. Him the Kid mounted, gripped with his knees, and slapped gently with the owner's own quirt.

If the slaying of the temerarious card-player had cast a cloud over the Kid's standing as a good and true citizen, this last act of his veiled his figure in the darkest shadows of disrepute. On the Rio Grande border if you take a man's life you sometimes take trash; but if you take his horse, you take a thing the loss of which renders him poor, indeed, and which enriches you not—if you are caught. For the Kid there was no turning back now.

With the springing roan under him he felt little care or uneasiness. After a five-mile gallop he drew in to the plainsman's jogging trot, and rode north-eastward toward the Nueces River bottoms. He knew the country well—its most tortuous and obscure trails through the great wilderness of brush and pear, and its camps and lonesome ranches where one might find safe entertainment. Always he bore to the east; for the Kid had never seen the ocean, and he had a fancy to lay his hand upon the mane of the great Gulf, the gamesome colt of the greater waters.

So after three days he stood on the shore at Corpus Christi, and looked out across the gentle ripples of a quiet sea.

Captain Boone, of the schooner *Flyaway*, stood near his skiff, which one of his crew was guarding in the surf. When ready to sail he had discovered that one of the necessaries of life, in the parallelogrammatic shape of

几匹顾客的没卸鞍的马。它们大多提起一支腿,耷拉着头,睡迷迷地在等着。但是有一匹长腿弯颈的杂毛马却在喷鼻子,踹草皮。小利亚诺跳上马背,两膝一夹,用马主人的鞭子轻轻打着它。

如果说,枪杀那个莽撞的赌牌人的行为,使小利亚诺正直善良的公民身份有所损害的话,那么盗马一事就足以使他名誉扫地。在格朗德河边境,你夺去一个人的生命有时倒无所谓,可是你夺去他的坐骑,简直就叫他破产,而你自己也并没有什么好处——如果你被逮住的话。不过小利亚诺现在也顾不得这些了。

他骑着这匹鲜蹦活跳的杂毛马,把忧虑和不安都抛到了脑后。他策马跑了五英里后,就像平原人那样款款而行,驰向东北方的纽西斯河床。他很熟悉这个地方——熟悉它那粗犷的荆棘丛林之间最艰苦、最难走的小路,熟悉人们可以在那里得到款待的营地和孤寂的牧场。他一直向东走去;因为他生平还没有见过海洋,很想抚摩一下那匹淘气的小马——墨西哥湾——的鬃毛。

三天之后,他站在科珀斯克里斯蒂①的岸上,眺望着宁静的海洋上的潾潾微波。

纵帆船"逃亡者号"的布恩船长站在小快艇旁边,一个水手守着小艇。帆船刚要起航的时候,他发觉一件生活必需品——口嚼烟草块——给忘了。他便派一个水手去采办

---

① 科珀斯克里斯蒂:得克萨斯州纽西斯河口上的城市。

plug tobacco, had been forgotten. A sailor had been dispatched for the missing cargo. Meanwhile the captain paced the sands, chewing profanely at his pocket store.

A slim, wiry youth in high-heeled boots came down to the water's edge. His face was boyish, but with a premature severity that hinted at a man's experience. His complexion was naturally dark; and the sun and wind of an outdoor life had burned it to a coffee-brown. His hair was as black and straight as an Indian's; his face had not yet been upturned to the humiliation of a razor; his eyes were a cold and steady blue. He carried his left arm somewhat away from his body, for pearl-handled .45s are frowned upon by town marshals, and are a little bulky when packed in the left armhole of one's vest. He looked beyond Captain Boone at the gulf with the impersonal and expressionless dignity of a Chinese emperor.

"Thinkin' of buyin' that'ar gulf, buddy?" asked the captain, made sarcastic by his narrow escape from the tobaccoless voyage.

"Why, no," said the Kid gently, "I reckon not. I never saw it before. I was just looking at it. Not thinking of selling it, are you?"

"Not this trip," said the captain. "I'll send it to you C.O.D. when I get back to Buenas Tierras. Here comes that capstan-footed lubber with the chewin'. I ought to 've weighed anchor an hour ago."

"Is that your ship out there?" asked the Kid.

"Why, yes," answered the captain, "if you want to call a schooner a ship, and I don't mind lyin'. But you better say Miller and Gonzales, owners, and ordinary plain, Billy-be-damned old Samuel K. Boone, skipper."

"Where are you going to?" asked the refugee.

那被遗忘的货物。与此同时,船长在沙滩上来回踱步,一面滥骂,一面嚼着口袋里的存货。

一个穿高跟马靴,瘦长结实的小伙子来到了海边。他脸上孩子气十足,不过还夹杂着一种早熟的严厉神情,说明他阅历很深。他的皮肤本来就黑,加上户外生活的风吹日晒,竟成了深褐色。他的头发同印第安人一样又黑又直;他的脸还没有受过剃刀的翻掘;他那一双蓝眼睛又冷酷,又坚定。他的左臂有点儿往外撇,因为警长们见到珍珠贝柄的四五口径手枪就头痛,他只得把手枪插在坎肩的左腋窝里,那未免大了些。他带着中国皇帝那种漠然无动于衷的尊严,眺望着布恩船长身后的海湾。

"打算把海湾买下来吗!老弟?"船长问道。他差点要做一次没有烟草的航行,心里正没有好气。

"呀,不,"小利亚诺和善地说,"我没有这个打算。我生平没有见过海。只是看看而已。你也不打算把它出卖吧?"

"这一次没有这个打算。"船长说。"等我回到布埃纳斯蒂埃拉斯之后,我把它给你运去,货到付款。那个傻瓜水手终于把烟草办来了,他跑得那么慢,不然我一小时前就可以启碇了。"

"那条大船是你的吗?"小利亚诺问道。

"嗯,是的,"船长回说,"如果你要把一条帆船叫做大船的话,我也不妨吹吹牛。不过说得正确些,船主是米勒和冈萨雷斯,在下只不过是老塞缪尔·凯·布恩,一个没什么了不起的船长。"

"你们去哪儿?"逃亡者问道。

"Buenas Tierras, coast of South America—I forget what they called the country the last time I was there. Cargo—lumber, corrugated iron, and machetes."

"What kind of a country is it?"asked the Kid—"hot or cold?"

"Warmish, buddy," said the captain. "But a regular Paradise Lost for elegance of scenery and be-yooty of geography. Ye're wakened every morning by the sweet singin' of red birds with seven purple tails, and the sighin' of breezes in the posies and roses. And the inhabitants never work, for they can reach out and pick steamer baskets of the choicest hothouse fruit without gettin' out of bed. And there's no Sunday and no ice and no rent and no troubles and no use and no nothin'. It's a great country for a man to go to sleep with, and wait for somethin' to turn up. The bananas and oranges and hurricanes and pineapples that ye eat comes from there."

"That sounds to me!"said the Kid, at last betraying interest. "What'll the expressage be to take me out there with you?"

"Twenty-four dollars," said Captain Boone; "grub and transportation. Second cabin. I haven't got a first cabin."

"You've got my company,"said the Kid, pulling out a buckskin bag.

With three hundred dollars he had gone to Laredo for his regular "blowout." The duel in Valdos's had cut short his season of hilarity, but it had left him with nearly $ 200 for aid in the flight that it had made necessary.

"All right, buddy,"said the captain. "I hope your ma won't blame me for this little childish escapade of yours." He beckoned to one of the boat's crew. "Let

"布埃纳斯蒂埃拉斯,南美海岸——上次我去过那里,不过那个国家叫什么名字我可忘了。船上装的是木材、波纹铁皮和砍刀。"

"那个国家是什么样的?"小利亚诺问道——"是热还是冷?"

"不冷不热,老弟。"船长说。"风景优美,山水秀丽,十足是个失乐园。你一早醒来就听到七条紫尾巴的红鸟在歌唱,微风在奇花异葩中叹息。当地居民从来不干活,他们不用下床,只消伸出手就可以采到一大篮一大篮最好的温室水果。那里没有礼拜天,没有冰,没有要付的房租,没有烦恼,没有用处,什么都没有。对于那些只想躺在床上等运气找上门的人来说,那个国家是再好没有的了。你吃的香蕉、橘子、飓风和菠萝就是从那里来的。"

"那倒正合我心意!"小利亚诺终于很感兴趣地说道。"我搭你的船去那里要多少船费?"

"二十四块钱,"布恩船长说,"包括伙食和船费。二等舱。我船上没有头等舱。"

"我去。"小利亚诺一面说,一面掏出了一个鹿皮袋子。

他去拉雷多的时候,带着三百块钱,准备像以前那样大玩一场。在伐尔多斯赌场里的决斗,中断了他的欢乐的季节,但是给他留下了将近两百元钱;如今由于决斗而不得不逃亡时,这笔钱倒帮了他的忙。

"好吧,老弟。"船长说。"你这次像小孩一样逃了出来,我希望你妈不要怪我。"他招呼一个水手说:"让桑切斯背你

Sanchez lift you out to the skiff so you won't get your feet wet."

Thacker, the United States consul at Buenas Tierras, was not yet drunk. It was only eleven o'clock; and he never arrived at his desired state of beatitude—a state where he sang ancient maudlin vaudeville songs and pelted his screaming parrot with banana peels—until the middle of the afternoon. So, when he looked up from his hammock at the sound of a slight cough, and saw the Kid standing in the door of the consulate, he was still in a condition to extend the hospitality and courtesy due from the representative of a great nation. "Don't disturb yourself," said the Kid easily. "I just dropped in. They told me it was customary to light at your camp before starting in to round up the town. I just came in on a ship from Texas."

"Glad to see you, Mr. — ," said the consul.

The Kid laughed.

"Sprague Dalton," he said. "It sounds funny to me to hear it. I'm called the Llano Kid in the Rio Grande country."

"I'm Thacker," said the consul. "Take that cane-bottom chair. Now if you've come to invest, you want somebody to advise you. These dingies will cheat you out of the gold in your teeth if you don't understand their ways. Try a cigar?"

"Much obliged," said the Kid, "but if it wasn't for my corn shucks and the little bag in my back pocket I couldn't live a minute." He took out his "makings", and rolled a cigarette.

"They speak Spanish here," said the consul. "You'll

到小艇上去，免得你踩湿靴子。"

美利坚合众国驻布埃纳斯蒂埃拉斯的领事撒克还没有喝醉。当时只有十一点钟；到下午三四点之前，他不会达到飘飘然的境界——到了那种境界，他就会用哭音唱着小曲，用香蕉皮投掷他那尖叫怪嚷的八哥。因此，当他躺在吊床上听到一声轻咳而抬起头来，看到小利亚诺站在领事馆门口时，仍旧能够保持一个大国代表的风度，表示应有的礼貌和客气。"请便请便。"小利亚诺轻松地说。"我只是顺道路过。他们说，开始在镇上逛逛之前，按规矩应当到你的营地来一次。我刚乘了船从得克萨斯来。"

"见到你很高兴，请问贵姓？"领事说。

小利亚诺笑了。

"斯普拉格·多尔顿。"他说。"这个姓名我自己听了都觉得好笑。在格朗德河一带，人家都管我叫小利亚诺。"

"我姓撒克。"领事说。"请坐到那张竹椅上。假如你来到这儿是想投资，就需要有人帮你出出主意。这些黑家伙，如果你不了解他们的作风，会把你的金牙齿都骗光。抽雪茄吗？"

"多谢，"小利亚诺说，"我不抽雪茄，不过如果我后裤袋里没有烟草和那个小包，我一分钟也活不下去。"他取出卷烟纸和烟草，卷了一支烟。

"这里的人说西班牙语，"领事说，"你需要一个译员。

need an interpreter. If there's anything I can do, why, I'd be delighted. If you're buying fruit lands or looking for a concession of any sort, you'll want somebody who knows the ropes to look out for you."

"I speak Spanish," said the Kid, "about nine times better than I do English. Everybody speaks it on the range where I come from. And I'm not in the market for anything."

"You speak Spanish?" said Thacker, thoughtfully. He regarded the Kid absorbedly.

"You look like a Spaniard, too," he continued. "And you're from Texas. And you can't be more than twenty or twenty-one. I wonder if you've got any nerve."

"You got a deal of some kind to put through?" asked the Texan, with unexpected shrewdness.

"Are you open to a proposition?" said Thacker.

"What's the use to deny it?" said the Kid. "I got into a little gun frolic down in Laredo, and plugged a white man. There wasn't any Mexican handy. And I come down to your parrot-and-monkey range just for to smell the morning-glories and marigolds. Now, do you *sabe*?"

Thacker got up and closed the door.

"Let me see your hand," he said.

He took the Kid's left hand, and examined the back of it closely.

"I can do it," he said, excitedly. "Your flesh is as hard as wood and as healthy as a baby's. It will heal in a week."

"If it's a fist fight you want to back me for," said the Kid, "don't put your money up yet. Make it gun work, and I'll keep you company. But no bare-handed scrapping, like ladies at a tea-party, for me."

我有什么地方可以效劳,嗯,我一定很高兴。如果你打算买果树地或者想搞什么租借权,你一定需要一个熟悉内幕的人替你出主意。"

"我说西班牙语,"小利亚诺说,"大概比说英语要好九倍。我原先的那个牧场上人人都说西班牙语。我不打算买什么。"

"你会西班牙语?"撒克若有所思地说。他出神地瞅着小利亚诺。

"你的长相也像西班牙人。"他接着说。"你又是从得克萨斯来的。你的年纪不会超出二十或者二十一。我不知道你有没有胆量。"

"你在打什么主意?"小利亚诺问道,他的精明出人意料。

"你有意思插一手吗?"撒克问。

"我不妨对你讲实话。"小利亚诺说。"我在拉雷多玩了一场小小的枪斗,毙了一个白人。当时没有凑手的墨西哥人。我到你们这个八哥和猴子的牧场上来,只是想闻闻牵牛花和金盏草。现在你明白了吗?"

撒克站起来把门关上。

"让我看看你的手。"他说。

他抓着小利亚诺的左手,把手背端详了好一会儿。

"我办得了。"他兴奋地说。"你的皮肉像木头一般结实,像婴孩儿一般健康。一星期内就能长好。"

"如果你打算叫我来一场拳头,"小利亚诺说,"那你可别对我存什么希望。换成枪斗,我一定奉陪。我才不喜欢像茶会上的太太们那样赤手空拳地打架。"

"It's easier than that,"said Thacker. "Just step here, will you?"

Through the window he pointed to a two-story white-stuccoed house with wide galleries rising amid the deep-green tropical foliage on a wooded hill that sloped gently from the Sea.

"In that house,"said Thacker, "a fine old Castilian gentleman and his wife are yearning to gather you into their arms and fill your pockets with money. Old Santos Urique lives there. He owns half the gold-mines in the country. "

"You haven't been eating loco weed, have you?" asked the Kid.

"Sit down again,"said Thacker, "and I'll tell you. Twelve years ago they lost a kid. No, he didn't die—although most of 'em here do from drinking the surface water. He was a wild little devil, even if he wasn't but eight years old. Everybody knows about it. Some Americans who were through here prospecting for gold had letters to Señor Urique, and the boy who was a favorite with them. They filled his head with big stories about the States; and about a month after they left, the kid disappeared, too. He was supposed to have stowed himself away among the banana bunches on a fruit steamer, and gone to New Orleans. He was seen once afterward in Texas, it was, but they never heard anything more of him. Old Urique has spent thousands of dollars having him looked for. The madam was broken up worst of all. The kid was her life. She wears mourning yet. But they say she believes he'll come back to her some day, and never gives up hope. On the back of the boy's left hand was tattooed a flying eagle carrying a spear in his claws.

"没那么严重。"撒克说。"请过来,好吗?"

他指着窗外一幢两层楼的、有宽回廊的白墙房屋。那幢建筑矗立在海边一个树木葱茏的小山上,在深绿色的热带植物中间显得分外醒目。

"那幢房屋里,"撒克说,"有一位高尚的西班牙老绅士和他的夫人,他们迫不及待地想把你搂在怀里,把钱装满你的口袋。住在那里的是老桑托斯·乌里盖。这个国家里的金矿有一半是他的产业。"

"你没有吃错疯草吧?"小利亚诺说。

"再请坐下来,"撒克说,"我告诉你。十二年前,他们丧失了一个小孩儿。不,他并没有死——虽然这里有许多人因为喝了淤水,害病死掉了。当时他只有八岁,可是顽皮得出格。大家都知道。有几个勘察金矿的美国人路过这里,同乌里盖先生打了交道,他们非常喜欢这个孩子。他们把许多有关美国的大话灌进了他的脑袋里;他们离开后一个月,这小家伙也失踪了。据人家揣测,他大概是躲在一条水果船的香蕉堆里,偷偷地到了新奥尔良。据说有人在得克萨斯见过他,此后就音讯杳然。老乌里盖花了几千块钱找他。夫人尤其伤心。这小家伙是她的命根子。她目前还穿着丧服。但大家说她从不放弃希望,认为孩子总有一天会回来的。孩子的左手背上刺了一只抓枪的飞鹰。那是老乌

That's old Urique's coat of arms or something that he in-
herited in Spain. "

The Kid raised his left hand slowly and gazed at it
curiously.

"That's it, "said Thacker, reaching behind the official desk for his bottle of smuggled brandy. "You're not
so slow. I can do it. What was I consul at Sandakan for?
I never knew till now. In a week I'll have the eagle bird
with the frog-sticker blended in so you'd think you were
born with it. I brought a set of the needles and ink just
because I was sure you'd drop in some day, Mr. Dalton. "

"Oh, hell, "said the Kid. "I thought I told you my
name!"

"All right, 'Kid, ' then. It won't be that long. How
does 'Señorito Urique' sound, for a change?"

"I never played son any that I remember of, "said
the Kid. "If I had any parents to mention they went over
the divide about the time I gave my first bleat. What is
the plan of your round-up?"

Thacker leaned back against the wall and held his
glass up to the light.

"We've come now, "said he, "to the question of how
far you're willing to go in a little matter of the sort. "

"I told you why I came down here, "said the Kid
simply.

"A good answer, "said the consul. "But you won't
have to go that far. Here's the scheme. After I get the
trade-mark tattooed on your hand I'll notify old Urique.
In the meantime I'll furnish you with all of the family
history I can find out, so you can be studying up points to
talk about. You've got the looks, you speak the Spanish,
you know the facts, you can tell about Texas, you've got

里盖家族的纹章,或是他在西班牙继承下来的标记。"

小利亚诺慢慢地抬起左手,好奇地瞅着它。

"正是,"撒克说着,伸手去拿藏在办公桌后面的一瓶走私运来的白兰地。"你脑筋不笨。我会刺花。我在山打根①当了一任领事有什么好处? 直到今天我才明白。一星期之内我能把那只抓着小尖刀的老鹰刺在你的手上,仿佛从小就有刺花似的。我这里备有一套刺花针和墨水,正因为我料到你有一天会来的,多尔顿先生。"

"喔,妈的。"小利亚诺说。"我不是把我的名字早告诉了你吗!"

"好吧,那么就叫你'小利亚诺'。这个名字也不会长了。换成乌里盖少爷怎么样?"

"从我记事的时候起,我从没有扮演过儿子的角色。"小利亚诺说。"假如我有父母的话,我第一次哇哇大叫时,他们就进了鬼门关。你的计划是怎么样的呀?"

撒克往后靠着墙,把酒杯对着亮光瞧瞧。

"现在的问题是,"他说,"你打算在这件小事里干多久。"

"我已经把我来这里的原因告诉你了。"小利亚诺简单地说。

"回答得好。"领事说。"不过你用不着呆这么久。我的计划是这样的:等我在你手上刺好商标之后,我就通知老乌里盖。刺花期间,我把我收集到的有关那个家族的情况讲给你听,那你谈吐就不会露出破绽了。你的长相像西班牙人,你能说西班牙语,你了解情况,你又能谈谈得克萨斯时

---

① 山打根:马来西亚城市。

the tattoo mark. When I notify them that the rightful
heir has returned and is waiting to know whether he will
be received and pardoned what will happen? They'll
simply rush down here and fall on your neck, and the
curtain goes down for refreshments and a stroll in the
lobby."

"I'm waiting."said the Kid. "I haven't had my saddle off in your camp long, pardner, and I never met you
before; but if you intend to let it go at a parental blessing, why, I'm mistaken in my man, that's all."

"Thanks."said the consul. "I haven't met anybody in
a long time that keeps up with an argument as well as
you do. The rest of it is simple. If they take you in only
for a while it's long enough. Don't give 'em time to hunt
up the strawberry mark on your left shoulder. Old Urique
keeps anywhere from $50,000 to $100,000 in his house
all the time in a little safe that you could open with a
shoe buttoner. Get it. My skill as a tattooer is worth half
the boodle. We go halves and catch a tramp steamer for
Rio Janeiro. Let the United States go to pieces if it can't
get along without my services. *Qué dice, señor?*"

"It sounds to me!"said the Kid, nodding his head.
"I'm out for the dust."

"All right, then,"said Thacker. "You'll have to keep
close until we get the bird on you. You can live in the
back room here. I do my own cooking, and I'll make you
as comfortable as a parsimonious government will allow
me."

Thacker had set the time at a week, but it was two
weeks before the design that he patiently tattooed upon
the Kid's hand was to his notion. And then Thacker
called a *muchacho*, and dispatched this note to the in-

的见闻,你有刺花。当我通知他们说,真正的继承人已经回来,想知道他能不能得到收容和宽恕时,那会发生什么事情? 他们一准立刻赶到这里,抱住你的脖子,这场戏也就结束,可以到休息室去吃些茶点,舒散舒散了。"

"我准备好了。"小利亚诺说。"我在你营地里歇脚的时间还不长,老兄,以前也不认识你;但如果你的目的只限于父母的祝福,那我可看错人了。"

"多谢。"领事说。"我好久没有遇到像你这样条理分明的人了。以后的事情很简单。只要他们接纳,哪怕是很短一个时期,事情就妥了。别让他们有机会查看你左肩膀上有没有一块红记。老乌里盖家的一个小保险箱里经常藏着五万到十万块钱,那个保险箱,你用一根铜丝都可以捅开。把钱搞来。我的刺花技术值其中的半数。我们把钱平分,搭一条不定期的轮船到里约热内卢去。如果美国政府由于少了我的服务而混不下去的话,那就让它垮台吧。你觉得怎么样,先生?"

"很合我的口味!"小利亚诺说。"我干。"

"那好。"撒克说。"在我替你刺上老鹰之前,你得躲起来。你可以住这里的后房。我是自己做饭的,我一定在吝啬的政府给我的薪俸所许可的范围之内尽量款待你。"

撒克估计的时间是一星期,但是等他不厌其烦地在小利亚诺手上刺好那个花样,觉得满意时,已经过了两个星期。撒克找了一个小厮,把下面的便条送达他准备暗算的人:

tended victim：

EL SEÑOR DON SANTOS URIQUE，
　La Casa Blanca，
MY DEAR SIR：
　I beg permission to inform you that there is in my house as a temporary guest a young man who arrived in Buenas Tierras from the United States some days ago. Without wishing to excite any hopes that may not be realized，I think there is a possibility of his being your long-absent son. It might be well for you to call and see him. If he is，it is my opinion that his intention was to return to his home，but upon arriving here，his courage failed him from doubts as to how he would be received. Your true servant，

THOMPSON THACKER.

　Half an hour afterward—quick time for Buenas Tierras—Señor Urique's ancient landau drove to the consul's door，with the bare-footed coachman beating and shouting at the team of fat，awkward horses.

　A tall man with a white moustache alighted，and assisted to the ground a lady who was dressed and veiled in unrelieved black.

　The two hastened inside，and were met by Thacker with his best diplomatic bow. By his desk stood a slender young man with clearcut，sunbrowned features and smoothly brushed black hair.

　Señora Urique threw back her heavy veil with a quick gesture. She was past middle age，and her hair was beginning to silver，but her full，proud figure and clear olive skin retained traces of the beauty peculiar to the

白屋

堂桑托斯·乌里盖先生

亲爱的先生：

请允许我奉告，数日前有一位年轻人从美国来到布埃纳斯蒂埃拉斯，目前暂住舍间。我不想引起可能落空的希望，但是我认为这人可能是您失踪多年的儿子。您最好亲自来看看他。如果他确实是您的儿子，据我看，他很想回自己家，可是到后不知道将会得到怎样的接待，不敢贸然前去。

汤普森·撒克谨启

半小时以后——这在布埃纳斯蒂埃拉斯还算是快的——乌里盖先生的古色古香的四轮马车，由一个赤脚的马夫鞭打和吆喝着那几匹肥胖笨拙的马，来到了领事住处的门口。

一个白胡须的高个子下了车，然后搀扶着一个穿黑衣服，蒙黑面纱的太太下来。

两人急煎煎地走进来，撒克以最彬彬有礼的外交式的鞠躬迎接了他们。他桌旁站着一个瘦长的年轻人，眉清目秀，皮肤黧黑，乌黑的头发梳得光光的。

乌里盖夫人飞快地把厚面纱一揭。她已过中年，头发开始花白，但她那丰满漂亮的身段和浅橄榄色的皮肤还保

Basque province. But, once you had seen her eyes, and comprehended the great sadness that was revealed in their deep shadows and hopeless expression, you saw that the woman lived only in some memory.

She bent upon the young man a long look of the most agonized questioning. Then her great black eyes turned, and her gaze rested upon his left hand. And then with a sob, not loud, but seeming to shake the room, she cried" *Hijo mio* !"and caught the Llano Kid to her heart.

A month afterward the Kid came to the consulate in response to a message sent by Thacker.

He looked the young Spanish caballero. His clothes were imported, and the wiles of the jewellers had not been spent upon him in vain. A more than respectable diamond shone on his finger as he rolled a shuck cigarette.

"What's doing?"asked Thacker.

"Nothing much,"said the Kid calmly. "I eat my first iguana steak to-day. They're them big lizards, you *sabe*? I reckon, though, that frijoles and side bacon would do me about as well. Do you care for iguanas, Thacker?"

"No, nor for some other kinds of reptiles," said Thacker.

It was three in the afternoon, and in another hour he would be in his state of beatitude.

"It's time you were making good, sonny," he went on, with an ugly look on his reddened face. "You're not playing up to me square. You've been the prodigal son for four weeks now, and you could have had veal for every meal on a gold dish if you'd wanted it. Now, Mr. Kid, do you think it's right to leave me out so long on a husk diet? What's the trouble? Don't you get your filial eyes

244

存着巴斯克妇女所特有的妍丽。你一见到她的眼睛,发现它们的暗影和失望的表情中透露出极大的哀伤,你就知道这个女人只是依靠了某种记忆才能生活的。

她带着痛苦万分的询问神情,向那年轻人瞅了好久。她一双乌黑的大眼睛转到了他的左手上。接着,她抽噎了一下,声音虽然不大,但仿佛震动了整幢房屋。她嚷道:"我的儿子!"紧接着便把小利亚诺搂在怀里。

过了一个月,小利亚诺接到撒克捎给他的信,来到领事馆。

他完全成了一位年轻的西班牙绅士。他的衣服都是进口货,珠宝商的狡黠并没有在他身上白费气力。他卷纸烟的时候,一枚大得异乎寻常的钻石戒指在他手上闪闪发光。

"怎么样啦?"撒克问道。

"没怎么样。"小利亚诺平静地说。"今天我第一次吃了蜥蜴肉排。就是那种大四脚蛇。你知道吗? 我却认为咸肉煮豆子也配我的胃口。你喜欢吃蜥蜴吗,撒克?"

"不,别的爬虫也不吃。"撒克说。

现在是下午三点钟,再过一小时,他就要达到那种飘飘然的境界了。

"你该履行诺言了,老弟。"他接着说,他那张猪肝色的脸上露出一副狰狞相。"你对我太不公平。你已经当了四星期的宝贝儿子,你喜欢的话,每顿饭都可以用金盘子来盛小牛肉。喂,小利亚诺先生,你说应不应该让我老是过粗茶淡饭的日子? 毛病在哪里? 难道你这双孝顺儿子的眼睛在白屋里面没有见到任何像是现款的东西? 别对我说你没有

on anything that looks like cash in the Casa Blanca?
Don't tell me you don't. Everybody knows where old
Urique keeps his stuff. It's U. S. currency, too; he don't
accept anything else. What's doing? Don't say 'nothing'
this time."

"Why. sure," said the Kid, admiring his diamond,
"there's plenty of money up there. I'm no judge of collat-
eral in bunches, but I will undertake for to say that I've
seen the rise of $ 50,000 at a time in that tin grub box
that my adopted father calls his safe. And he lets me carry the key sometimes just to show me that he knows I'm
the real little Francisco that strayed from the herd a long
time ago."

"Well, what are you waiting for?" asked Thacker
angrily. "Don't you forget that I can upset your apple-
cart any day I want to. If old Urique knew you were an
impostor, what sort of things would happen to you? Oh,
you don't know this country, Mr. Texas Kid. The laws
here have got mustard spread between 'em. These people
here'd stretch you out like a frog that had been stepped
on, and give you about fifty sticks at every corner of the
plaza. And they'd wear every stick out, too. What was
left of you they'd feed to alligators."

"I might as well tell you now, pardner," said the
Kid, sliding down low on his steamer chair, "that things
are going to stay just as they are. They're about right
now."

"What do you mean?" asked Thacker, rattling the
bottom of his glass on his desk.

"The scheme's off," said the Kid. "And whenever
you have the pleasure of speaking to me address me as
Don Francisco Urique. I'll guarantee I'll answer to it.

见到。谁都知道老乌里盖藏钱的地方。并且还是美国货币；别的钱他不要。你究竟怎么啦？这次别说'没有'。"

"哎，当然，"小利亚诺欣赏着他的钻石戒指说，"那里的钱确实很多。至于证券之类的玩意儿我可不懂，但是我可以担保说，在我干爸爸叫做保险箱的铁皮盒子里，我一次就见到过五万元现款，有时候，他把保险箱的钥匙交给我，主要是让我知道他把我当做那个走失多年的真的小弗朗西斯科。"

"哎，那你还等什么呀？"撒克愤愤地问道。"别忘了只要我高兴，我随时随地都可以揭你的老底。如果老乌里盖知道你是骗子，你知道会出什么事？哦，得克萨斯的小利亚诺先生，你才不了解这个国家。这里的法律才叫辣呢。他们会把你绑得像一只被踩扁的蛤蟆，在广场的每一个角上揍你五十棍。棍子都要打断好几根。再把你身上剩下来的皮肉喂鳄鱼。"

"我现在不妨告诉你，伙计，"小利亚诺舒适地坐在帆布椅子里说，"事情就按照目前的样子维持下去，目前很不坏。"

"你这是什么意思？"撒克问道，把酒杯在桌子上碰得格格直响。

"计划吹啦。"小利亚诺说。"以后你同我说话，请称呼我堂弗朗西斯科·乌里盖。我保证答应。我们不去碰乌里

We'll let Colonel Urique keep his money. His little tin safe is as good as the time-locker in the First National Bank of Laredo as far as you and me are concerned. "

"You're going to throw me down, then, are you?" said the consul.

"Sure,"said the Kid, cheerfully. "Throw you down. That's it. And now I'll tell you why. The first night I was up at the colonel's house they introduced me to a bedroom. No blankets on the floor—a real room, with a bed and things in it. And before I was asleep, in comes this artificial mother of mine and tucks in the covers. 'Panchito,'she says, 'my little lost one, God has brought you back to me. I bless His name forever.' It was that, or some truck like that, she said. And down comes a drop or two of rain and hits me on the nose. And all that stuck by me, Mr. Thacker. And it's been that way ever since. And it's got to stay that way. Don't you think that it's for what's in it for me, either, that I say so. If you have any such ideas keep 'em to yourself. I haven't had much truck with women in my life, and no mothers to speak of, but here's a lady that we've got to keep fooled. Once she stood it; twice she won't. I'm a low-down wolf, and the devil may have sent me on this trail instead of God, but I'll travel it to the end. And now, don't forget that I'm Don Francisco Urique whenever you happen to mention my name.

"I'll expose you to-day. you—you double-dyed traitor,"stammered Thacker.

The Kid arose and, without violence, took Thacker by the throat with a hand of steel, and shoved him slowly into a corner. Then he drew from under his left arm his pearl-handled. 45 and poked the cold muzzle of it against

盖上校的钱。就你我两人来说,他的小铁皮保险箱同拉雷多第一国民银行的定时保险库一样安全可靠。"

"那你是想出卖我了,是吗?"领事说。

"当然。"小利亚诺快活地说。"出卖你。说得对。现在我把原因告诉你。我到上校家的第一晚,他们领我到了一间卧室里。不是在地板上铺一张床垫——而是一间真正的卧室,有床有家具。我入睡前,我那位假母亲走了进来,替我掖好被子。'小宝贝,'她说,'我的走失的小宝贝,天主把你送了回来。我永远赞美他的名。'她说了一些诸如此类的废话。接着落了几点雨,滴在我的鼻子上。这情形我永远忘不了,撒克先生。那以后一直是这样,将来也是这样。我说这番话,别以为我为自己的好处打算。你不要以小人之心度君子之腹。我生平没有跟女人多说过话,也没有母亲可谈,但是对于这位太太,我们却不得不继续瞒下去。她已经忍受了一次痛苦;第二次她可受不了。我像是一条卑贱的野狼,送我走上这条路的可能不是上帝,而是魔鬼,但是我要走到头。喂,你以后提起我的名字时,别忘了我是堂弗朗西斯科·乌里盖。"

"我今天就揭发你,你——你这个双料叛徒。"撒克结结巴巴地说。

小利亚诺站了起来,并不粗暴地用他有力的手掐住撒克的脖子,慢慢地把他推到一个角落去。接着,他从左腋窝下抽出他那支珍珠贝柄的四五口径手枪,用冰冷的枪口戳

the consul's mouth.

"I told you why I come here," he said, with his old freezing smile. "If I leave here, you'll be the reason. Never forget it, partner. Now, what is my name?"

"Er—Don Francisco Urique," gasped Thacker.

From outside came a sound of wheels, and the shouting of someone, and the sharp thwacks of a wooden whipstock upon the backs of fat horses.

The Kid put up his gun, and walked toward the door. But he turned again and came back to the trembling Thacker, and held up his left hand with its back toward the consul.

"There's one more reason," he said, slowly, "why things have got to stand as they are. The fellow I killed in Laredo had one of them same pictures on his left hand."

Outside, the ancient landau of Don Santos Urique rattled to the door. The coachman ceased his bellowing. Señora Urique, in a voluminous gay gown of white lace and flying ribbons, leaned forward with a happy look in her great soft eyes.

"Are you within, dear son?" she called, in the rippling Castilian.

"*Madre mía, yo vengo* [mother, I come]," answered the young Don Francisco Urique.

着领事的嘴巴。

"我已经告诉过你,我怎么会来到这里的。"他露出以前那种叫人心寒的微笑说。"如果我再离开这里,那将是由于你的缘故。千万别忘记,伙计。喂,我叫什么名字呀?"

"呃——堂弗朗西斯科·乌里盖。"撒克喘着气说。

外面传来车轮声,人的吆喝声和木鞭柄打在肥马背上的响亮的啪啪声。

小利亚诺收起手枪,向门口走去。但他又扭过头,回到哆嗦着的撒克面前,向领事扬起了左手。

"这种情况为什么要维持下去,"他慢慢地说,"还有一个原因。我在拉雷多杀掉的那个人,左手背也有一个同样的刺花。"

外面,堂桑托斯·乌里盖的古色古香的四轮马车咔嗒咔嗒地驶到门口。马车夫停止了吆喝。乌里盖太太穿着一套缀着许多花边和缎带的漂亮衣服,一双柔和的大眼睛里露出幸福的神情,她向前探着身子。

"你在里面吗,亲爱的儿子?"她用银铃般的西班牙语喊道。

"妈妈,我来啦。"年轻的堂弗朗西斯科·乌里盖回答说。

The Roads We Take

TWENTY miles west of Tucson the "Sunset Express" stopped at a tank to take on water. Besides the aqueous addition the engine of that famous flyer acquired some other things that were not good for it.

While the fireman was lowering the feeding hose, Bob Tidball, "Shark" Dodson, and a quarter-bred Creek Indian called John Big Dog climbed on the engine and showed the engineer three round orifices in pieces of ordnance that they carried. These orifices so impressed the engineer with their possibilities that he raised both hands in a gesture such as accompanies the ejaculation "Do tell!"

At the crisp command of Shark Dodson, who was leader of the attacking force, the engineer descended to the ground and uncoupled the engine and tender. Then John Big Dog, perched upon the coal, sportively held two guns upon the engine driver and the fireman, and suggested that they run the engine fifty yards away and there await further orders.

Shark Dodson and Bob Tidball, scorning to put such low-grade ore as the passengers through the mill, struck out for the rich pocket of the express car. They found the messenger serene in the belief that the "Sunset Express" was taking on nothing more stimulating and dangerous than aqua pura. While Bob was knocking this idea out of his head with the butt-end of his six-shooter Shark Dodson was already dosing the express-car safe with dynamite.

252

我们选择的道路

"落日快车"在塔克森①以西二十英里的一座水塔旁边停下来加水。那列著名的快车的车头除了水之外,还加了一些对它不利的东西。

火夫放下输水管的时候,三个人爬上了车头:鲍勃·蒂德博尔、"鲨鱼"多德森和有四分之一克里克印第安血统的约翰·大狗。他们把带在身边的三件家伙的圆口子对准了司机。司机被这样口子所暗示的可能性吓得举起了双手,仿佛要说:"不至于吧!"

进攻队伍的头儿,鲨鱼多德森,利索地发了一个命令,司机下了车,把机车和煤水车同列车卸开。接着,约翰·大狗蹲在煤堆上,开玩笑似地用两支手枪分别对着司机和火夫,吩咐他们把车头开出五十码,在那里听候命令。

鲨鱼多德森和鲍勃·蒂德博尔认为旅客是品位不高的矿石,没有筛选的价值,便直奔特别快车的富矿。他们发现押运员正自得其乐地认为"落日快车"除了清水之外,没有添加危险刺激的东西。鲍勃用六响手枪的枪柄把这个念头从他脑袋里敲了出去,与此同时,鲨鱼多德森已经动手用炸药炸开了邮车的保险柜。

---

① 塔克森:美国阿利桑那州南部城市。

The safe exploded to the tune of $30,000, all gold and currency. The passengers thrust their heads casually out of the windows to look for the thunder-cloud. The conductor jerked at the bell rope, which sagged down loose and unresisting, at his tug. Shark Dodson and Bob Tidball, with their booty in a stout canvas bag, tumbled out of the express car and ran awkwardly in their high-heeled boots to the engine.

The engineer, sullenly angry but wise, ran the engine, according to orders, rapidly away from the inert train. But before this was accomplished the express messenger, recovered from Bob Tidball's persuader to neutrality, jumped out of his car with a Winchester rifle and took a trick in the game. Mr. John Big Dog, sitting on the coal tender, unwittingly made a wrong lead by giving an imitation of a target, and the messenger trumped him. With a ball exactly between his shoulder blades the Creek chevalier of industry rolled off to the ground, thus increasing the share of his comrades in the loot by one-sixth each.

Two miles from the tank the engineer was ordered to stop.

The robbers waved a defiant adieu and plunged down the steep slope into the thick woods that lined the track. Five minutes of crashing through a thicket of chaparral brought them to open woods, where the three horses were tied to low-hanging branches. One was waiting for John Big Dog, who would never ride by night or day again. This animal the robbers divested of saddle and bridle and set free. They mounted the other two with the bag across one pommel, and rode fast and with discretion through the forest and up a primeval, lonely gorge. Here

保险柜炸开后，发现有三万元之多，全是金币和现钞。旅客们漫不经心地从窗口探出头去看看哪里有雷雨云。列车员急忙拉铃索，可是先被割断的绳索一拉就软绵绵地脱落下来。鲨鱼多德森和鲍勃·蒂德博尔把他们的战利品装进一只结实的帆布袋。跳出邮车朝车头跑去，高跟的马靴使他们在奔跑时有些蹒跚。

司机正生着闷气，人却不傻，他遵照命令把车头迅速驶离不能动弹的列车。然而在车头开出之前，押运员已经从鲍勃·蒂德博尔使他退居中立的一击下苏醒过来。他抓起一支温彻斯特来复枪，参加了这场游戏。坐在煤水车上的约翰·大狗先生无心中走错一着，成了打靶的目标，被押运员钻了空子。子弹恰恰打进他两片肩胛骨中间，这个克里克的骗子一个跟头栽到地上，让他的伙伴每人多分到六分之一的赃款。

车头开到离水塔两英里时，司机被命令停车。

两个强盗大模大样地挥手告别，然后冲下陡坡，在路轨旁边的密林中消失了。他们在矮橻树林里横冲直闯了五分钟之后，到了稀疏的树林里，那儿有三匹马给拴在低垂的树枝上。其中一匹是等候约翰·大狗的，但是无论白天黑夜，他再也骑不成马了。两个强盗卸掉这头牲口的鞍辔，放了它。他们跨上另外两匹马，把帆布袋搁在一匹马的鞍头上，审慎而迅速地穿过树林，驰进一个原始的荒凉的峡谷。在

the animal that bore Bob Tidball slipped on a mossy boulder and broke a foreleg. They shot him through the head at once and sat down to hold a council of flight. Made secure for the present by the tortuous trail they had traveled, the question of time was no longer so big. Many miles and hours lay between them and the spryest posse that could follow. Shark Dodson's horse, with trailing rope and dropped bridle, panted and cropped thankfully of the grass along the stream in the gorge. Bob Tidball opened the sack, and drew out double handfuls of the neat packages of currency and the one sack of gold and chuckled with the glee of a child.

"Say, you old double-decked pirate," he called joyfully to Dodson, "you said we could do it—you got a head for financing that knocks the horns off of anything in Arizona."

"What are we going to do about a hoss for you, Bob? We ain't got long to wait here. They'll be on our trail before daylight in the mornin'."

"Oh, I guess that cayuse of yourn'll carry double for a while," answered the sanguine Bob. "We'll annex the first animal we come across. By jingoes, we made a haul, didn't we? Accordin' to the marks on this money there's $ 30,000 — $ 15,000 apiece!"

"It's short of what I expected," said Shark Dodson, kicking softly at the packages with the toe of his boot. And then he looked pensively at the wet sides of his tired horse.

"Old Bolivar's mighty nigh played out," he said, slowly. "I wish that sorrel of yours hadn't got hurt."

"So do I," said Bob, heartily, "but it can't be helped. Bolivar's got plenty of bottom—he'll get us both far

这里,鲍勃·蒂德博尔的坐骑在一块长满苔藓的岩石上打了滑,摔折了前腿。他们立刻朝它脑袋开了一枪,坐下来讨论怎样远走高飞。由于他们所走的路径盘旋曲折,暂时可保安全,时间的问题不像先前那么严重了。追踪而来的搜索队,即使矫健非凡,在时间和空间上同他们还隔着一大段距离。鲨鱼多德森的马已经松开笼头,拖着缰绳,喘着气在峡谷的溪流边上大吃青草。鲍勃·蒂德博尔打开帆布袋,双手抓起扎得整整齐齐的现钞和一小袋金币,像小孩一般咯咯笑起来。

"喂,你这个双料强盗,"他快活地招呼多德森,"你说我们准能行——在金融事业上,你的头脑可真行,整个阿利桑那州找不到你的对手。"

"你没有坐骑怎么办呢,鲍勃?我们不能在这里多耗时间。明早天没亮,他们就会来追缉的。"

"哦,我想你那匹小野马暂时驮得动我们两个人。"乐天派的鲍勃回答说。"路上一见到马,我们就征用一匹。天哪,我们发了一笔财,可不是吗?看钱上的标签,一共三万,每人一万五!"

"比我预料的要少。"鲨鱼多德森说,用靴尖轻轻踢着钞票捆。接着,他沉思地瞅着他那匹跑累的马的汗水淋漓的胁腹。

"老博利瓦差不多要累垮啦。"他慢吞吞地说。"我真希望你的栗毛马没有摔伤。"

"我也这样希望。"鲍勃无忧无虑地说,"不过那也是没有办法的事。博利瓦的脚力很健——它能把我们驮到可以

enough to get fresh mounts. Dang it, Shark, I can't help
thinkin' how funny it is that an Easterner like you can
come out here and give us Western fellows cards and
spades in the desperado business. What part of the East
was you from, anyway?"

"New York State," said Shark Dodson, sitting down
on a boulder and chewing a twig. "I was born on a farm
in Ulster County. I ran away from home when I was sev-
enteen. It was an accident my comin' West. I was walkin'
along the road with my clothes in a bundle, makin' for
New York City. I had an idea of goin' there and makin'
lots of money. I always felt like I could do it. I came to a
place one evenin' where the road forked and I didn't
know which fork to take. I studied about it for half an
hour and then I took the left-hand. That night I run into
the camp of a Wild West show that was travelin' among
the little towns, and I went West with it. I've often wondered if I wouldn't have turned out different if I'd took
the other road."

"Oh, I reckon you'd have ended up about the same,"
said Bob Tidball, cheerfully philosophical. "It ain't the
roads we take; it's what's inside of us that makes us turn
out the way we do."

Shark Dodson got up and leaned against a tree.

"I'd a good deal rather that sorrel of yourn hadn't
hurt himself, Bob," he said again, almost pathetically.

"Same here," agreed Bob; "he sure was a first-rate
kind of a crowbait. But Bolivar, he'll pull us through all
right. Reckon we'd better be movin'on, hadn't we,
Shark? I'll bag the boodle ag'in and we'll hit the trail
for higher timber."

Bob Tidball replaced the spoil in the bag and tied

换新坐骑的地方。妈的，鲨鱼，我想起来就纳闷，像你这样的一个东部人来到这里，在这些横行不法的勾当中居然胜过我们西部人。你究竟是东部哪里的人？"

"纽约州。"鲨鱼多德森说着在一块岩石上坐下，嘴里嚼着一根小树枝。"我出生在厄斯特县的一个农庄里，十七岁的时候，从家里逃了出来。我来到西部完全是一个偶然的机遇。当时我挎着一小包衣服，沿路走去，想到纽约市。我打算到那里去挣大钱。我觉得我能行。一天傍晚，我到了一个三岔路口，不知道该走哪一条路。我琢磨了半个小时，终于选择了左面的一条。就在那天晚上，我遇到一个在乡镇旅行演出的西部戏班子，我跟着他们来到了西部。我常想，如果当时我选择了另一条路，会不会成为另一种人。"

"哦，我想你结果还是一样。"鲍勃·蒂德博尔愉快而带有哲理地说。"我们选择的道路关系不大；我们成为哪一种人，完全由本质决定。"

鲨鱼多德森站起来，靠在一株树上。

"我真不愿意你那匹栗毛马摔伤，鲍勃。"他又说了一遍，几乎有点儿伤感。

"我何尝愿意，"鲍勃附和说，"它确实是匹头挑的快马。但是博利瓦准能帮我们渡过难关的。我们还是赶紧上路为好，对不对，鲨鱼？我把钱装好，我们上路找一个妥当的地方吧。"

鲍勃·蒂德博尔把抢来的钱重新装进帆布袋，用绳索

the mouth of it tightly with a cord. When he looked up the most prominent object that he saw was the muzzle of Shark Dodson's. 45 held upon him without a waver.

"Stop your funnin'," said Bob, with a grin. "We got to be hittin' the breeze."

"Set still," said Shark. "You ain't goin' to hit no breeze, Bob. I hate to tell you, but there ain't any chance for but one of us. Bolivar, he's plenty tired, and he can't carry double."

"We been pards, me and you, Shark Dodson, for three years," Bob said quietly. "We've risked our lives together time and again. I've always give you a square deal, and I thought you was a man. I've heard some queer stories about you shootin' one or two men in a peculiar way, but I never believed 'em. Now if you're just havin' a little fun with me, Shark, put your gun up, and we'll get on Bolivar and vamose. If you mean to shoot—shoot, you blackhearted son of a tarantula!"

Shark Dodson's face bore a deeply sorrowful look.

"You don't know how bad I feel," he sighed, "about that sorrel of yourn breakin' his leg, Bob."

The expression on Dodson's face changed in an instant to one of cold ferocity mingled with inexorable cupidity. The soul of the man showed itself for a moment like an evil face in the window of a reputable house.

Truly Bob Tidball was never to "hit the breeze" again. The deadly. 45 of the false friend cracked and filled the gorge with a roar that the walls hurled back with indignant echoes. And Bolivar, unconscious accomplice, swiftly bore away the last of the holders-up of the "Sunset Express", not put to the stress of "carrying double".

But as Shark Dodson galloped away the woods

扎紧袋口。他抬起头时看到的最扎眼的东西,是鲨鱼多德森手里握得四平八稳的、对准他的四五口径的枪口。

"别开玩笑。"鲍勃咧着嘴说。"我们还得赶路呢。"

"别动。"鲨鱼说。"你不必赶路了,鲍勃。我不得不告诉你,我们中间只有一个人有机会逃脱。博利瓦已经够累的了,驮不动两个人。"

"鲨鱼多德森,你我搭档已有三年,"鲍勃平静地说,"我们一起出生入死,也不止一次。我一向同你公平交易,满以为你是条汉子。我也曾听到一些古怪的传说,说你不光明地杀过一两个人,但是我从不相信。如果你同我开小玩笑,鲨鱼,那就收起你的枪,让我们骑上博利瓦赶路。如果你存心要枪杀我——那就杀吧,你这个毒蜘蛛养的黑心小子!"

鲨鱼多德森的神色显得十分悲哀。

"你不了解,鲍勃,"他叹了一口气说,"你那匹栗毛马摔折了腿,叫我多么难过。"

刹那间,多德森换了一副凛冽的凶相,还夹杂着一种冷酷的贪婪。那个人的灵魂透露了一会儿,像一幢外观正派的房屋的窗口出现了一张邪恶的脸庞。

一点儿不假,鲍勃·蒂德博尔不必再赶路了。那个不仗义的朋友的致命的四五口径手枪呼的一声,在山谷间布满了吼号,石壁响起了愤愤不平的回音。博利瓦,那个不自知的同谋者,驮着抢劫"落日快车"的强盗中最后的一个飞快地驰走,没有被强迫"驮两个人"。

在鲨鱼多德森疾驰而去时,他眼前的树林似乎逐渐消

seemed to fade from his view; the revolver in his right hand turned to the curved arm of a mahogany chair; his saddle was strangely upholstered, and he opened his eyes and saw his feet, not in stirrups, but resting quietly on the edge of a quartered-oak desk.

I am telling you that Dodson, of the firm of Dodson & Decker, Wall Street brokers, opened his eyes. Peabody, the confidential clerk, was standing by his chair, hesitating to speak. There was a confused hum of wheels below, and the sedative buzz of an electric fan.

"Ahem! Peabody," said Dodson, blinking. "I must have fallen asleep. I had a most remarkable dream. What is it, Peabody?"

"Mr. Williams, sir, of Tracy & Williams, is outside. He has come to settle his deal in X. Y. Z. The market caught him short, sir, if you remember."

"Yes, I remember. What is X. Y. Z. quoted at to-day, Peabody?"

"One eighty-five, sir."

"Then that's his price."

"Excuse me," said Peabody, rather nervously, "for speaking of it, but I've been talking to Williams. He's an old friend of yours, Mr. Dodson, and you practically have a corner in X. Y. Z. I thought you might—that is, I thought you might not remember that he sold you the stock at 98. If he settles at the market price it will take every cent he has in the world and his home too to deliver the shares."

The expression on Dodson's face changed in an instant to one of cold ferocity mingled with inexorable cupidity. The soul of the man showed itself for a moment like an evil face in the window of a reputable house.

"He will settle at one eighty-five." said Dodson. "Bolivar cannot carry double."

失了;他右手里的枪变成了桃花心木椅子的弯扶手;他的马鞍奇怪地装上了弹簧,他睁眼一看,发现自己的脚并没有踩在马镫上,而是安详地搁在那张直纹橡木办公桌的边上。

我告诉各位的是这么一回事:华尔街经纪人,多德森—德克尔公司的多德森睁开了眼睛。机要秘书皮博迪站在他的椅子旁边,嗫嗫嚅嚅地正想说话。楼下传来杂乱的车轮声,屋里是电风扇催人欲眠的营营声。

"嘿嗨!皮博迪,"多德森眨着眼睛说,"我准是睡着了。我做了一个非常奇怪的梦。有什么事吗,皮博迪?"

"特雷西—威廉斯公司的威廉斯先生等在外面。他是来结算那笔艾克斯·淮·齐股票账目的。他抛空失了风,你大概还记得吧,先生。"

"对,我记得。今天艾克斯·淮·齐是什么行情,皮博迪?"

"一块八毛五,先生。"

"那就按这个行情结账好啦。"

"对不起,我想说一句,"皮博迪局促不安地说。"我刚才同威廉斯谈过。多德森先生,他是你的老朋友,事实上你垄断了艾克斯·淮·齐股票。我想你也许——呃,你也许不记得他卖给你的价钱是九毛八。如果要他按市场行情结账,那他就得倾家荡产,变卖掉一切才能交割。"

刹那间,多德森换了一副凛冽的凶相,还夹杂着一种冷酷的贪婪。那个人的灵魂透露了一会儿,像一幢外观正派的房屋的窗口出现了一张邪恶的脸庞。

"他得按一元八毛五的行情结账。"多德森说。"博利瓦驮不动两个人。"

名著名译英汉对照读本

《哈姆莱特》

〔英〕莎士比亚 著 朱生豪 译

《黑暗的心》

〔英〕康拉德 著 黄雨石 译

《简·爱》

〔英〕夏洛特·勃朗特 著 吴钧燮 译

《凯撒和克莉奥佩特拉》

〔英〕萧伯纳 著 杨宪益 译

《理想丈夫》

〔英〕王尔德 著 文 心 译

《马克·吐温短篇小说选》

〔美〕马克·吐温 著 叶冬心 译

《名利场》

〔英〕萨克雷 著 杨 必 译

《欧·亨利短篇小说选》

〔美〕欧·亨利 著 王永年 译

《一间自己的房间》

〔英〕弗吉尼亚·吴尔夫 著 贾辉丰 译

《伊坦·弗洛美》

〔美〕伊迪丝·华顿 著 吕叔湘 译

A Series of
Fine Translation of Classics

HAMLET
William Shakespeare

HEART OF DARKNESS
Joseph Conrad

JANE EYRE
Charlotte Brontë

CAESAR AND CLEOPATRA
Benard Shaw

AN IDEAL HUSBAND
Oscar Wilde

SELECTED SHORT STORIES
OF MARK TWAIN
Mark Twain

VANITY FAIR
William Thackeray

SELECTED SHORT STORIES
OF O. HENRY
O. Henry

A ROOM OF ONE'S OWN
Virginia Woolf

ETHAN FROME
Edith Wharton